BED &
BREAKFAST
COAST TO COAST

Bed & Breakfast Coast to Coast

Bernice Chesler

THE STEPHEN GREENE PRESS
LEXINGTON, MASSACHUSETTS

Copyright © Bernice Chesler, 1986
All rights reserved

First published in 1986 by The Stephen Greene Press, Inc.
Published simultaneously in Canada by Penguin Books Canada Limited
Distributed by Viking Penguin Inc., 40 West 23rd Street, New York, NY 10010.

LIBRARY OF CONGRESS CATALOGING IN PUBLICATION DATA
Chesler, Bernice.
Bed and breakfast coast to coast.
Includes index.
1. Bed and breakfast accommodations—United States—
Directories. I. Title.
TX907.C5528   1986   647′.9473   85-27182
ISBN 0-8289-0583-5

Printed in the United States of America by
R. R. Donnelley & Sons, Harrisonburg, Virginia
Set in Century Schoolbook

Design by Mary A. Wirth
Maps by Deborah Perugi and Jane Simon

To David

◊ ◊ ◊

It is like being cared for by your favorite aunt who happens to have a darned good data bank.
—Alaska Private Lodgings' guest from California

The hosts went beyond the call of duty in using their car to help us, in providing extra snacks, and in just being nice people. It is a fine service you offer.
—Guests from Oregon of
Be Our Guest, Bed & Breakfast, Ltd., Massachusetts

Among our first-timers were three lawyers who thought they would try something different from a hotel. They used our service for three nights a week for six months, until their case ended. I am pretty sure they love B&B.
—Maxine Kates, Nutmeg Bed & Breakfast, Connecticut

Contents

◇ ◇ ◇

Introduction

This book is mostly about thousands of little-known, wonderful places to stay. They are private homes and small inns where gracious and friendly people share both their homes and their knowledge of an area, often over tea, sherry, a cool drink, breakfast.

Since the concept of bed and breakfast arrived in America (finally) about a decade ago, it has flourished. As more travelers discover this alternative style of lodging, B&Bs with signs and some form of advertising have sprouted from coast to coast. Yet about 85 percent of the thousands of B&Bs in North America exist because of the phenomenon known as a *bed and breakfast reservation service*. Essentially, the B&B reservation service has been created as a small personalized agency to screen hosts, inspect their homes, and then to book screened guests into those homes. Most of the hosts are anonymous to the public. After the service makes a match according to needs (and often interests, too), the hosts' names and addresses are given to the guest.

There are many differences among reservation services. The purpose of this book is to detail those differences, so that you are not only familiar with the "where" of the B&Bs listed with each service, but the "what" and even the "who." This handbook fully explains what each service is, how it works, what it offers, and the kinds of experiences that happen with personalized travel arrangements.

Although many reservation services limit their listings to private homes that accept paying houseguests, some also arrange stays at B&B inns, small public lodging places that are usually owner-occupied with about 10 or 12 guest rooms. Other variations on listings might include short-term (interim) lodging, particularly for house hunters and relocating executives. Car rentals, sightseeing tours, and theater tickets are some of the expanded services available through a limited number of reservation services.

Each reservation service determines its territory. Some offer homes in a small area. Others may cover an entire region. Many are beginning to network with other services in their state, their region, or even throughout the continent.

Each reservation service sets its own standards. Beyond the facilities available, reservation services tend to be very careful about the hosts, choosing people who enjoy meeting others. Whenever I am asked who the hosts are, I think of the hotel executive, one who hosts B&B guests in his own lovely home, and his suggestion that the answer should be "People you would like to know."

Having stayed at hundreds of B&Bs and having spent the last three years in B&B research, interviewing hosts, guests, and reservation services, I am among the hundreds of thousands who appreciate the addition of a reservation service to the B&B scene. I am quite comfortable with the conclusion that there is plenty of room for the complementary existence of the reservation service and the independent B&B owner who enjoys the full operation from initial booking to collecting fees. Thanks to reservation services, countless travelers have been able to stay with local residents in major cities, in farmhouses located where there is no hotel or motel, and in resort areas too. How nice to be welcomed (and expected) in a residential neighborhood just 10 minutes off an interstate highway. How nice to be able to stay away from the highway entirely and just explore the country roads by going from B&B to B&B. The big city feels a bit smaller (and more familiar) when you come "home" rather than to a large establishment. Nonsmokers appreciate staying in a residence with nonsmokers. Special diets are catered to. Although arranging a B&B visit (as many people call their stays) takes a little more work than calling a toll-free number of a major hotel chain, a reservation service can save the B&B traveler time, money, and gas too. Reservation services provide not only a part-time occupation for frustrated innkeepers and a supplementary income for people who enjoy sharing their lifestyle, but a valuable service to the community—and the traveler.

Reservation services find that there are some interesting variations in travelers' tastes. While B&B guests usually remember the hosts at least as much as the antiques or the decor, some established services are being asked more often for "the nicest place you have." Some notice more requests for a private bath, for pampering, for a full breakfast, or for amenities. Cost is not always the major consideration. Many reservation services observe that the business traveler has come to appreciate the nonstandardized accommodations of B&Bs. At the same time, the number of experienced B&B travelers is balanced by a large number of first-timers, people who often write about being "won over" by hosts who are so caring.

In addition to corresponding with all of the reservation service owners in this book, I have had extensive telephone conversations with most of them and met many of them while traveling and at conferences. They have all answered dozens of detailed questions. Their joy in making perfect matches is evident. Although some service owners are also hosts, most of them express the feeling that the one missing element in their business is the opportunity to meet the traveler in person. They have all agreed to respond to any rare complaint.

Technology does not eliminate all paperwork. For her cheerful and thoughtful assistance with organization as well as the interpretation of some handwritten letters, my thanks to Jo Madden. My thanks, too, to the staff of the Tourism Division of the Canadian Consulate General in Boston, Massachusetts. As editor, Jay Howland is a whiz at knowing what I really did intend to say. My anchor through the whole project has been my husband; David manages to support and encourage, listen and evaluate, and share in the adventure of meeting new hosts.

While we all settle into an era of computerization, it feels good to be able to wish travelers many happy discoveries.

Bernice Chesler

No one can pay or is paid to be in this book.

All about
Bed & Breakfast
and
Reservation
Services

BED AND BREAKFAST IS an overnight accommodation in a private home or small inn. Breakfast is included in the package rate. *Hospitality is the keynote.*

It is such a wonderful concept, one that is well established in the British Isles, that now some B&B inns (over 300 in California alone) are small personalized full-fledged businesses. Some larger lodging places such as hotels or motels have begun to offer package B&B rates.

A BED AND BREAKFAST RESERVATION SERVICE IS a North American phenomenon based on the idea that many individuals would like to host on a part-time basis in their own residences. The service (a private agency) selects hosts, screens guests, and arranges bookings. Each service is autonomous. It sets its own standards and policies, decides whether to include B&B inns on its roster, deals with any zoning issues that may arise, and defines its own territory.

Some services have basic requirements that are filled by a wide range of homes. Some reservation services feature historic properties, luxurious homes, or "comfort and cleanliness at a relatively inexpensive rate." Most require that a guest room be just that, even though guests are (often) made to feel part of the family.

Most private homes registered with a service have 2 or 3 rooms available. (A B&B inn might have 10 or 12 guest rooms, and some with even more rooms have taken on the B&B label too.) Private homes are usually available as B&Bs only through a service, an arrangement that provides the host(s) the option of being anonymous to the general public.

A reservation service may be owned and run by one person (who certainly finds the need to use an answering machine at some hours), by a married couple, or by two or three friends who have become business partners. About 20 percent hire full or part-time staff. Some reservation services are owned and run by natives who know an area. Some are owned and run by relative newcomers who appreciate and explore the area. Some are owned and run by people who are also hosts themselves; many by career changers, by people who like the idea of an at-home business, and by sensitive listeners who are competent and experienced organizers. Although a few service owners tend to work very quickly with "just the facts," most personalize their service. When they say that they care or worry, they really do!

RATES: The average rate is about $40 a night for two. The range runs from quite inexpensive ($30 for two including breakfast) to over $100 in very unusual and elegant settings.

Rates at private home B&Bs available through a reservation service are usually set after the service inspects the home, meets the hosts, and comes to an agreement with the host.

Rates are determined by location and facilities. Private bath arrangements are more expensive than shared bath.

In large cities B&Bs cost less than major hotels. Suburban homes (with parking included) may be less than in-town locations. In some areas rates at budget motels may compete with B&Bs; the main difference, of course, is the hospitality and personalized environment offered at a B&B.

If you are comparing rates with commercial establishments, the inclusion of breakfast should be remembered.

Rates quoted to the traveler include the service's commission. In almost all B&B inns available through a service, the service's commission (20–30 percent) is added on to the established rate of the inn—and included in the quoted rate. There are a few services that charge the same rate for inns as the inns charge for direct bookings. Other fees could include taxes (where applicable) and/or a one-night surcharge. Occasionally, B&Bs that serve continental breakfast offer the option of a full breakfast for an extra charge. And if there is a guest membership fee for using the service, that information, too, is included in this book.

In private homes and small family-owned and -operated B&B inns, tips are not customary unless there is hired help. However, hosts notice that when their "built-in" help (younger family members) receive the smallest acknowledgement, those understanding guests are held in the highest regard! Universally, thank-you notes are considered treasures.

PAYMENTS: Payment arrangements usually require a deposit. Foreign travelers should send deposit amounts in U.S. currency.

Some services require full prepayment; some suggest paying on arrival. As Stratford and Area Visitors' and Convention Bureau in Ontario states, "You and your host will find it easier to do business while you are still strangers."

If payment is made directly to the host, payment should be made with cash or travelers' checks. Some inns accept credit cards. Check the entries in this book for each reservation service's credit-card policy.

CANCELLATION POLICIES differ. Please see the details with each listing. Most services charge a nominal fee for cancellation. There is more than money involved, however. Ruth Taylor of Bed & Breakfast of Birmingham says, "I would like guests to understand that a last-minute cancellation has to be relayed to hosts who may have cleaned up especially well, baked bread or such, maybe gone out to buy (or cut) fresh flowers, fruit, wine, and perhaps altered their own plans in order to offer their best hospitality."

LOCATIONS: B&Bs can be found—thanks to reservation services—in much of North America. They are not only in areas where some hotels and motels are, but they are away from traffic and highways, near convention centers, in residential neighborhoods, and in interesting communities that are still close to travelers' destinations.

On both coasts, particularly in the Northeast, in Florida and on the West Coast, B&Bs through reservation services are available almost everywhere. In between there are thousands, and surely many more to come because the B&B movement is still growing. As indicated on the following pages, some B&Bs are located in marvelous areas that are still considered "undiscovered."

Inquiries from travelers are sometimes responsible for the establishment of additional B&Bs. Mike Warner of Bed & Breakfast of St. Louis/River Country of Missouri and Illinois uses an inquiry for an uncharted location as a reason to interview some of her potential hosts sooner, rather than later.

Most reservation services designate coverage in a specific geographical area, usually one where they can travel to meet hosts and personally inspect homes.

Zoning can be an issue, but a most uneven one. Even where there are safety and health regulations to conform to, there may not be any specific bed and breakfast regulations. A few have been written recently in some states or cities and towns. Often the issue is that town fathers—or neighbors—do not understand the concept of B&B. There have been cases where B&B has been officially recognized as a home occupation. Occasionally, restraints, in the form of fees, extensive requirements, or interpretation of the law have made it impossible to establish B&Bs in a community. And then there are situations where the town itself has encouraged the establishment of B&Bs to begin with.

B&Bs throughout the United States, but not necessarily in every destination of the traveler, are available through:

American Historic Homes Bed and Breakfast, page 45
Bed & Breakfast Hospitality, page 66

—and through other services that have decided to network
with each other.

BREAKFAST can be at a set time or ready at an hour agreed upon
the night before. It may be simple or rather elegant. It can be
served in the kitchen with the family or in the dining room by
candlelight; near a fireplace or next to a picture window with
mountain views. Or it may be eat-and-run, depending on your own
plans. Occasionally it is a help-yourself arrangement, particularly
in cities where the hosts work. Many hosts do not join guests unless they are invited. B&B innkeepers have observed that breakfast time is when the magic of the inn happens. Breakfast can be a
time of great camaraderie; if leisurely, it is often the most memorable part of the stay or trip.

A HOST IS the person who greets you and offers hospitality, but
hosts do more than that. Many times—because they welcome
guests as old friends—hosts surprise themselves by doing more
than they ever would have anticipated or agreed to when they
decided to begin hosting. They have been known to offer to drive
someone to a job interview or do laundry for a business guest who
has a sudden change of route.

Hosts are a good source for all sorts of information and local
contacts. Some keep guests' comment books about restaurants and
tourist attractions.

Hosts are just as concerned about "the type of guests" as travelers are about hosts. Hosts depend on their agents who run services to screen guests. Out of thousands of guests to date, there is
not one—or perhaps just one—who would not be welcome again. I
sometimes wonder if that unpleasant one, usually described as a
demanding person, is traveling from B&B to B&B!

Reservation service hosts in private homes host on a part-time
basis. Some look forward to guests as often as possible. Others host
infrequently. The listings change depending on circumstances in
hosts' private lives. Some of the original hosts who started 10 years
ago in Charlottesville, Virginia with Sally Reger's service, Guesthouses, are still with her—and still enthusiastic.

Among hosts are mayors, lawyers, farmers, artists, architects,
tour guides, and community activists. They know (or quickly learn)
how to be sensitive to guests' needs—together with their own.

◇ ◇ ◇

Reservation service hosts are responsible to the service and its requirements of cleanliness, comfort, and cordiality. (Some services have a long list of requirements.) Hosts are visited by reservation services before they are listed. Some service owners arrive as a team of two for an interview with a potential host. A few employ representatives to screen hosts at more distant places. Some take pictures for their own reference files. In small communities, hosts and reservation service owners may be neighbors and friends and see each other frequently. Some services begin by visiting hosts annually, but may reinspect only if there is a (rare) complaint. If there are constant rave reviews for a particular host and home, a revisit may seem unnecessary.

Among the reasons a service might reject a potential host:
- Too few requests for the location.
- Too much emphasis on the potential income. (They may be told to consider a regular boarder.)
- "It's not the kind of place I would want to stay in."
- Too much clutter.

Hosting in a private home usually provides supplementary income. Although many B&B inns are businesses (sometimes seasonal) and the primary source of income for owner-occupants, most private homes registered with reservation services find that the income helps to pay for refurbishing or maintenance, the mortgage or the heating bill. In some locations, guests arrive infrequently. That may change as B&B traveling becomes even more popular. (Still, there will always be homes with hosts who wish to limit the guest nights.) Some reservation services that operate year round report that their busiest hosts in prime locations make far above the average—about $10,000 a year.

Reservation hosts also host as a way to bring the world to their doorstep—at the hosts' convenience. As one New York City host said, "We wouldn't do it without getting paid, but it is not possible to make a living this way. It is a fascinating way to meet people you would not meet otherwise." Friendships are often formed. Ruth Young of Mi Casa–Su Casa in Arizona wrote, "Many of our hosts are invited to their guests' homes."

B&B GUESTS ARE experienced B&B travelers (abroad and/or here); first-timers; tourists; wedding guests; visiting parents of college students; house hunters (75 percent of Helen Denton's business in Tennessee); business men and women—just about anyone who can be at home in someone else's home. B&B guests enjoy the opportunity to have a glimpse at another person's way of life. Guests are often inspired to return home and become hosts themselves.

B&B guests realize that most B&Bs are private homes and do not have desk clerks. Phones are not manned at all times.

B&B guests are prepared to tell the reservation service their place of employment, a driver's license number, perhaps the name of someone to contact in an emergency.

If you have need for standardized accommodations that include unlimited use of the telephone, or if you wish to travel anonymously, to come and go at all hours, to entertain guests, or to have someone at your beck and call, bypass B&B!

TO MAKE A RESERVATION THROUGH A SERVICE: Write or call as much in advance as possible, particularly for high-demand locations or for high season or holiday weekends. Check (in this book) to see if the service takes last-minute reservations.

If you call a service and get a taped message, leave as much information as possible on the tape. Be specific—with dates, destination, price range. "We (who? how many?) are coming to . . ." isn't enough. Say if you have ever traveled B&B before. Give your reason for traveling. Tell a little about yourself (and anyone you are traveling with). Specify your need and preferences about
Location of B&B
Size of bed
Private (off the hall or adjacent to room) or shared bath
Location of room (front, back, up, down)
Parking space
Public transportation
Breakfast
Surroundings (elegant, homey, in-between)
Privacy (physical arrangement of each home varies)
Facilities for children or pets
Air conditioning
Smoking—by residents or guests
Languages spoken
After you have made the reservation, keep the host informed about arrival time and any changes in it.

Confirmations arrive in various forms. Some may be accompanied by a map to the home together with written directions, a map of the area, and even with sightseeing information.

BEYOND THE BASICS, if you have some expectation—or fantasy— about what your B&B will be, let the reservation service know. The experience of Joyce Meiser and Ken Mendis of Bed & Breakfast of Rhode Island is that "Most people want something special at their B&B—whether it is a romantic setting, a historic home, a relaxing getaway, or just a touch of the region."

Are you visualizing a canopied bed with mints on the pillow? Do you want to be able to eat and run? Is your idea of a B&B some place that is clean and comfortable, with reasonable rates? Or pure luxury? Does "country" to you mean genuine (and isolated) rural surroundings or 1980s designer style? Do you hope to meet other guests or wish to be the only one(s)?

Because of all the press attention given to "extras" offered by many hosts, at least one big-city host reports that guests arrive asking about amenities. "My well-located lovely apartment does not feature a pool or evening meals, but I do offer comfortable accommodations and a continental breakfast," she says. It is true that in other locations travelers may have use of a bicycle or canoe, the pool, the patio, or maybe the kitchen or laundry. The use of the living room (at least) is usually available to guests. Whatever, sometimes there are surprises and bonuses; express your expectations and check on what you consider your basic needs or desires.

A PEOPLE-TO-PEOPLE BUSINESS is a time-consuming enterprise with expenses. Those services that personalize matches say that an hour (at least) is a good estimate for time spent on one reservation. That is one of the reasons why some services require a two-night minimum or a one-night surcharge. One-night reservations are rarely profitable for reservation services.

Most reservation services charge each host a membership fee to help with advertising, printing, and office expenses.

Postage and phone charges can be a problem for a service. Good press coverage can produce enough inquiries to result in an impossible postage bill for many services. When guests initially request information by mail, it helps if a business-sized, self-addressed stamped envelope (SASE) is enclosed. There is even a trend to requiring a SASE. An international reply coupon should accompany foreign inquiries. (*Bed and Breakfast Coast to Coast* has all the information of most service brochures—and much more!) Messages on reservation service answering machines usually say how return telephone calls are paid for; they are usually made collect.

DIRECTORIES of listings available through reservation services are seldom required for reservations. (The few that are—mostly in Canada—publish the names, addresses, and phone numbers of hosts so that you make your own reservations directly with the host.)

Directories have evolved to respond to the need of the advance planner who wants to know what the options might be with any particular service. Anne Diamond of Bed and Breakfast Brookline/ Boston reminds guests that if you write for a directory just two weeks in advance, choices will be minimal and confirmation cannot be mailed with confidence. Sometimes your choice is unavailable because the host is already booked or may not be hosting at that time. According to some services, if the traveler has the directory in hand, it is easier to discuss options on the telephone.

Some services that do not publish any directory feel that they could not possibly keep up with the changes that occur in their listings—or they feel that the directory is unnecessary. As with B&Bs themselves, reservation services are not standardized!

Included in *Bed and Breakfast Coast to Coast* are sample directory descriptions so that you have an idea of the extent of information given in any one directory. Formats range from a simple sheet of paper to spiral-bound books with photographs. They may be coded, filled with detail, or quite brief. Directories can be relatively expensive to produce, but depending on the charge (usually a few dollars—see each listing in this book), they may be self-supporting. They can be very helpful. Upon release, they are as up-to-date as possible. There are always changes.

EVALUATIONS: A reservation service appreciates feedback. Although hosts frequently hear from guests, services, too, sometimes receive letters of appreciation. The many services that issue evaluation cards to guests are sincerely soliciting our response. The cards can be as simple as a form to be checked. They are important because they are a good follow-up for the service that is not able to visit hosts regularly or to stay overnight as you have.

"If you like our service, please tell others. If not, please tell us," suggests Kate Peterson of Bed & Breakfast—Rocky Mountains (Colorado).

Services rarely receive criticism, but they aim to please and stand ready to follow up on any such communication.

B&Bs
in the
United States

Alabama

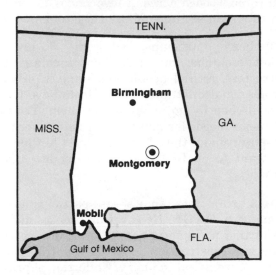

BED & BREAKFAST BIRMINGHAM, INC.

RUTH TAYLOR
P.O. BOX 3138
BIRMINGHAM, AL 35222

PHONE: 205/591-6406
   Live Monday and Wednesday 9:30–5:30. Tuesday, Thursday, Friday, variable hours. Answering machine other times.
OPEN: Year round. ("Hosts in private homes tend to be scarce during traditional holiday seasons.")

ACCOMMODATIONS
B&Bs
Hosted private residences: 50.
Most have air conditioning.   All have private baths.

OTHER SERVICES: Pickup at airport possible if requested in advance.

LOCATIONS   *Most are in Greater Birmingham area. A few listings in smaller cities: Auburn, Cullman, Decatur, Dothan, and Heflin.*

SETTINGS: Range from a cozy remodeled mill-village cottage to a white-and-glass architectural modern prizewinner with sauna and pool sited on three wooded acres. A few condos. Some contemporaries. Some in suburban settings. Many close to downtown.

HOSTS: Symphony musicians, bankers, a lawyer-and-artist couple, market researcher, metals broker, psychiatric and oncology nursing instructors, retired people and some in private business, and one "professional dilettante"! . . . "Hosts have their own lives to live and will cheerily go about living them. They are all very sensitive to guests' needs for privacy and quite talented at offering help and hospitality and then leaving guests to their own devices. People who want to do B&B are generally attentive to others' moods, I think."

GUESTS COME FOR: Art shows—as participants and judges. Sports reasons such as PGA, NCAA. Conferences. Relocation. University of Alabama at Birmingham. Sloss Furnace National Historic Landmark reconstruction of early pig iron furnace, which records history of iron/steel industry. Collection of preserved Victorian and Art Deco buildings. "Business people—including representatives from brokerage and realty investment firms—are discovering that our places can be convenient and modern, not just charming old relics with blackberry jam."

BREAKFAST: "We guarantee only a continental breakfast, though most hosts embellish. Their doing so depends on their time and mood. Guests desiring a full breakfast should request it in advance. Might get Cajun omelet, special waffles, eggs Benedict, fresh-laid eggs with grits, home-baked breads."

RESERVATIONS
Two weeks in advance preferred. If arrangements can be made, will accept last-minute reservations.
Groups: Equipped to handle up to 40, but depends on whether guests must be close together.
Also sometimes available through travel agents.

RATES
$34–$75. A few $80–$150.
One-night surcharge: $5.
Deposit required: First night's lodging fee required or $40.
Cancellation policy: Refunds made less $10 service fee if cancellation is received at least five days before the date of reservation.

Just Like Home

One guest, the husband of a middle-aged couple, noticed that the bathroom door was dragging. He told his hostess that if she would get some screws, he would fix it. And he did.

Ambassador

"In the midst of a growingly sophisticated city culture, Birmingham has managed to hold on to the slower-paced, down-home warmth of the Southern agricultural past. Birmingham is really a highly individualistic town, warm and fun to visit. I probably spend an undue amount of effort to match guests and hosts; I know from evaluations received from B&B guests that it pays off for the city."

—Ruth Taylor

BED & BREAKFAST MOBILE

ANNE WRIGHT AND LYNN ROBERTS
P.O. BOX 66261
MOBILE, AL 36606

PHONE: 205/473-2939
Live after 5 p.m. on weekdays. Answering machine at other times.
OPEN: Year round.

ACCOMMODATIONS
B&Bs
Hosted private residences: 20.
All have air conditioning and private baths.
Plus
One guest cottage available for short-term housing.

LOCATIONS *Mobile, Spanish Fort, and Daphne—all within a 10-mile radius of downtown.*

SETTINGS: Breakfast in bed on a silver service in a home built before the Civil War, or privacy in a guest cottage with its own kitchen. Many historic homes.

GUESTS COME FOR: University of South Alabama, United States
Sports Academy, Mobile College. Mardi Gras in February; azaleas
in March; Mobile Bay, Gulf Shores, and Dauphin Island in summer; Senior Bowl in autumn; hunting and sailing in winter. More:
antebellum homes, Junior Miss pageant, Bellingrath Gardens and
Home, Mobile Greyhound Park, Fairhope, and Point Clear.

BREAKFAST: All serve continental.

RESERVATIONS
Two weeks in advance preferred. If possible, last-minute accepted.
Also available through travel agents.

DIRECTORY: A few pages complete with pictures or sketches. No
charge. *Sample description:*

> Contructed in 1897, the Old Monterey House is built in the
> Queen Anne style and filled with Victorian furnishings.
> There are nine fireplaces in this beautiful old home, and
> the rooms proudly display many collectibles, such as per-
> fume bottles and English redware. The family is in the
> process of finishing the antique toy room. There are two
> bedrooms available: one with double bed and connecting
> bath—$38.50 per night; one with double bed and bath
> down the hall—$35 per night; washer, dryer, and iron
> available for use; continental breakfast included.

RATES
Singles $24–$32. Doubles $28–$40. A few $62–$80.
Weekly and monthly rates are available.
Deposit required: $20.
Cancellation policy: Deposit is refunded less $5 if cancellation is
received within three days of reservation.

How to Talk to an Answering Machine
*"It is very helpful if travelers would leave dates, locations (if
known), and an approximate price of home desired when
leaving a message on our B&B recording machine."*

BED & BREAKFAST MONTGOMERY

HELEN P. MAIER
P.O. BOX 886
MILLBROOK, AL 36054

PHONE: 205/285-5421
  Live almost all the time; answering machine at other times.
OPEN: Year round except Christmas.

ACCOMMODATIONS
B&Bs
Hosted private residences: At least 15.
All have air conditioning and private baths.
Plus
Some hosted short-term housing available for two to three weeks.

LOCATIONS *Montgomery, Prattville, Millbrook—all within a 15-mile radius of the center of Montgomery.*

SETTINGS: Range from an antebellum home on an historical ridge to a farmhouse with a pool to an architecturally significant house right in town.

HOSTS: Most are professionals and include retired schoolteachers, social workers, clergy, doctor. . . .

BREAKFAST: Varies from help-yourself to an elaborate meal.

RESERVATIONS
Advance reservations preferred. If arrangements can be made, will accept last-minute reservations.

RATES
Singles $24–$36. Doubles $28–$48.
Deposit required: $20.
Cancellation policy: Refunds made less $5 service charge if cancellation is received at least three days before expected arrival date.

Less than a half hour's drive from Montgomery is an historical village with a dozen noted homes on the main street. The restoration of that village is Helen's major volunteer interest. Professionally, she has established her B&B service with beautiful homes that are owned and lived in by residents who enjoy meeting travelers.

Alaska

ALASKA BED & BREAKFAST ASSOCIATION

PAT DENNY
526 SEWARD STREET
JUNEAU, AK 99801

PHONE: 907/586-2929
  Monday–Friday 8 a.m.–noon, 5–10 p.m.
OPEN: Year round.

ACCOMMODATIONS
B&Bs
Hosted private residences: 20.

OTHER SERVICES: Sometimes able to pick up at ferry. "We like to accommodate our guests, but we cannot provide full travel agency services such as fishing outings."

LOCATIONS   *All in southeastern Alaska. Locations range from isolated Indian village to a home next door to the State Capitol.*

SETTINGS: Rustic cabins, boats, old miner's home, log cabin included.

HOSTS: Retired public employees, gun shop owner, social workers, health educator, Tlingit Indian woman. . . .

GUESTS COME FOR: Fishing, sightseeing, glaciers, wildlife, mountains, hiking, kayaking. Government business. Conferences.

BREAKFAST: All full. Examples—sourdough babies, shrimp omelet (fresh shrimp), blueberry sourdough hot cakes.

RESERVATIONS
Advance reservations preferred. If arrangements can be made, will accept last-minute reservations.
Also available through travel agents.

DIRECTORY: None available. Inquiries are answered with a brochure that has a map of area covered, a description of service, and a guest reservation form.

RATES
Singles $30–$40. Doubles $35–$50.
Weekly and monthly rates available only in off season (before May 15 and after September 15).
Deposit required: $25.
Cancellation policy: If notice received 24 hours before expected arrival date, deposit returned less $7 handling fee.

> *"Julie and Bob made me feel as if I were at home, and Bob always prepared a delicious breakfast. In addition, they and their son-in-law were very helpful. The son-in-law carried two friends and me to Mendenhall Glacier on Sunday when the buses were not operating, and Bob insisted on driving me to the airport on the morning of my departure for Cordova. During my three weeks in Alaska, I fell in love with your beautiful state and its friendly people."*
>
> *—A guest from Georgia*

ALASKA PRIVATE LODGINGS
SUSAN HANSEN
P.O. BOX 110135 SOUTH STATION
ANCHORAGE, AK 99511

PHONE: 907/345-2222
Live 8:30 a.m.–8:30 p.m. Answering machine at other times.

OPEN: Year round except Thanksgiving, Christmas, January 1, half day on July 4th.

ACCOMMODATIONS
B&Bs
Hosted private residences: 35.
Plus
Some hosted short-term (maximum six months in the winter) housing.

OTHER SERVICES: Car rentals. Pickup at train.

LOCATIONS   *Anchorage, Homer, Kenai, Palmer, Seward, Talkeetna, and Willow. Downtown Anchorage B&Bs are all within walking distance of major attractions. Others are on bus routes or in rural settings that require transportation.*

SETTINGS: Some luxurious, most are a home-away-from-home. All have scenic views.

HOSTS: Attorneys, teachers, antique dealers, art studio proprietor, grocer, college professor, museum staff, a jeweler, computer whiz. . . .

GUESTS COME FOR: "Two thousand square miles filled with history, wilderness, glaciers, fishing and skiing. The visitor can literally raft a wild river (sighting moose, beaver, maybe bear) in the morning and attend the theatre at night. Salmon fishing. Tallest peak (Denali) in North America."

BREAKFAST: About half serve continental; half serve a full meal. Could include Scotch eggs, sour-cream coffee cake, lingonberry (picked locally) muffins, sourdough flapjacks, fresh eggs (gather your own at some places), buttermilk walnut bread, German pancakes.

RESERVATIONS
At least three days in advance preferred. If arrangements can be made, will accept last-minute reservations.
Also available through travel agents.

DIRECTORY: A sampler sent on request (please enclose a self-addressed stamped envelope) that describes some of the B&Bs.
Sample:

Experience bed and breakfast at a Matanuska Valley Farm. We provide simple accommodations here with a friendly family who have farmed and resided in the Valley for more than 30 years. Guests can observe Alaska farming and gardening techniques. There's a lovely lawn for relaxing while enjoying the duck pond and breathtaking view of Pioneer Peak. A small trout stream crosses the acreage. The hostess says if you catch 'em and clean 'em, she'll serve them for your breakfast. A short distance from the farm are the Matanuska Glacier, the University of Alaska Extension Service Experimental Farm (free tours), many great fishing lakes, Hatcher Pass, and Independence Mine. Still another nice excursion from this B&B is a drive to Mt. McKinley Overlook. Full breakfast served. Bath is shared. Other farm meals available at an additional charge. Single $33. Double occupancy $40.

RATES
Singles $30–$50. Doubles $40–$65. A few are higher.
One-night surcharge: $5.
Weekly rates and monthly rates available October through April.
Deposit required: $25 per B&B booked.
Credit cards accepted: MasterCard and VISA.
Cancellation policy: Deposit refunded less $10 service fee if notice received 48 hours before reservation date.

A We-Try-Hard-Tale

"I received a very rushed call from Denali National Park early one afternoon. The caller quickly explained that she and her friend were headed for Anchorage on the train—and that same train was about to pull away from the Park's depot. No time for congeniality: "Just bare-bones bed and breakfast," she said. I hurriedly solicited essential information and guaranteed her a room on their arrival. She screamed that the train was starting to pull out. "We'll meet you at the station," I yelled. "What do you look like?" The reply: "Two ladies. One tall. One short. Both with grey hair." And the phone went dead. I was left with visions of a senior lady sprinting down the tracks after the caboose. We met them that evening. They were delightful guests and their B&B hosts enjoyed them for several nights."

"We specified a private bath as a must and had a most luxurious suite. . . . They are professional without being impersonal. It is like being cared for by your favorite aunt who happens to have a darned good data bank."
—Guests from Whittier, California

STAY WITH A FRIEND
IRENE PETTIGREW
3605 ARCTIC BOULEVARD—BOX 173
ANCHORAGE, AK 99503

PHONE: 907/274-6445
   Monday–Saturday 9–7.
OPEN: Year round. Basic season is June 1–September 15.
   Downtown area homes accept guests year round. (March is a hectic month for the office.)

ACCOMMODATIONS
B&Bs
Hosted private residences: 44.   B&B inns: 4.
Almost all have fireplaces. Some have sauna, jacuzzi, and redwood hot tubs.

OTHER SERVICES: Some hosts will meet guests at point of arrival.

LOCATIONS   *Anchorage, Palmer, Alyeska, around the Kenai Peninsula, and in Nome.*

SETTINGS: The range of possibilities includes homes overlooking bays, some in the mountains, or lodging on a private lake with boat and fishing gear available.

HOSTS: Social worker, artist, realtor, lawyers, nurses, engineers, mining people, many teachers, railroad men, military and home-steaders. . . . (Most homes list with Irene in the spring when their own summer plans are known.)

GUESTS COME FOR: Spectacular scenery—from Mt. McKinley to Valdez or Homer. Calving glaciers, flowering hillsides, unexpected views of bird, sea, and wildlife. "Chance to land a hundred-pound halibut, get a picture of an eagle watching you. Clean, fresh air and long, long days."

BREAKFAST: About 75 percent serve continental. Full breakfast more likely on Sunday when hosts not working; might include Alaskan sausage, smoked salmon, fresh berries if in season or in the gardens, sourdough pancakes.

RESERVATIONS
Advance reservations preferred. Will accept last-minute reservations.

Groups: The maximum number depends on date of arrival and advance notice.

Also available through travel agents.

A special note from Irene: Alaska mail can be slow. In the past, even second or third choices would be gone with a delayed response from guest, so matches of guest to host are now made by Irene on the basis of the guest's request for location, price range, type of bed, and a sense of general compatibility.

DIRECTORY: None published, but inquiries (please enclose a self-addressed stamped envelope) are answered with a Cheechako Guide, a booklet that gives full information about the service and an introduction to Alaska. A few samples of homes may be included in the mailing. *Sample:*

> #G020: Real estate broker enjoys extensive involvement in professional and civic organizations, with a special interest in performing arts. Home layout affords privacy and yet easy conversation with this 23-year resident of Alaska. In one room is double bed. Family room has a queen foldout sofabed. Private bath for guests. Beautiful two-story home located in a fine area, just a few blocks from the Seward Highway with access to downtown within a few minutes. TV and laundry available.

RATES

Singles $29–$49. Doubles $35–$52. Suites $49–$59.

Apartment $52–$62. The higher rates are for peak season.

Family rates available. Prereserved get lower rate for stay of three consecutive nights.

Weekly and monthly rates available.

Deposit required: $25 single, $35 double, or cost of one night's stay.

Credit cards: MasterCard and VISA accepted through service office.

Cancellation policy: All but one night's lodging refunded with 15 days' notice for bookings of three or more nights. For a booking of one night or two consecutive nights, refund made less $10 service charge with 15-day notice; $20 service charge with 15-day notice.

Why All the Questions?

"Guests often ask me why I request so much information from them. It helps us to place them in congenial surroundings to make a vacation truly a memorable and exciting experience."

KETCHIKAN BED & BREAKFAST
SHIRLEY CARLIN AND MARILYN WRIGHT
P.O. BOX 7735
KETCHIKAN, AK 99901

PHONE: 907/225-3860 or 225-9277
   Live 24 hours a day.
OPEN: May 1–September 30.

ACCOMMODATIONS
B&Bs
Hosted private residences: Six.
Two are accessible to handicapped.

OTHER SERVICES: "We pick up and deliver all our guests."

LOCATIONS *Five homes are within walking distance to downtown Ketchikan. One home is eight miles out of town on the beach.*

SETTINGS: All are comfortable "homey" (not fancy) homes.

HOSTS: "We are all homebodies who used to work outside the home."

GUESTS COME FOR: Sightseeing, walking and bus tours, flightseeing. Some are just passing through.

BREAKFAST: Varies according to host. Ranges from hot coffee and rolls to hearty cooked meals.

RESERVATIONS
Advance reservations are preferred, but not mandatory. If arrangements can be made, will accept last-minute reservations.
Also available through travel agents.

RATES
Singles $40. Doubles $45.
Deposit required: $25.

Arizona

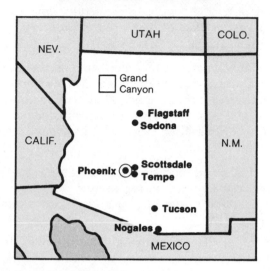

BED AND BREAKFAST IN ARIZONA

BESSIE LIPINSKI
8433 NORTH BLACK CANYON, SUITE 160
PHOENIX, AZ 85021

PHONE: 602/995-2831
   Live: 8–5, Monday–Friday, 8–1 Saturday. Answering machine at other times.
OPEN: Year round.

ACCOMMODATIONS
B&Bs
Hosted private residences: 240.   B&B inns: 12.
All have air conditioning and/or heating depending on location and climate. All have private baths. Homes in Phoenix, Tucson, and Scottsdale have pools.
Many are accessible to handicapped. Some can stable horses.
Plus
Short-term (three to four months) housing with or without breakfast.

OTHER SERVICES: Car rentals. Pickup at airport, bus, or train. Theater tickets. Bus tours. River rafting and boat tours.

LOCATIONS *"Flagstaff, Sedona, Phoenix, Scottsdale, and Tucson are our most popular places so we have more homes in these areas because of need, but listings are statewide."*

SETTINGS: The wide range includes some on the National Register of Historic Places, some luxurious and some that are just clean, attractive homes-away-from-home. They are surrounded by wonderful scenery and are near good restaurants, museums, art and theater centers, universities, rodeos, fair grounds, and national monuments.

HOSTS: Principals and teachers, artists, caterer, violinist, lawyer, antique dealer, realtor, cancer researcher, gourmet cooks, doctor, librarian, author, and a lion hunter and concert violinist who live on a 10-acre ranch. . . .

GUESTS COME FOR: House hunting. A vacation. Colleges and universities. Business and professional reasons. Conferences. The scenery and climate. Museums, art, theaters, rodeos . . . and friendly people.

BREAKFAST: Varies from help-yourself to an elaborate meal. All are full.

RESERVATIONS
Two weeks in advance preferred. If possible, last-minute reservations accepted.
Minimum stay of two nights required.
Groups: Maximum size is 12.

DIRECTORY: Please send a self-addressed stamped envelope if you would like a description of 75 of Bessie's B&Bs. *Samples:*

In Window Rock, on the Indian reservation near New Mexico on way to California or Colorado. Rustic guest cabin. Great hosts. $30 single, $40 double.

In Paradise Valley near Scottsdale: beautiful estate home, terraced gardens, gazebo, rose and herb gardens, large pool, stream, putting green, tennis court. Guest room has private patio, a changing room with kitchen and fountain, privacy. Charm! $90 single, $100 double.

RATES
Singles $25–$90. Doubles $35–$110. Seventh night free.

Deposit required: $25 for single, $35 double, $45 family.
Credit cards accepted: MasterCard, VISA, AMEX.
Cancellation policy: Once booking is confirmed, the deposit is non-refundable.

A Personalized Service

"Our hosts know each other, meet for breakfast periodically, help with B&B teas and open houses, and host Chamber of Commerce functions. They know their area and are a source of information and help for guests."

MI CASA–SU CASA BED AND BREAKFAST
RUTH YOUNG
P.O. BOX 950
TEMPE, AZ 85281

PHONE: 602/990-0682
Live 8 a.m.–8 p.m. daily. Answering machine at other times.
OPEN: Year round.

ACCOMMODATIONS
B&Bs
Hosted private residences: 102.   B&B inns: 10.
"Almost all have air conditioning (and private baths); northern mountain homes don't need air conditioning!"
Plus
Some unhosted private residences for overnight or weekend lodging.
Some short-term (up to two or three months) housing.

OTHER SERVICES: Car rentals. Pickup at airport, bus, and train for a reasonable fee. Theater, concert, and festival tickets.

LOCATIONS   *In Arizona: Flagstaff, Sedona, Prescott, Payson, Show Low, Phoenix, Scottsdale, Tempe, Mesa, Fountain Hills, Chandler, Glendale, Maryvale, Sun City, Sun City West, Tucson, Yuma, Sierra Vista, Nogales, Cochise, Sasabe, Wickenburg.*
In California: San Diego, La Jolla, Catalina Island, and Placerville.
In Utah: St. George.

SETTINGS: Metro patio to luxury homes in scenic areas. Country mini-ranches to large working ranches. Guest house on citrus farm. Mountain getaway near fishing.

HOSTS: Business and professional people: architect, building contractors, phone directories' publisher, large restaurant owner, realtors, computer company officer, executive secretaries, doctors, lawyers, teachers, stained-glass artist, university administrator, systems analyst, engineers, museum director, hunting guide. . . .

GUESTS COME FOR: A vacation and touring—Grand Canyon, national parks, sports events, theater, concerts, art galleries, art and Indian museums, international and ethnic restaurants, snow skiing, water skiing, fishing, surfing, prehistoric cliff dwellings, fine arts and crafts centers and shows, ethnic festivals, world-class zoos, planetariums. Conferences, relocation, and colleges and universities also bring many B&B guests here.

BREAKFAST: Varies from help-yourself to an elaborate meal.

RESERVATIONS
One week in advance requested. If arrangements can be made, will accept last-minute reservations.
Also available through travel agents.

DIRECTORY (not required for reservations): $3. *Sample descriptions:*

> #20–94 Northeast Tucson. Large home decorated with items from world travels. Hostess enjoys cooking. Large breakfasts included in rates. Are members of nearby country club with full sports activity complex, minimal charge for guests, minimal greens fee. Has Olympic-size pool, nine-hole golf course, tennis, racquet ball, nautilus workout room, etc. Are close to Reddington Pass (hiking and falls), Colossal Cave, Saguaro National Monument. Hostess in clothing business (boutique importer), host is civil engineer. No pets in home. Host couple speak English and Tagalog. Children welcome. #1 Queen bed, full bath (adjacent) $40. #2 Smaller room, queen bed, adjacent hall bath $35. #3 Overflow room, double bed, sharing full bath with room #2 $35. Seventh night free.

> #13–131 Tempe. Convenient, attractive home minutes from ASU, Mesa Community College, two large shopping malls, central Mesa, Tempe, Scottsdale. Midway between

Mesa and Tempe Adult Recreation Centers. Trolley access at end of street. Five minutes from Superstition Freeway; close to numerous restaurants and churches. Home has tranquil, pleasant atmosphere with pool and fireplace. Light cooking privileges, nonsmokers preferred. No pets in home. Host is a lawyer and hostess enjoys cooking and making superior bagels. Room #1 King bed, adjacent full bath. Private entrance to pool, outside, through arcadia doors. S/D $45. Room #2 Twin bed. Room #3 Double bed. Rooms #2 and #3 share hall bath. S/D nightly $35.

RATES
Singles $25–$100. Doubles $30–$125.
One-night surcharge: $5.
Weekly and monthly rates available.
Deposit required: $25.
Cancellation policy: Full refund made less $10 service fee if notified at least three days before confirmed arrival date.

What peace, comfort, and luxury. How we wish that more people could be advised of this incomparable bed and breakfast spot. Not a single detail was left to chance; all was exquisitely orchestrated so that Peter and I are leaving— with our work done, with our souls rested and nourished (as well as our bodies)!

—Guests from Maine

B&B: A People-to-People Program

One hostess discovered the lost branch of her family in a visiting guest from the Chicago area. . . . A hostess who was born and raised in Indiana discovered that her best friend in high school was the college roommate in Missouri of her guest. . . . Another hostess had as guests a couple from New Jersey and their parents from Florida. They became very good friends, with guests and hostess taking each other out to dinner. Those two couples have adopted their hostess into their family. They send her cards, gifts, or flowers on special days and have even called her just to talk. . . .

BED & BREAKFAST—SCOTTSDALE
LOIS O'GRADY
P.O. BOX 624
SCOTTSDALE, AZ 85252

PHONE: 602/998-7044
  Usually 7–7, but 7–noon is best, Monday–Saturday.
OPEN: Year round.

ACCOMMODATIONS
B&Bs
Hosted private residences: 12.
All have air conditioning, private baths, and unheated pools. One in Cave Creek is accessible to handicapped.
Plus
Hosted and unhosted short-term housing available for winter season.

OTHER SERVICES: Car rentals. Pickup at airport. Theater tickets.

LOCATIONS   *Most are in the heart of Scottsdale close to everything, within 5- to 10-minute drive to all local points of interest. Others are in Cave Creek, Fountain Hills, Pinnacle Peak, and Paradise Valley.*

SETTINGS: Some are private guest units that are attached suites with private entrance. Others are detached guest cottages. "All are self-contained, different, sometimes slightly offbeat, unique accommodations."

HOSTS: Most are artists or craftsmen, not nine-to-fivers. Many are involved in real estate in some way. Most are native Arizonans or long-time residents. "My hosts are friends. I feel they are an extension of myself."

GUESTS COME FOR: Fifth Avenue shops, art galleries, museums, botanical gardens, zoo, The Borgata, dining, sidewalk cafes, parks, golf. For guests staying more than a week: Old mining towns, red rock country of Sedona, high country towns of Prescott or Payson, are all within a two-hour drive. Water sports on lakes. "Our guest list is not limited, but we do place mostly professional people: doctors, dentists, bankers, vintners, classic auto collectors, and many guests who come to show or purchase Arabians."

BREAKFAST: A help-yourself arrangement (with special treats or baked goods provided) unless specified as a served full breakfast.

RESERVATIONS
Minimum stay of three days required in February and March. Advance reservations preferred. If arrangements can be made, will accept last-minute reservations.
Also available through travel agents.

DIRECTORY: Sent without charge. *Sample:*

Unique, rustic, and comfortable, with the allure of a romantic bygone era. Its 1,200 square feet encompass a living room with a native-stone fireplace, piano, cable TV, and fully equipped kitchen. Floor plan is such that it can be used as a three-bedroom/two-bath or a two-bedroom/one-bath plus private-entrance bedroom with bath. Decorated with antiques and "a touch of country," this guest house sits on two acres at the base of Squaw Peak Mountain Reserve Park. Hiking, golf, shopping, and fine dining are only minutes away in the towns of Paradise Valley, Scottsdale, and Phoenix. Guests have use of the large grassy courtyard for sunbathing. Continental breakfast fixings provided along with special goodies fresh out of the oven. The hosts reside in the main house, formerly an inn. They have restored and refurbished it and are delighted to show guests what they have done. The hostess, a potter, hand made and set all the tile in the kitchens and bathrooms of both buildings. The host has a PhD in music and teaches real estate and investment counseling. Three-bedroom/two-bath $125 per day. Two-bedroom/one-bath $90 per day. Private-entrance bedroom with bath $40. Discount for stay of seven days or more.

RATES
$35–$75. Three-bedroom guest houses are higher.
One-night surcharge: $5.
Some weekly rates available.
Deposit required is 50 percent of total bill.
Cancellation policy: If notice received at least 15 days before arrival, refund made minus one day's deposit.

"The location was ideal for our purposes. Close to all the places we wanted to be. Your map was so perfect, we felt we were residents of long standing. Thanks!!"
　　　　　　　　—Bed & Breakfast—Scottsdale guests

BARBARA'S BED & BREAKFAST

BARBARA POLLARD
P.O. BOX 13603
TUCSON, AZ 85732

PHONE: 602/886-5847
  Monday–Friday, 9–7.
OPEN: Year round.

ACCOMMODATIONS
B&Bs
Hosted private residences: 25. One B&B inn.
Almost all have air conditioning. One is accessible to handicapped.
Plus
Hosted short-term (about a month) housing.

OTHER SERVICES: Possible pickup at airport. Some hosts offer additional meals and guided trips to local points of interest.

LOCATIONS *Homes are in Tucson proper and close to the desert. Some are in outlying towns.*
In California: A few are in Los Angeles and San Diego.

SETTINGS: They range from "nothing pretentious" to foothills elegance and charm. Most fall in the comfortable middle range.

HOSTS: Photographers, teachers, caterer, restaurant owner, retirees. . . .

GUESTS COME FOR: Arizona Sonora Desert Museum, Indian missions, University of Arizona, Pima Community College, golf, the weather, and Nogales, Mexico.

BREAKFAST: Varies from help-yourself to an elaborate meal.

RESERVATIONS
Advance reservations preferred. If necessary, last-minute accepted.

DIRECTORY: Inquiries are answered with a host list (no charge, but please send business-sized self-addressed stamped envelope) that includes a brief description of each home. *Samples:*

> #32—Northwest apartment. Living room with sleeper sofa, dining room, kitchenette, bedroom with double bed. Can accommodate up to five people. Private entrance. $38 double.

#39—North central foothills. Multilevel home with city views. Lots of privacy. King-sized bed with private bath and patio. Queen-sized bed with private bath. Full-sized water bed with private bath. Pool table. Hosts love to entertain. One mile from lovely city park with tennis courts and outdoor swimming pool. $30 single, $40 double.

RATES

Singles $20–$45. Doubles $30–$75.
Weekly and monthly rates available.
Deposit required is 25 percent of total stay.
Cancellation policy: Refunds, less a $5 service charge, made with notice of at least seven days.

Barbara says: "Several people call and ask for 'a typical Arizona home'. There is nothing that we think of as 'typical'. I like all of my homes, so I could easily place someone in any of them, but the main thing is for you to like your accommodations, so tell me what you like."

Arkansas

B&Bs in Eureka Springs and in Pindall are represented by Ozark Mountain Country Bed & Breakfast Service, page 208.

Some others in Arkansas are represented by Louisiana Hospitality Services, page 137.

California

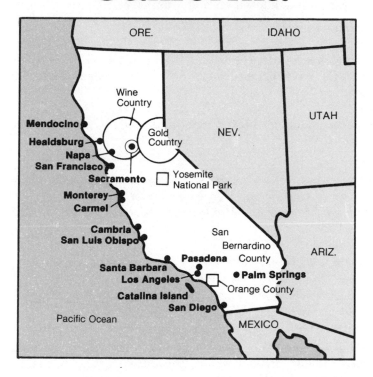

California was the first stronghold of the bed and breakfast concept in America. Although there appears to be wide representation by reservation services, additional services are still being created. Many of the *California-based bed and breakfast reservation services* below will match guests with hosts in more than one area. As much as possible, they are *listed here starting with those that cover the whole state, followed by those that focus on a particular area, going from north to south.*

BED & BREAKFAST INTERNATIONAL

JEAN BROWN
151 ARDMORE ROAD
KENSINGTON, CA, 94707
PHONE: 415/525-4569

Live Monday–Friday 8:30–5, Saturday 8:30–noon. Answering machine at other times.

OPEN: Year round. Closed on major holidays.

ACCOMMODATIONS

B&Bs

Hosted private residences: 300.   B&B inns: 4.

Most B&Bs have private baths. "Where needed" most have air conditioning.

Plus

Short-term housing, hosted and unhosted, available for one to three months.

LOCATIONS   *Most are in San Francisco and the Bay Area. Others in California: Mendocino Coast, Napa Valley, Sierra Nevada Mountains, Monterey Peninsula, Santa Barbara, Los Angeles, Southern California beaches, San Diego, Palm Springs.*

Outside of California: Las Vegas, Seattle, Hawaii, New York City, and Washington, D.C.

And still elsewhere in the United States: Reservations arranged through cooperating agencies.

SETTINGS: Range includes townhouses, estates, houseboats, and historical homes. In California, they are located in city centers, near the ocean, in the mountains, in desert areas, and near wine and gold country.

BREAKFAST: A full breakfast is served by all hosts.

RESERVATIONS

Two weeks in advance preferred. Last-minute reservations can sometimes be made.

Minimum stay requirement: Two nights.

Groups: Maximum size is 10.

Also available through travel agents.

RATES

Single $24–$80. Double $30–$96.

Discounts available for single travelers, families with children, and reservations of more than one week.

Deposit required: $25.

Credit cards accepted: MasterCard, VISA, AMEX, Diners Club. (If for entire fee, 4 percent credit-card charge is added.)

Cancellation policy: Deposit is nonrefundable after reservation has been confirmed.

Should It Be Called "Breakfast And Bed?"

Guests from Kansas City, Missouri wrote: "Recently we dropped off five children and three adults, our children and grandchildren, during a special birthday celebration in San Francisco, at the Wileys'. They absolutely loved the house, sleeping arrangements, and the food. (They almost missed their return flight due to a sumptuous breakfast.)"

Where It All Began

"When we started in January 1978, we were the first to use the magic words 'Bed & Breakfast' for a private home reservation service name. The publicity that we received nationwide started the B&B in the United States."

—Jean Brown

CoHost, America's Bed & Breakfast
COLEEN DAVIS
P.O. BOX 9302
WHITTIER, CA 90608

PHONE: 213/699-8427
Live 6 a.m.–9 p.m. daily. Answering machine at other times.
OPEN: Year round.

ACCOMMODATIONS
B&Bs
Hosted private residences: 100.   B&B inns: 25.
Almost all have air conditioning and private baths. Many have memberships (that can be used with/by guests) in health spas, tennis courts, golf courses, country clubs. Some homes are accessible to handicapped.
Plus
Some unhosted private residences for overnight or weekend lodging. Some short-term (two to three weeks) hosted housing.

OTHER SERVICES: Car rentals. Pickup at airport, bus, train, Theater tickets.

Special attention given to providing accommodations to specific groups such as students who need a home away from home while they are interviewing or looking for a place to live while going to school, and to the elderly, handicapped, or ethnic or religious groups.

Home exchanges arranged between owners in the United States and England.

LOCATIONS *Throughout the state of California in both surburban and urban areas.*

Others throughout the United States and in England are arranged through a cooperative or networking system with other reservation services.

HOSTS: Restauranteurs, professors, teachers, world travelers, artists, photographers, tour guides. . . .

BREAKFAST: Most serve a full breakfast. Specialties might be Danish aebleskiver (similar to a doughnut), Scotch eggs, omelets, johnny cakes, souffles, fondues, parfaits, cheesecake, turnovers, cinnamon rolls, coffee cake. . . .

RESERVATIONS
Two weeks in advance preferred. If arrangements can be made, will accept last-minute reservations.
Minimum stay requirement: Two nights.
Groups: "We are ready to handle wedding parties and other celebrations by placing guests in several area homes."
Also available through travel agents.

DIRECTORY: A sampler of about 20 homes is sent in response to requests that include a business-sized self-addressed stamped envelope. *Sample:*

Whittier: The large patio, with its private entrance, is surrounded by lovely plants. You will enjoy the privacy and the sunny breakfast table here, or you may choose for your breakfast spot the deck overlooking the city. It, too, is secluded and has a spectacular view and exotic plants. The two bedrooms feature extra-long twins in one and a king-sized bed in the other. Each has its own private bath. A gourmet full breakfast awaits your pleasure, and the hostess, a licensed tour director, will assist with your travel plans. Although you are removed from the hustle and bustle of city life, you are less than five minutes from the 605 freeway. Disneyland and Knotts Berry Farm are close, as is the Queen Mary. Beaches, Universal Studios, and Hollywood are just a few minutes away. The luxurious private suite which is yours to enjoy is beautifully decorated and spacious. $35–$55 double.

RATES
Singles $20–$50. Doubles $30–$60. A very few are higher.
One-night surcharge: $10.
Weekly and monthly rates available.
Deposit required: $25.
Cancellation policy: If notice received at least three days before confirmed arrival date, refund minus a $10 service charge is made.

From a South African guest: "The tranquility of the garden and marvelous comfort of home set me up to enjoy the sightseeing—not to mention, of course, the warmth and never-ending help of the host."

CALIFORNIA HOUSEGUESTS INTERNATIONAL, INC.
TRUDI ALEXY
18533 BURBANK BOULEVARD, BOX 190
TARZANA (LOS ANGELES), CA 91356

PHONE: 818/344-7878
Usually live. Answering machine at other times. Best time to call: early morning, before 8.
OPEN: Year round.

ACCOMMODATIONS
B&Bs
Hosted private residences: around 750. B&B inns: 250.
Many have air conditioning, private baths, and pools.
Plus
Some unhosted private residences available for short-term rentals (with host providing maid service).

OTHER SERVICES: Airport, bus, train pickup. Guided tours, babysitting, kitchen privileges, and extra meals.

LOCATIONS *About 100 communities in state are represented.*

SETTINGS: Some "just plain home," many very special, some luxurious estates, a few historic.

HOSTS: Teachers, artists, retirees, single people, many well-traveled professionals who have experienced B&B elsewhere. . . .

BREAKFAST: Most serve a continental breakfast. Often includes homemade breads, jams, or even quiche, cheese, fruit, and always a fresh flower.

RESERVATIONS
Minimum stay of two nights required.
Advance notice preferred. If arrangements can be made, will accept last-minute reservations.
Groups: Maximum size is 50.
Also available through travel agents.

RATES
Membership fee: $5 for one year.
Singles $30–$80. Doubles: $35–$85. A few are higher.
One-night surcharge: $20.
Weekly and monthly rates available.
Deposit required: $25.
Cancellation: All but deposit and membership fee refunded if notice received seven days before reservation date.

How Did Your List Get So Big, Trudi?

Many of our newer hosts found out about B&B during the Olympics and then elected to stay on because they love the concept and enjoy meeting new friends.

Have You Any Special Needs?

A guest asked us to recommend a romantic B&B to get her boyfriend to propose. She called next day to let us know it worked! (They are now married.)

EYE OPENERS BED & BREAKFAST RESERVATIONS
RUTH JUDKINS AND BETTY COX
P.O. BOX 694
ALTADENA, CA 91001

PHONE: 213/684-4428 or 818/797-2055
  Monday–Saturday 9–6.
OPEN: Year round.

ACCOMMODATIONS
B&Bs
Hosted private residences: 80. B&B inns: 20.
About half have private baths. Many have air conditioning and several have pools and hot tubs.
Plus
Two unhosted private residences available for overnight or weekend lodging.

OTHER SERVICES: Pickup at local bus stops from airport, bus, and train. Tour assistance.

LOCATIONS *All in California from San Diego to San Francisco.*

HOSTS: School principal, yoga teacher, school teachers, industrial designer, secretaries, university professor, small business owners, ministers, and veterinarian. . . .

BREAKFAST: Varies from help-yourself to an elaborate meal.

RESERVATIONS
Two weeks in advance preferred. If arrangements can be made, will accept last-minute reservations.

DIRECTORY: Two or three descriptions mailed or phoned after Eye Openers assesses requirements of guest.

RATES
Guest membership fee of $5 is a one-time fee.
Singles $30–$55. Double $35–$60.
Some weekly and monthly rates available.
Deposit required: $25.
Credit cards accepted: MasterCard and VISA (with slight surcharge) for entire fee only.
Cancellation policy: If notice received seven days before expected arrival date, refund minus a $10 bookkeeping charge is made.

The Happy Guest Department

"We liked the response of the newspaper reporter covering the Rose Bowl game. He was especially pleased with his lovely and spacious accommodations at $60, and was overwhelmed by our successful follow-up on his request for finding a local marathon."

"We are still receiving letters and phone calls from an Italian student who found his first visit to the U.S. a wonderful experience. His original two-night reservation extended to five. He later returned for another B&B stay, and recommended us to three other students we placed while they were involved in market research studies."

CHRISTIAN BED & BREAKFAST OF AMERICA

DEBORAH SAKACH
BOX 388
SAN JUAN CAPISTRANO, CA 92693

PHONE: 714/496-7050
Live Monday–Friday 9–5. Answering machine at other times.
OPEN: Year round except for last two weeks of December.

ACCOMMODATIONS
B&Bs
Hosted private residences: 350. B&B inns: 25.
Plus
Some hosted and unhosted short-term (up to three months) housing. A few homes are accessible to handicapped.

LOCATIONS *Predominantly in California, but others are throughout the United States (a few in most states). Some in Bolivia, England, France, Germany, and in Amsterdam, Netherlands.*

SETTINGS: Range from the home of a lobsterman on the coast of Maine to an oceanfront guest room in a mansion on the coast of California.

HOSTS: "Because of the distances involved, we have them screened by other hosts or local reservation services." Full range of occupations represented.

RESERVATIONS
Three weeks in advance preferred. If arrangements can be made, will accept last-minute reservations.
Groups: Some conference centers can book 100.

DIRECTORY: A few sample descriptions of listings and a full list of nationwide locations is sent in answer to all inquiries. Please enclose a business-sized self-addressed stamped envelope. *Samples:*

California, Napa: Queen Anne Victorian on the National Register has eight guest rooms, many with private baths. The tower suites are especially romantic. Full breakfasts. $48 and up for two.

Washington, D.C. Charming. On woodsy two acres just 30 minutes from downtown D.C. and 45 minutes to Annapolis. This home has a piano, swimming pool, and patio graced with a fountain. Wood floors and elevators are suitable for the handicapped. $25 double.

RATES
Singles $15–$50. Doubles $20–$75.
Some weekly and monthly rates available.
Deposit required: $25.
Cancellation policy: Refund made if notice given at least five days before expected arrival date.

MEGAN'S FRIENDS
BILL AND FREDA MURPHY
1768 ROYAL WAY
SAN LUIS OBISPO, CA 93401

PHONE: 805/544-4406
Live 3:30–8:30 p.m. on school days. Non-school days, 7:30 a.m.–6 p.m. Answering machine at other times.
OPEN: Year round.

ACCOMMODATIONS
B&Bs
Hosted private residences: 14.
All have private baths.

LOCATIONS *Spread throughout the state in rural, subur-
ban, and urban areas. Bookings made in Carmel, King
City, Cambria, Los Osos, San Luis Obispo, Shell Beach,
Solvang, Glendora, and Pleasanton. (Referrals are made to
B&Bs in Santa Barbara, Orosi, San Diego, Angwin,
Pebble Beach, Laguna, Niguel, El Cajon, Incline Village,
La Palma, Rancho Palos Verdes, San Francisco, and Los
Angeles in California. Referrals also made to B&Bs and
reservation services in other states including Hawaii, Ari-
zona, and Washington.)*

SETTINGS: Most are attractive homes-away-from-home. One is
very elegant. One is an Austrian decorated guest house. Among
the referrals is a houseboat in Sausalito.

HOSTS: Physicist, college teachers, banker, realtors, electronics
and office workers, retired Austrian castle curator, teachers, nurse,
parks and beaches director, and railroad worker. Many are world
travelers. Some are Dutch, German, English, Chinese. . . .

BREAKFAST: Varies from help-yourself to an elaborate meal. All
are full and could include eggs Benedict, Dutch babies (oven pancakes with berries), Holland waffles, scrambled eggs and ham,
scrambled eggs with cheese, bran muffins, or apricot nut bread.

RESERVATIONS
Advance reservations preferred. If arrangements can be made, will
accept last-minute reservations.
Also available through travel agents.

DIRECTORY: Answers to inquiries include two pages of descriptions. *Sample:*

Los Osos Area. Coastal, small town 12 miles west of San
Luis Obispo. Hillside house in prestige neighborhood, stunning view of valley, mountains, bay, and ocean. Two miles
from sand dunes and Montana de Oro State Park. European
grace extends to the welcoming entry lined with flower baskets against a woodsy background. Meticulous Dutch house-
keeping and hospitality. Upstairs, queen or twin bedroom.
$45 for two. Downstairs, family suite with king bed, shower
bath, color TV, glass doors to patio. $45 for two. $35 for one.
Child in sleeping bag, own sheet (downstairs only) $10.

RATES
Membership fee (one-time payment): $10.
Singles $30–$50. Doubles $35–$50. A few are higher.
Weekly and monthly rates available.
Deposit required is 20 percent of each night's stay.
Cancellation policy: No refunds given on membership fee or deposit. If cancellation is at least two days before expected arrival date, deposit can be applied to a new reservation if made within 30 days.

AMERICAN HISTORIC HOMES BED AND BREAKFAST
SUE DUGGAN AND DEBORAH SAKACH
P.O. BOX 336
DANA POINT, CA 92629

PHONE: 714/496-6953
Monday–Friday, 9–5.
OPEN: Year round. Closed for the last two weeks in December.

ACCOMMODATIONS
B&Bs
Hosted private residences: 350.   B&B inns: 350.
Plus
Some homes are available, hosted or unhosted, for short-term (up to two or three months) housing.

OTHER SERVICES: "In California, we help plan California tours up and down the coast, in gold country and in wine country, using bed and breakfast stays all along the way. Tours may also be arranged in some other areas of the country, including Boston, Massachusetts, and in the state of Louisiana."

LOCATIONS *All over America in country houses, farmhouses, oceanfront estates, in cities and in resort areas too. "All are considered historically significant by their communities, including Washington, D.C.; Orlando, Florida; Boston, Massachusetts; Atlanta, Georgia; Los Angeles and San Francisco in California; and Seattle, Washington. Where we do not have a B&B, we make referrals to other reservation services and information centers."*

HOSTS: Mayor, university administrator, pediatrician, city planner, nursing administrator, geologist, psychologist, professor, airline pilot, theater director, orthopedic surgeon, dentists, teachers, secretaries, and "Moms" and Grandmas and Grandpas. . . .

BREAKFAST: Varies from help-yourself to an elaborate meal.

RESERVATIONS

Advance reservations preferred. Resort and vacation destinations in popular areas should be arranged 8–12 weeks ahead for best choice. If possible, last-minute reservations will be made.

Minimum stay required: Two-night minimum if guests are staying on a Saturday night during peak seasons.

Groups: Depending on location, arrangements can be made for 8–45 people.

Also available through travel agents.

RATES

Singles $20–$95. Doubles $25–$165. A few higher.

Some weekly and monthly rates available.

Deposit required: First night's lodging fee.

Cancellation policy: If cancellation is received five days before expected arrival date, a complete refund is made.

Hints for the Traveler

"Be sure to inquire whether the bed and breakfast you are booking is an inn (with three or more guest rooms) or a private homestay. Some folks envision a romantic inn where they might meet other couples at breakfast, but the accommodation we are describing may be a homestay with only one guest room. Other travelers really want to stay with a family, get to know the hosts, and talk about the area and do not want an inn. Many travelers enjoy either type of stay as long as the location or price is right.

"Because most of our hosts are not desk clerks manning the phone all day, and many do not have answering machines, it sometimes takes us several calls before we get through to them, but our guests find that the extra time it may take to book a bed and breakfast well worth while!"

BED & BREAKFAST HOMES AWAY FROM HOME—WEST COAST

DIANE KNIGHT
P.O. BOX 591
CUPERTINO, CA 95015

PHONE: 408/996-0668
Live most of the time. Answering machine at other times.

ACCOMMODATIONS
B&Bs
Hosted private residences: 173. B&B inns: 10, all small and owner-occupied.

OTHER SERVICES: Some hosts pick up at transportation points. Some obtain theater tickets.

LOCATIONS *Spread throughout California, Oregon, and Washington.*
In Nevada: Genoa.
In British Columbia: In Nanaimo, Surrey, Vancouver.

SETTINGS: Urban, suburban, and rural. On the ocean, among vineyards, in the heart of cities, and in historic houses in gold rush towns.

HOSTS: Journalist, dentist, artist, teacher, magician, veterinarian, educators, park ranger, rancher, executive, small business owner. . . .

BREAKFAST: Varies according to host. Diane says that her most memorable one was in Los Angeles: fresh-squeezed orange juice, fresh strawberries with cream, Scotch eggs with creamy mild-flavored mustard sauce, and old-fashioned bread pudding accompanied by plenty of rich, almond-flavored coffee.

RESERVATIONS
Booked directly with host by guest.
Some hosts accept last-minute reservations.

DIRECTORY: $8.95. Each full-page description includes a sketch of the home. Diane visits every place. She features reasonably priced small B&Bs that are allowed to set their own rates; her selection, however, is based in part on her opinion about just how the specified rate matches the home. Cleanliness and friendliness, of course, count too. Almost half of the (member) listings are exclusive with Diane.

RATES

Singles $20–$50. Doubles $30–$60. A few are higher.

> *Guests wrote: "We stayed in Lake Tahoe on our honeymoon. . . . Our car broke down and had to be repaired. . . . Walt Genest let us use his. . . . He served the best breakfast. . . .*

HOSPITALITY PLUS

DEBORAH SAKACH, TAMMY CANTU

P.O. BOX 388

SAN JUAN CAPISTRANO, CA 92693

PHONE: 714/496-7050
   Monday–Friday 9–5. Toll free for California only:
   1-800-CAL-INNS.
OPEN: Year round. Closed last two weeks of December.

ACCOMMODATIONS

Listings: 454. Included are hosted private residences, B&B inns, hotels, and motels. Almost all B&Bs have private baths.
Plus
Some unhosted private residences are available for overnight or weekend lodging.
Short-term housing available includes many oceanfront summer rentals in Laguna, Newport, and Malibu and cottages near the beach for senior citizens during the winter months.
B&B examples
In Capistrano Beach between Los Angeles and San Diego, a classic Spanish house built in 1929 stands on a bluff overlooking Dana Point. Full breakfast, ocean views, jacuzzi, and pool. $65 for two with private bath. . . . In San Diego next to Balboa Park and close to fine restaurants and theater is a friendly little B&B with brass and antique beds and down quilts. Wine, cheese, and crackers served in the evening. Full breakfasts on weekends; continental on weekdays. Hostess has a law degree but prefers running her bed and breakfast. $40 and up for two, depending on room choice.

LOCATIONS *All over California in 80 communities. Disneyland area, beach locations, wine country, gold country, Yosemite area, in cities including San Francisco, Los Angeles, and San Diego.*

HOSTS: A French chef, magician at the Magic Castle in Hollywood, Emmy-award winning screen writer, novelist. . . .

BREAKFAST: Varies from help-yourself to an elaborate meal according to host.

RESERVATIONS
Three weeks in advance preferred. "We do our best to accommodate last-minute calls."
Minimum stay required: Two nights on summer weekends.
Groups: Maximum size is 60.
Also available through travel agencies.

RATES
Singles $20–$90. Doubles $30–$95. A few higher.
Cancellation policy: Five-day notice required for a full refund.

A Service Is More than a Booking Agent

"It is helpful to know why a guest is traveling, e.g. business trip but wants to meet locals, sunning on the beach, seeing the sights, wish to meet people knowledgeable about history of the area, so that we are able to make a match in selecting accommodations for the guest."

ACCOMMODATION REFERRAL
YOUNTVILLE, CA 94599

PHONE: 707/944-8891
    Live 7 a.m.–9 p.m. daily.
OPEN: Year round except Christmas Eve and Christmas Day.

ACCOMMODATIONS
B&Bs
Hosted private residences: About 25.   B&B inns: 85. Almost all have air conditioning. Some are accessible to handicapped.

Plus
Some unhosted private residences for overnight or weekend lodging also available.
Some resorts, golf clubs, and hotels.

LOCATIONS *All are in the heart of Napa Valley wine country, where there are 30 miles of vineyards and 40 wineries. Located one hour north of San Francisco.*

SETTINGS: Creek sides, near Napa River, surrounded by vineyards and old stone wineries.

HOSTS: College president, architect, accountant. . . .

BREAKFAST: All serve continental.

RESERVATIONS
Advance reservations preferred.
Groups can be accommodated. (Some places can provide meeting rooms.)
Also available through travel agents.
Because of the variety of types of accommodations available through this telephone service, they strongly suggest that you call knowing exactly what you want. "Be specific," they say. "When you call with dates and amenities desired, specify a rate range." Example: "We wish to lodge nearby several wineries on May 17 and 18. Two people in our party. Would like to stay within the $50–$80 price range per night and prefer a room in a B&B with a private bath and a jacuzzi."
Or: "Party of three needs July 4, 5, and 6 with a first-class lodging in a resort setting with tennis courts. A suite needed for extra bedroom for a four-year-old. Also needed: Baby-sitting service, TV, and phone."
As a caller, you are put through to a lodging facility during the one call. There is no charge to the traveler for this service.

RATES: $35–$400.

THE BED AND BREAKFAST EXCHANGE
NANCY JENKINS AND CAROLYN STANLEY
P.O. BOX 88
ST. HELENA, CA 94574

PHONE: 707/963-7756
Monday–Saturday, 9–5.
OPEN: Year round. Closed major holidays.

ACCOMMODATIONS
B&Bs
Hosted private residences: 61.   B&B inns: 32.
Some have air conditioning. Most have private baths. Some are
accessible to handicapped.
Plus
Some unhosted private residences for overnight or weekend lodging.
Some unhosted short-term (up to several months) lodging available.

OTHER SERVICES: Arrangements can be made for pickup at airport, wine tours, and balloon rides.

LOCATIONS   *Almost all (98 percent) are in California Napa
and Sonoma Valleys, in the country but within 5–10 minutes of center city. Communities with accommodations: Cal-
istoga, St. Helena, Yountville, Rutherford, Oakville, Napa,
Sonoma, Healdsburg as well as Bodega Bay, Santa Rosa,
Sausalito, Lake Tahoe.*

SETTINGS: Most are luxurious. Very few are "just plain." The
innkeepers have given special attention to decor; several are historic sites.

HOSTS: Internationally known restaurant owner, winemaker,
physical therapist, former mayor, artist, realtor, grape grower, attorney, photographer, entrepreneur, physician, teacher, accountant, pilot, antique shop owner. . . .

BREAKFAST: Varies. Most are continental but some could include
Belgian waffles with fresh whipped cream and strawberries, or
Danish aebleskiver with homemade jam, flavored with cardamom.

RESERVATIONS
Some hosts have a two-night minimum. Advance reservations
strongly advised, one to two weeks off season and four to six weeks
in season. Twenty-five to 30 percent of inns listed require a two-
night minimum during the peak season of March–October.
Last-minute reservations accepted.
Equipped to handle groups.

DIRECTORY: "In planning stages."

RATES

Singles $60–$85. Doubles $40–$180. A few higher, up to $310. Quoted inn rates are the same as what inns charge direct bookings. Some weekly and monthly rates available.

Deposit required: First night's lodging.

Credit cards: Some accepted by some inns.

Cancellation policy: Usually a 48-hour notice required for full refund.

Who Runs the Show?

"We have a very homey, personal business that started with one private home, and soon friends suggested friends as hosts. Both of us know the hosts from multiple personal visits. The Valley is small, and we are likely to drop by and chat with an innkeeper on our way home from work. Since our innkeepers call in their bookings daily, we have learned first hand the joys and sorrows of innkeeping. This keeps us sympathetic and very well informed. Travelers might be surprised to know how much time, effort, and thought go into the management of a bed and breakfast inn. We are convinced that we could never handle it, and we both lead rather hectic lives ourselves. Rates are agonized over, breakfasts lovingly prepared (we are amazed at how many innkeepers would not think of serving the same fare two days in a row!), and room decor is reviewed with a critical eye. Guests are gone after and retrieved when lost. I drove by once to visit and found one of our innkeepers patrolling her street at dusk, worried her guests couldn't find her. These are warm, lovely people with lots of energy; few hotels could offer this kind of talent and quality."

AMERICAN FAMILY INN/BED & BREAKFAST SAN FRANCISCO

SUSAN AND RICHARD KREIBICH

P.O. BOX 349

SAN FRANCISCO, CA 94101

PHONE: 415/931-3083
   Monday–Friday 9–5.
OPEN: Year round.

ACCOMMODATIONS
B&Bs
Hosted private residences: 98.   B&B inns: 2.
About half have private baths. One in Monterey and one in San Francisco are accessible to handicapped.
Plus
Some unhosted private residences for overnight or weekend lodging. Short-term housing, hosted and unhosted.

OTHER SERVICES: Car rentals; pickup at bus; theater tickets; sightseeing arrangements; and recommendations by "experts in San Francisco restaurants."

LOCATIONS   *Almost all are centrally located in San Francisco. Others are in the wine country, in Monterey/Carmel, the gold country, and Hollywood.*

SETTINGS: Romantic Victorians, country cottages, homes with views, with access to the area's famous cable cars, Chinatown, Union Square, and Fisherman's Wharf.

HOSTS: Professional French chef, doctors, lawyers, opera singer, retired professional ice skaters. . . .

BREAKFAST: Full breakfast is always served.

RESERVATIONS
Advance reservations preferred. If arrangements can be made, will accept last-minute reservations.
Groups: Maximum number is eight at any one location but more can be booked into a neighborhood.
Also available through travel agents.

RATES
Singles $40–$75. Doubles $50–$85. Yachts $100 per night and up.
One-night surcharge: $5.
Monthly rates available.
Deposit required: One night's lodging or credit card number.
Credit cards accepted: AMEX, VISA, and MasterCard.
Cancellation policy: One night's lodging fee charged. If enough advance notice given, refund minus $10 service fee is made.

UNIVERSITY BEDS & BREAKFASTS

JOHN AND ALICE MICKLEWRIGHT
1387 SIXTH AVENUE
SAN FRANCISCO, CA 94122

PHONE: 415/661-8940 or 753-3474
Live 9–5 weekdays. Answering machine at other times.
OPEN: Year round.

ACCOMMODATIONS
B&Bs
Hosted private residences: 10.
A couple are accessible to handicapped.
Plus
Some unhosted private residences for overnight or weekend lodging.
Some hosted and unhosted short-term (up to several months) housing available.

LOCATIONS *"Most of our homes are near University of California Medical Center/Golden Gate Park. They all offer easy access to all San Francisco attractions."* University Beds & Breakfasts was created because accommodations are difficult to find in the Medical Center area of San Francisco. The Micklewrights were hosts for more than a year before they took over the service.

HOSTS: Social work professor, teacher, writer, doctor, translator, nurse. . . .

GUESTS COME FOR: "Our small agency caters primarily to the U.C. Medical Center. Our guests include many doctors and relatives of patients at U.C., as well as those just enjoying the sights of the city."

BREAKFAST: All serve continental.

RESERVATIONS
Advance preferred. If possible, last-minute reservations made.
Also available through travel agents.

DIRECTORY: None available. Inquiries are answered with information about the service, approximate cab fares, and some details about other transportation available.

RATES
Singles $35–$65. Doubles $45–$85. Seventh night free in winter.
Monthly rates available.

RENT A ROOM
ESTHER MACLACHLAN
11531 VARNA STREET
GARDEN GROVE, CA 92640

PHONE: 714/638-1406
   Live 8 a.m.–10 p.m. daily.
OPEN: Year round.

ACCOMMODATIONS
B&Bs
Hosted private residences: 50.

OTHER SERVICES: Pickup at bus.

LOCATIONS   *Los Angeles to San Diego. Many along the coast. Many in the Anaheim-Disneyland area.*

SETTINGS: At the top of the Laguna hills with magnificent views of Catalina and the Pacific . . . on a quaint lane in the heart of Brentwood, convenient to Santa Monica, UCLA, or Westwood . . . on quaint Balboa Island in Newport Bay . . . five minutes to Sea World in San Diego.

HOSTS: Clergyman, engineer, teachers, retired businessmen, journalists, self-employed manufacturers. . . .

RESERVATIONS
Minimum stay of three nights required.
Advance reservations preferred but will accept last-minute reservations.
Also sometimes available through travel agents.

BREAKFAST: Varies from simple to elaborate.

RATES
Singles $25–$40. Doubles $30–$55. A few are higher.
Deposit required: $30.
Cancellation policy: One half of deposit charged if cancellation received one week or less before arrival date.

The Matchmaking Service of a Reservation Service

"A girl from the South of France carried on a long correspondence before coming in the summer of 1983. Since returning home, she has continued to write, call, and send

*lovely gifts and refers to her hostess as her American
mother. She has arranged to come again this summer and
will stay nearly two weeks. She remembers everything about
her original visit and looks forward to meeting all her hostess's friends again. To me, this is the bonus of B&B."*

WINE COUNTRY BED & BREAKFAST

HELGA POULSEN
P.O. BOX 3211
SANTA ROSA, CA 95403

PHONE: 707/578-1661
Live Monday–Friday 10–6. Answering machine at other times.
OPEN: Variable season. If closed, announced on tape.

ACCOMMODATIONS
B&Bs
Hosted private residences: 15.   B&B inns: 3.
Almost all have air conditioning and private baths. Some have
pools or hot tubs.

OTHER SERVICES: Restaurant reservations. Mud bath reservations. Arrangements for hot-air balloon rides. "We have even
helped a client find a musical instrument."

LOCATIONS *All are in Northern California within a
35-mile radius of Santa Rosa in Santa Rosa, Healdsburg,
Sebastopol, Sonoma, St. Helena, and Occidental. The inns
are in Sonoma, Napa Valley, and Santa Rosa. (Note that
public transportation in these areas is minimal; car travel is
a necessity.)*

SETTINGS: Some are in towns; others are out in the country.

HOSTS: Teachers, doctor, insurance agent, accountant, several
retirees, some Europeans who have chosen this area as home. . . .

RESERVATIONS
Advance reservations preferred. If arrangements can be made, will
accept last-minute reservations.
Also available through travel agents.

BREAKFAST: All full and may include an assortment of egg dishes, fresh-baked muffins or breads, or fresh fruits; each host has their own specialties.

DIRECTORY: None available, but inquiries are answered with a couple of described B&Bs. *Sample:*

> A country home on several acres completely surrounded by vineyards. Nice bedroom with double bed and private bath plus private entrance. They have a pool that guests may use. There are several wineries just up the road; some are open to the public. Good country breakfast, often with their own fresh eggs and home-grown fruit. $50 per night for two, including breakfast.

RATES

Singles $40–$50. Doubles $45–$65.

Inns tend to be higher than private homes. One Napa Valley inn's top rate is $125.

Deposit required: First night's lodging fee.

Credit cards accepted by inns only.

Cancellation policy: Seven days' notice prior to arrival for a refund of deposit less $10 processing fee.

Parents Enjoy a Home-Away-from-Home Too

Guests wrote: "Enjoyed staying with you in your lovely home—we feel that we have made new friends. We were happy to see our daughter settled into college and the next time we visit her, would like to stay with you again."

BayHosts

DON STANKE
1155 Bosworth Street
SAN FRANCISCO, CA 94131

PHONE: 415/334-7262

Live Monday–Friday 5:30–10. Answering service at other times.

SEASON: Year round except Thanksgiving and Christmas.

ACCOMMODATIONS

B&Bs

Hosted private residences: 70.

Most have private baths.

Plus
Some short-term (up to 30 days) hosted housing.

OTHER SERVICES: Pickup at airport or station. Theater tickets. Discount tickets when available.

LOCATIONS   *In California—many districts of San Francisco, Berkeley and Sausalito, Los Angeles, and San Diego. In Arizona: Phoenix. Also on the islands of Maui and Hawaii (big island).*

SETTINGS: Homes, condos, apartments, flats, yachts and floating homes. They range from the modest to the luxurious.

HOSTS: Architects, doctors, dentists, real estate brokers, professors, barbers, tour guides, civil rights activists (nonradical), photographers. . . .

BREAKFAST: All serve continental.

RESERVATIONS
Advance reservations required. Written reservations strongly preferred. Five to 10 days for California cities. Thirty days for Phoenix and Hawaii.

DIRECTORY: A sheet of descriptions is sent on request. *Samples:*

#222 Richard, David: Walk to Castro. Quiet street off 17th. 2 rms avail. 1 at back of huge flat faces yd, queen bed; 1 at front has queen sofabed. No smoking. Have cat. Tours available. Ask.

#051 Sarah: Haight Distr. 1892 Victorian home. 3 rms. avail. Can sleep 5. Queen and 3 twin beds. A cat and dog. Does not smoke.

RATES
Singles $26–$39. Doubles $33–$46.
Deposit required: $5–$9 per night depending on occupancy choice.
Cancellation policy: Deposit refunded less 20 percent.

"We are a gay/lesbian reservation service (nongays are welcome guests too) that started in 1981 in San Francisco before expanding to other areas. Current expansion plans include several cities including Washington, D.C."

BED & BREAKFAST HOMESTAY

ALEX LAPUTZ
P.O. BOX 326
CAMBRIA, CA 93428

PHONE: 805/927-4613
  Daily 7:30 a.m.–10:30 p.m. Toll free in California:
  1-800-44ROOMS
OPEN: Year round.

ACCOMMODATIONS
B&Bs
Hosted private residences: 40.
Referrals (not bookings) made to 10 B&B inns.
(A B&B inn in Cambria is accessible to handicapped.)
Plus
Short-term hosted housing.
Tourist homes with no breakfast or kitchen.
Vacation homes with kitchen.

OTHER SERVICES: Some hosts pick up at airport. Tickets for
Hearst Castle and Monterey Aquarium.
Requests filled (please send a self-addressed stamped envelope) for
tourist information about Cambria's history, points of interest and
special events in a specific area. Alex also offers his own information sheet, complete with hints for activities, what not to miss, and
where to eat, for a scenic day trip from Pt. Lobos to Hearst Castle.

LOCATIONS *Monterey, Carmel, Pebble Beach, Pacific
Grove. Most are within 10-mile radius of city center. A few
are in urban areas. Some are near public transportation;
others are in suburban communities. Some have ocean
views.*
*In Cambria, San Simeon, Morro Bay, San Luis Obispo,
Pismo Beach, the listings range from oceanfront to hillside
secluded cottages. Most are within two- to three-mile radius
of city center, some with public transportation.*
*In Santa Barbara, Montecito, Carpenteria, most are within
10–15 miles from city center. Some are close to public
transportation, some have ocean or valley views.*

HOSTS: Wine merchant, real estate broker, retired deputy sheriff,
electrologist, retired school teachers, school administrators. . . .

59

BREAKFAST: Varies from simple to elaborate. Could include souffles, waffles, omelets, eggs Benedict, croissants.

RESERVATIONS

Reservations accepted no more than 90 days in advance. If possible, last-minute reservations may be accommodated.

Minimum stay: Some hosts require more than one night during holidays and in July, August, and September.

Groups: Maximum size is 20.

Also available through travel agents.

DIRECTORY: None available, but the following could be a sample description sent in answer to inquiries:

B&B1. Cambria. High on the side of Happy Hill, secluded in the Monterey pines with an expansive view of the Pacific, one can relax in the private hot tub while observing the surfers, shell, and rock collectors on Moonstone Beach, or watch the formations of birds or migrating whales. Make yourself at home in the quaintly decorated apartment with your own private entrance, bedroom with queen bed, living room/dining room with color TV and video player, fireplace, outside deck, full kitchen, large bath with tub/shower. How about a menu? Select your gourmet breakfast, prepared upstairs by your hosts and served to you whenever you are ready. The best of two worlds—a quality B&B home *and* a secluded vacation home. A delight for special occasions. On a scale of 0–5, this B&B scores a solid 10!

RATES

B&Bs—Singles $30–$65. Doubles $40–$70. Some give a discount for two or more nights.

Vacation homes—Singles $45–100. Doubles $60–100. Add $5 per each additional person.

Weekend, weekly, and monthly rates available.

Deposit required: Thirty to 90 days prior—50 percent. Balance due 30 days prior to stay. Reservations made less than 30 days before arrival date: full prepayment.

Credit cards accepted: MasterCard and VISA.

Cancellation policy: Within 31–89 days, half of deposit forfeited. Within 15–30 days, half of payment refundable. Within 14 days of reserved dates, no refund unless unit rerented.

More than B&Bs Here

Because Alex offers a wide variety of accommodations, including other than B&Bs, he is often called upon to find

housing for vacationers who have not made advance ar-
rangements. He writes, "My greatest thrill is finding just
one more accommodation. When all motels are booked
within a two- to three-hour drive of Cambria, I begin to get
heavy overflow. When I am 'full', it is time to go back over
the lists of hosts, would-be hosts, possibles, sometimes avail-
ables, and even the rarely availables."

As much as possible, California-based reservation services
are listed with those that cover the whole state at the begin-
ning, followed by services that focus on a particular area,
going from north to south.

BED AND BREAKFAST APPROVED HOSTS
CLARA HUTTON
10890 GALVIN
VENTURA, CA 93004

PHONE: 805/647-0651
  Monday–Friday, 8 a.m.–noon, 6–9 p.m.
OPEN: November 1–September 1.

ACCOMMODATIONS
B&Bs
Hosted private residences: Eight. B&B inns: Two.
Plus
Two unhosted private residences available for overnight or week-
end lodging.
Hosted and unhosted short-term (one to two weeks) housing avail-
able.

LOCATIONS *North of Los Angeles in Ventura, Oxnard,*
Ojai, Camarillo, and Thousand Oaks.

SETTINGS: From plain and comfortable to luxurious.

HOSTS: Teachers, military wives, tour directors. . . .

BREAKFAST: Most hosts serve a full breakfast. Specialties might
include fried apples or gravy biscuits.

61

RESERVATIONS

Advance reservations preferred. If possible, will accept last-minute reservations.

Also available through travel agents.

DIRECTORY: None available, but inquiries are answered with a one-page sheet that describes some homes. *Sample:*

> Ojai hilltop: Eat breakfast by the pool, served by hostess who lived in Europe many years. King-sized bed, private bath; double bed with bath in hall. $50, $45.

RATES

Singles $28–$45. Doubles $35–$58.

A deposit is required.

Credit card accepted: VISA.

Cancellation policy: If notice received at least three days before expected arrival date, refund minus 15 percent of first night's charge made.

BED AND BREAKFAST OF LOS ANGELES

PEG MARSHALL AND ANGIE KOBABE
32074 WATERSIDE LANE
WESTLAKE VILLAGE, CA 91361

PHONE: 818/889-7325 or 889-8870
  Live Monday–Friday,
  8 a.m.–10 p.m. Answering machine at other times.
OPEN: Year round.

ACCOMMODATIONS

B&Bs

Hosted private residences: 130.   B&B inns: 20.

Plus

Hosted short-term (three to four months or longer) housing in some areas.

OTHER SERVICES: Car rentals.

Locations *All areas of greater Los Angeles. Hosts in private homes are also in Palm Springs. B&B inns are located along the California coastline between San Diego and San Francisco. A few inland listings.*

SETTINGS: Everything from a 15-room 1930s mansion in the Hollywood hills to private homes with guest rooms that have either private or shared baths.

HOSTS: Doctors, teachers, realtors, actors, business people, retirees . . . "everything!"

BREAKFAST: Most serve a continental breakfast.

RESERVATIONS
At least one week in advance preferred. If arrangements can be made, will accept last-minute reservations.
Minimum stay: Some hosts require two days.
Groups: Maximum size is 20.
Also available through travel agents.

DIRECTORY (not required for bookings): $1. Describes all listings.
Samples:

> Studio City: High in the Hollywood Hills, with magnificent views of the San Fernando Valley from the private terrace of this cute little studio apartment. Twin beds, full kitchen and bath, TV. Steep driveway to parking area in front. Spa outside for guests' use. Over 16. Car essential. Good location for Hollywood or the studios. Two-night minimum. Apartment for 2 $40, weekly rate $250.

> Anaheim: Maximum—6 guests. Limited kitchen use. Eight children grew up in the substantial home, one of the original homes in the area and on the 1983 Historical Society Tour. Three upstairs bedrooms have a shared bath, one with queen bed, the other with twins. The downstairs guest room has a private entrance, shared bath, and twin beds. All ages welcome. TV shared with the family. Large yard with pool. Room for 2, $35. Extra person, same group $10.

RATES
Singles $18–$50. Doubles $30–$125.
One-night surcharge: A few charge 10 percent.
Weekly and monthly rates available.
Deposit required is 20 percent plus $5 reservation fee.
Cancellation policy: Full refund minus $5 reservation fee made if cancellation received five days before reservation date.

It's Just Like Home
"Among the few guests we were able to send to a host who lives 'way out in the suburbs where few tourists want to go'

was a transferred couple who got along so well with the hosts that they bought the house next door."

BED & BREAKFAST CALIFORNIA SUNSHINE

MIRIAM ALTMAN
22704 VENTURA BLVD., SUITE 1984
WOODLAND HILLS, CA 91364

PHONE: 818/992-1984 or 213/174-4494
Live Monday–Saturday 8–6. Answering machine at other times.
OPEN: Year round.

ACCOMMODATIONS
B&Bs
Hosted private residences: 100.   B&B inns: 25.
Almost all have air conditioning, private baths, and pools.

OTHER SERVICES: Car rentals, pickup at airport bus drop-off point.

LOCATIONS   *All are in Southern California, from Calla-bassas south to San Diego. Most are in the Los Angeles area.*

SETTINGS: Range from cozy clean cottages to prestigious and palatial homes. Some are quiet and secluded; others are within the heart of the city.

HOSTS: International trade consultant, fashion designer, architect, doctor, dentist, lawyer, author, principal, teachers, nurse. . . . Several are multilingual.

BREAKFAST: Varies from simple to elaborate according to host.

RESERVATIONS
One week in advance preferred. If arrangements can be made, will accept last-minute reservations.
Also available through some travel agents.

RATES
Singles $35–$55. Doubles $45–$70.
Weekly rates available.
Deposit required: $50.
Cancellation policy: If notice is received at least two weeks in ad-

vance, full refund is made. Within two weeks of expected arrival date, refund, less one night's lodging, is made.

Southern California Hospitality
"One of our guests who was moving from England to California wanted to be in an area with good schools. We placed him in a home where the Mrs. was a teacher and the Mr. a principal. Needless to say, he found plenty out about our educational system—plus about baseball, football, soccer, scouting. . . . After the family arrived in California, the two families became fast friends.

CAROLYN'S BED & BREAKFAST HOMES IN SAN DIEGO
CAROLYN MOELLER
P.O. BOX 84776
SAN DIEGO, CA 92138

PHONE: 619/435-5009
Live hours vary. Answering machine at other times.
OPEN: Year round.

ACCOMMODATIONS
B&Bs
Hosted private residence: 50.   B&B inns: 2.
Plus:
A few unhosted private residences for overnight or weekend lodging.

OTHER SERVICES: Some hosts will pick up at airport, bus, and train.

LOCATIONS   *San Diego, La Jolla, Clairemont, El Cajon, La Mesa, Coronado, Del Mar, Carlsbad, Oceanside, Vista, Dulzura, Ramona, Rancho Bernardo, Anaheim, San Clemente, Santa Paula, Santa Monica, Lake Arrowhead, Hollywood, Pasadena, Ojai, Catalina Island.*

SETTINGS: Range from a farmhouse with handmade quilts and rugs to an oceanfront home in La Jolla, from a townhouse to a ranch.
BREAKFAST: All hosts serve continental.

RESERVATIONS

Advance reservations preferred. If arrangements can be made, will accept last-minute reservations.
Groups: Maximum size is 10.
Also available through travel agencies.

RATES

Singles $20–$60. Doubles $30–75. $10–$15 for extra person in room. $55–125 for suite or cottage.
Deposit required: Half of total cost.
Cancellation policy: If notice received seven days before expected arrival date, refund minus $10 service charge made.

BED & BREAKFAST HOSPITALITY

RICHARD CIRKA
P.O. BOX 2407
OCEANSIDE, CA 92054

PHONE: 619/722-6694
OPEN: Year round.

ACCOMMODATIONS
B&Bs
Hosted private residences: 100$^+$.   B&B inns: 20$^+$.
Most have private baths.
Plus
Some unhosted private residences for overnight or weekend lodging. Hosted and unhosted short-term (one month) housing.

OTHER SERVICES: In San Diego area: pickup at transportation points; theater tickets; arrangements for all kinds of customized and package tours, which could be a weekend with hot-air ballooning, winery tours, walking tours, and/or tide-pool lectures.
For travelers going to Europe and Israel: Information about B&Bs there that you can book directly or through Bed & Breakfast Hospitality.

LOCATIONS *Most are in the San Diego area within a radius of 30 miles of city center. Others are throughout California. Still others are elsewhere in the United States—as B&Bs listed with this service or through other reservation services in the country.*

SETTINGS: Urban, rural on farms and ranches, in the mountains, on beaches.

HOSTS: Musicians, decorators, travel agents, fashion designer, museum docents, educators, tour guides, microbiologists, actors. . . .

BREAKFAST: About half of the hosts serve continental. Others serve a full meal that could include specialties such as Belgian waffles, omelets, cottage cheese pancakes, Dutch babies (a type of popover), assorted homemade breads, muffins, preserves.

RESERVATIONS
Advance reservations preferred. If arrangements can be made, will accept last-minute reservations.
Minimum stay requirement: Two nights at most private homes.
Groups: Maximum size is about 12.
Also available through travel agents.

DIRECTORY (not required for reservations): $10 includes newsletter published at least twice a year. *Sample:*

CA–#121—A large, restored turn-of-the-century home located in one of San Diego's older neighborhoods, close to downtown, freeways to transport you easily and quickly to beaches, shopping, Mexico, other attractions. Three blocks from San Diego Zoo, Balboa Park.
Originally built in 1900, the house was renovated in 1932 by a French architect who added French doors and balconies to the existing Spanish arches, thus providing an interesting combination of architectural designs. Hosts have painstakingly renovated and decorated their home, filling the house with antiques, china, and years of acquired collectibles and family treasures. A lovely sitting room with fireplace and games awaits the weary traveler. Refreshments are served on arrival and a liqueur at bedtime is standard fare. A full breakfast (selections depend upon the mood of the hostess!) is served in your room, on one of the balconies, sun porches, or in the dining room on china and silver—at whatever time you choose. Some Spanish spoken; airport/Amtrak pickup by prior arrangement. Smoking permitted; no children or guests' pets; hosts' cats on premises.
The rooms (three with shared bath, one with private bath): Garden—cozy room with double bed, white wicker, lace and eyelet.

Western—warm and comforting with patchwork quilt on antique double four-poster bed.

Country—Cheery room filled with dolls, teddy bears, and toys, two twin beds (can be joined together to form king-size bed); balcony.

Bride & Groom—Elegant extra-large room decorated in shades of raspberry and burgundy with an antique cro-cheted bedspread on king-size bed; balcony; private bath. Rates: Garden—$50/night single or double; Western $60/night; Country—$75/night; Bride & Groom—$95/night. Rates do not include local tax.

RATES

Singles $25–$130. Doubles $35–$130. One-night surcharge: $5 at some places. Many offer "seventh night free." Weekly and monthly rates available.

Deposit required: Payment in full prior to stay, but half as deposit if reservation made two months in advance.

Credit cards accepted: MasterCard and VISA for confirmation only. Will not be charged except in cases of "no show." Cancellation policy: Full refund less 10 percent service charge if at least seven days' notice given. With less than a seven-day notice, forfeit of first night's lodging fee plus 10 percent service charge.

DIGS WEST

JEAN HORN
8191 CROWLEY CIRCLE
BUENA PARK, CA 90621

PHONE: 714/739-1669
Usually live Monday–Friday, 6–8:30 a.m. Answering machine at most times.
OPEN: Year round.

ACCOMMODATIONS
B&Bs:
Hosted private residences: 63.   B&Bs inns: The list is growing.
Plus:
Hosted short-term housing.

OTHER SERVICES: In Orange County, pickup at airport and train. Car rentals. Tours arranged for a small fee.

LOCATIONS *Most are in Southern California. Many in Orange County, in Los Angeles area, in Hollywood area, in Valley Side, Torrance, Palos Verdes. In San Diego area: central and north San Diego, La Jolla, Carlsbad, and some other southern coastal cities. A few in San Francisco area, Santa Barbara area, Carmel, Monterey.*

SETTINGS: They range from modest family homes to beach cottages and include condominiums, apartments, artists' studios, and an elegant beachfront property. "Throughout California, excepting San Francisco perhaps, an automobile is a real asset for visitors."

HOSTS: Computer analyst, travel agent, artist, realtor, gourmet cook, retirees, teacher, magician, interior decorator, housewife, writer. . . .

BREAKFAST: Varies from help-yourself to an elaborate meal.

RESERVATIONS
One month in advance recommended. If arrangements can be made, will accept last-minute reservations.
Also available through travel agents.

RATES
Singles $25–$60. Doubles $30–$75. A few are higher.
Deposit required: One night's lodging fee or $25.
Some weekly and monthly rates available.
Cancellation policy: Refunds, less a $15 service charge, made for cancellations received up to two weeks before expected arrival date.

Travel Is Jean's Business
"We try to fill travelers' needs as closely as possible. If we don't have what they want, we say so. I have been expanding my B&B listings for six years. In addition, I am a full-time travel professional, so I can help with all types of arrangements."

As much as possible, California-based reservation services are listed with those that cover the whole state at the beginning, followed by services that focus on a particular area, going from north to south.

TRAVELERS BED & BREAKFAST

LUCILLE GOULD
P.O. BOX 1368
CHINO, CA 91710

PHONE: 714/591-4647
  Live daily, usually 8–4.
OPEN: Year round.

ACCOMMODATIONS
B&Bs
Hosted private residences: 55.
B&B inns: Many throughout California.
Almost all have air conditioning and private baths. Some are accessible to handicapped.
Plus   .
Some unhosted mountain cabins and Palm Springs condos available for overnight or weekend lodging.
Some short-term (up to two months) hosted private homes available.

OTHER SERVICES: Pickup at airport.

LOCATIONS   *In San Bernardino County (east of Los Angeles), including Arrowhead, Big Bear, Chino, Palm Springs, Riverside, Ontario, Upland. Many are within walking distance of beach, shops, and parks.*
Others: Throughout California.
Across the country: Those represented by Miriam in other parts of the country are in communities that are convenient for cross-country drivers and business people and include Tulsa, Oklahoma; Dayton, Ohio; and Boston, Massachusetts.

SETTINGS: Those in San Bernardino County are mostly modern. Some are exquisitely furnished with antiques. Some include use of jacuzzi, tennis courts, country club. Many are down-to-earth, pleasant, comfortable homes.

HOSTS: Many teachers, both active and retired. Social workers, former horse trainer, antique dealer, doctors, therapist, nurse. . . .

BREAKFAST: Varies from continental to full, depending on host.

RESERVATIONS
At least two days in advance preferred. For holiday periods, two to

three weeks' advance notice strongly recommended. If arrangements can be made, will accept last-minute reservations.
Groups: Maximum size is 17.
Also available through travel agents.

DIRECTORY: None available, but requests are filled for a free list of 200 cities in the United States—and ten countries in Australia, South America, Europe, and Asia, where Lucille can book you into private homes or inns.

RATES
Singles $25–$35. Doubles $45–$75.
Booking fee: $5 per reservation.
Deposit required: At least 20 percent.
Credit cards accepted: VISA, MasterCard, AMEX.
Cancellation policy: If notice received at least 48 hours before expected arrival date, half of deposit is refunded.

Until five years ago, Lucille lived in New York. Her experiences of driving across country led her to find private homes that are now on her registry. Some of those other-than-California hosts are people who moved from Lucille's west coast territory or who, as official representatives, have screened new hosts.

SAN DIEGO BED & BREAKFAST
BEVERLY MCGAHEY
P.O. BOX 22948
SAN DIEGO, CA 92122

PHONE: 619/560-7322
Usually live after 7 p.m. Answering machine at other times.

ACCOMMODATIONS
B&Bs
Hosted private residences: 10 (and growing).
All have private guest baths.
Plus
Some furnished apartments for overnight or weekend lodging.
Some hosted short-term arrangements can be made.

Locations *All within 15–30 minutes of beaches and other attractions.*

Settings: Not elaborate, but "with a California flair." Range from homes overlooking the bay to a condo with a swimming pool.

Hosts: Teacher, editor, hospital administrator, Navy couple, business people, musician. . . .

Breakfast: At least a hearty continental.

Reservations
Advance reservations preferred. If arrangements can be made, will accept last-minute reservations.
Also available through travel agents.

Rates
Singles $30–$55. Doubles $35–55.
Monthly rates available.
Deposit required: $20.
Cancellation policy: If notice received at least 48 hours before expected arrival date, refund minus $5 service charge made.

The What-Did-You-Forget-to-Pack Department

Guest's thank-you note: "Thanks so much for your casual, heartfelt invitation to be ourselves in your comfortable and soothing atmosphere. . . . Quin told me just to leave Karen's borrowed slip and she would pick it up here. Please let her know it is freshly laundered."

Colorado

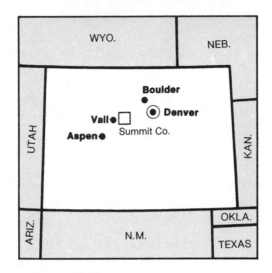

BED AND BREAKFAST COLORADO

RICK MADDEN
P.O. BOX 20596
DENVER, CO 80220

PHONE: 303/333-3340
   Live Monday–Friday, 1–6 p.m. Answering machine at other times.
OPEN: Year round. Closed federal and state holidays and December 15 through January 2.

ACCOMMODATIONS
B&Bs
Hosted private residences: 55 (depending on season).
B&B inns: 9.
Almost all have private baths. Some have hot tubs.
Plus
Some unhosted private residences for overnight or weekend lodging.
Short-term (one week to six months) leisure homes and cottages.

OTHER SERVICES: Pickup at airport in Denver, at train in Glenwood Springs. One host has a sleigh for winter rides and also offers carriage rides in the summer.

LOCATIONS *Throughout Colorado.*

SETTINGS: Forty-eight percent are contemporary mountain homes; 48 percent are historic homes. The others are farms or ranches.

HOSTS: Ski instructor, retired naval officer, teacher, architect, social worker, university professor, silversmith, aerospace engineer. . . .

GUESTS COME FOR: Vacations. The Rocky Mountains, Mesa Verde and Rocky Mountain National Parks, Durango Silverton Narrow Gauge Train, Air Force Academy, Denver Mint. Skiing. Conferences. Professional reasons. University of Denver, University of Colorado, Colorado College.

BREAKFAST: About half serve continental. Full breakfasts might include individual quiches, (mushroom, spinach, bacon); breakfast yogurts, Philadelphia eggs and popovers, Belgian waffles. One host serves farm fresh milk and two offer farm fresh eggs.

RESERVATIONS
Advance reservations preferred but will accept last-minute reservations.
Groups: Equipped to handle groups up to 20 in inns.
Also available through travel agents.

DIRECTORY (not required for reservations): $2. *Samples:*

Breckenridge: Summit House. This contemporary mountain home features peaceful quietness, a hot tub, sun room, and a hearty full breakfast. It is centrally located to all the major ski areas in Summit County, including Keystone and Copper Mountain. Summer travelers can enjoy fishing and horseback riding in the area. The hosts particularly enjoy skiing and hiking.
Location: Two and one-half miles from downtown Breckenridge. Good access to I-70.
Facilities: Main floor king bed with private bath. Second floor twin beds, share bath. No smokers or pets. Two resident cats. Children over 12.
Rates: $38 single; $44 double.

Denver: Beverly House. This elegant turn-of-the-century mansion is only 20 blocks from the famed Capitol building. Period antiques fill this large home, and natural oak and stained glass make it a very special place to visit. The hosts enjoy travel and theater. A continental breakfast is left on the sideboard to enjoy, or have it served in your room. Excellent restaurants are just a stone's throw.
Location: Central Denver in the Capitol Hill area. Excellent transportation and off-street parking available. Five blocks to Cheeman Park and the Botanical Gardens.
Facilities: Second floor king size bed, private adjacent bath. Second floor queen bed, share bath across the hall.
No pets.
Rates: From $35 single to $50 double.

RATES
Single $24–$42. Double $28–$50. Inns run up to $95. Seventh night free in some homes.
Weekly and monthly rates available.
Deposit required: $25.
Credit cards accepted: VISA, MasterCard, and AMEX.
Cancellation policy: Refund of room deposit will be made only with one week's notice or if B&B Colorado is unable to fill your request. In ski areas, the cancellation notice period is 30 days in advance.

Rick writes: "Our service is highly personalized. I try and talk with each prospective guest for at least 15 minutes before a decision is made about placement. I have a totally reliable group of host (most have hosted for over three years) who meet our high standards."

A lawyer from Seattle, Washington wrote: "In the past we have enjoyed the hospitality of world-class hostelries in Hong Kong, in Tokyo, in Munich, but never a more enjoyable stay or delightful host than Paul. The 15-minute walk past the Capitol grounds each morning and evening on our way to and from the headquarters hotel was just about right for a spot of exercise. We recommended it to some of the other attendees who, I am sure, were somewhat envious of our good luck."

BED & BREAKFAST—ROCKY MOUNTAINS

KATE PETERSON
P.O. BOX 804
COLORADO SPRINGS, CO 80901

PHONE: 303/630-3433
   Live 1–6 weekdays; answering machine at other times.
OPEN: Year round.

ACCOMMODATIONS
B&Bs
Hosted private residences: 76$^+$.   B&B inns: 42$^+$.
Almost all have private baths and some have hot tubs or saunas.
Plus
Short-term, hosted housing for up to 30 days available.
Referral service for ski condominiums (winter only).

OTHER SERVICES: Some hosts pick up at airport. Car rentals and theater tickets arranged.

LOCATIONS   *Colorado, Montana, Wyoming, New Mexico, Utah.*

SETTINGS: Urban, suburban, and very rural. Varied. From modest to elegant and include quarter-horse ranch on 1,000 acres, cattle ranches, ski chalets, a romantic cabin, and carriage houses.

HOSTS: Banker, ex-military, pilots, ski instructors, attorney, stained-glass artist, glass blower, landscape architects, ranchers, special-needs teacher, gourmet chefs. . . .

GUESTS COME FOR: Skiing, mountain scenery, colleges and universities, high-tech industry, military, house hunting, conferences.

BREAKFAST: Most serve a full breakfast. Specialties include quiches, home-baked breads, award-winning breakfast cookies, banana buckwheat pancakes, poached pears.

RESERVATIONS
Reservations made on the phone can be put on a five-day hold pending receipt of the deposit.
Two weeks in advance preferred. If arrangements can be made, will accept last-minute reservations.
Minimum stay: Just a few hosts require two nights.

Groups: A few small inns handle groups up to 20. Two inns can host up to 40.

Also available through travel agents.

DIRECTORY (not required for reservations): $3. Describes over 100 homes and inns in five Rocky Mountain states. *Sample*:

> (L-M) Summit County (Breckenridge area). What a view. Two bedrooms, private bath between, in private "upstairs" (2nd flr) of cute little chalet. Two and one-half miles to free shuttle to all four ski areas. Double bedroom has marvelous view of Breckenridge Ski Slopes. Second room has twin beds, large enough for third person. A "best buy." Location: One and one-half miles from town of Breckenridge. Own transportation required. Amenities: Use of club house with ping-pong, pool table, indoor heated swimming pool, jacuzzi, and sauna. In summer, two tennis courts. Breakfast: Full. Rates: Single, $33, double $43, second bedroom, $15 per person. Seventh night free. Hosts: Congenial retired couple, very active. Hostess, a semiprofessional photographer, enjoys cooking. Both ski (Alpine and Nordic). Restrictions: No children under 10. No pets please.

RATES

Singles $20–$65. Doubles $23–$95. Exceptional ski accommodations up to $174.

Some hosts have a one-night surcharge: $5.

Gift certificates available for honeymoons, anniversaries, and birthdays.

Deposit required: First night's occupancy, except ski areas require deposit of 50 percent entire fee between November 15 and April 15.

Cancellation policy: Full refund, less $15 service charge, for cancellations received at least 7 days before expected arrival date; at least 30 days before booking during ski season.

Kate, a skier and four-generation native, has much information to share about the territory she covers.

BED AND BREAKFAST OF BOULDER INC.

LOIS LACROIX
BOX 6061
BOULDER, CO 80306

PHONE: 303/442-6664
   Monday–Friday, 8–5.
OPEN: Year round. Closed major holidays and two weeks at Christmas.

ACCOMMODATIONS
B&Bs
Hosted private residences: 25.
Almost all have private baths.
Plus
Some unhosted private residences for overnight or weekend lodging.
Some short-term housing (up to four months) available.

LOCATIONS   *Most are in the city of Boulder. All are within a 10-mile radius of center city.*

HOSTS: Architects, restaurant owners, city council person, labor consultant, dentist. . . . They cater to nonsmokers.

GUESTS COME FOR: University of Colorado. Naropa Institute. Business—IBM, Ball Brothers, NBI, NeoData, STC. House hunting. Conferences. Festivals. Bicycle and jogging trails. Climate.

BREAKFAST: Varies from simple to elaborate.

RSERVATIONS
Advance reservations requested. If possible, last-minute reservations made.

RATES
Singles $22.50–$32. Doubles $29.50–$40.
Among those few that are higher is a honeymoon cottage with sauna, hot tub, fireplace, half-kitchen.
One-night surcharge: $5.
Weekly and monthly rates available.
Deposit required: $25 or VISA or MasterCard number.
Credit cards: VISA and MasterCard accepted for deposit or entire fee.
Cancellation policy: Minimum cancellation fee is $25. For no-shows the entire deposit is nonrefundable.

BED & BREAKFAST, VAIL VALLEY

KATHY FAGAN
P.O. BOX 491
VAIL, CO 81658

PHONE: 303/476-1225
  Summer, 9–6 daily. Winter, 10–9 daily. Answering machine at other times.
OPEN: Year round, except May during "mud month" in Vail.

ACCOMMODATIONS
B&Bs
Hosted private residences: 26.
All have private baths. Some listings are accessible to handi-capped.
Plus
Some unhosted private residences for overnight or weekend lodging.

OTHER SERVICES: Pickup at airport, bus, and train. Arrange-ments with limousine service.
Telephone information about proximity to ski slopes, lift ticket prices, road conditions, tennis, golf, hiking, rafting, costs of trans-portation to and from Denver Airport, restaurants, and check-in hours.

LOCATIONS *All homes are within 7–10 miles of downtown Vail, and most accessible by a free bus to the mountain. Some are close to the base of the mountain and others are "nestled away from the ski crowd."*

SETTINGS: All are attractive homes-away-from-home and a few are luxurious.

HOSTS: TV announcer, business people, store owners, restauran-teur, ski instructor, doctor, school teacher, professional cowboy. . . . "I personally visit each host three times a year."

GUESTS COME FOR: Skiing and seminars-plus-skiing in winter. Sleigh rides. Tennis, golf, hiking, rafting in summer.

BREAKFAST: Varies from simple to an elaborate meal.

RESERVATIONS
Advance reservations preferred. If arrangements can be made, will accept last-minute reservations.

79

Groups: Maximum size 8–10.

Also available through travel agents.

DIRECTORY: A sampler is sent without charge. *Sample descriptions*:

> The Guesthouse at Vail. Less that one mile west of the gondola, this gracious modern guest house is a bed and breakfast experience. A skylit living room with fireplace, formal dining, and exercise loft and apres ski fun. Accommodations for three individual parties or a family of eight. Two terrace-level bedrooms with private entry, queen beds, and tiled baths. The Paintbrush Suite features a private entrance, fireplace, queen bed, soaking tub, and loft with king bed. A morning shuttle service to the gondola is provided. A continental breakfast is served to all guests. $100. Suite: $150.

> #2. This newly built, contemporary decorated duplex in Eagle Fall is a wonderful hideaway for a family or two traveling companions. Available to the guests are two bedrooms with a queen bed, electric blankets, private bath, and a large living room exclusively for the use of guests. With a large downstairs area, the guests have adequate room to mingle and visit with the other guests. Full or continental breakfast is provided. After a hard day on the slopes, a warmed jacuzzi or steam room is available upon request. Food and gas facilities are also readily available. $40–$60.

RATES

Winter: Singles $25–$40. Doubles $40–$60.

Summer: Singles $25–$35. Doubles $40–$45.

Deposit required is 50 percent of total cost. On a one- or two-night stay, payment is due in full prior to arrival.

Connecticut

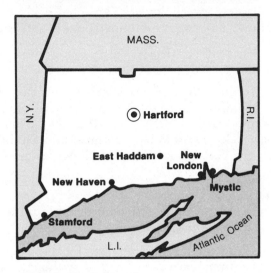

BED AND BREAKFAST, LTD.

JACK ARGENIO
P.O. BOX 216
NEW HAVEN, CT 06513

PHONE: 203/469-3260
Live 4–9 p.m. weekdays, anytime on weekends. Answering machine at other times.
OPEN: Year round.

ACCOMMODATIONS
B&Bs
Hosted private residences: 125.   B&B inns: 2.
Almost all have private baths.
Plus
Some unhosted private residences for overnight or weekend lodging.
Hosted short-term housing also available.

OTHER SERVICES: Pickup at airport, bus, or train may be arranged at a negotiated fee.

LOCATIONS   *Throughout Connecticut.*

SETTINGS: Some are luxurious and elegant. Some are historic. Some are modest.

HOSTS: Professors, psychologists, antique dealers, real estate people, attorneys, artists, aerobic instructors, self-employed business people. . . .

BREAKFAST: Vary from simple to elaborate.

GUESTS COME FOR: Business reasons. A vacation. House hunting. Schools including Yale University, Trinity College, Wesleyan University, Connecticut College, and the Coast Guard Academy. Mystic Seaport. The Long Wharf, Palace, and Shubert Theaters. Barnum Museum. Antiquing. Beaches. State parks.

RESERVATIONS
Advance reservations preferred.
If arrangements can be made, will accept last-minute reservations.
Also available through travel agents.

DIRECTORY: "We prefer to fill requests by speaking to guests on the phone." The sampler directory, sent without charge to those who send a business-sized self-addressed stamped envelope, includes:

New Haven: This 14-room estate is considered one of New Haven's most beautiful houses. Federal style, white clapboard, black shutters. Parklike setting. Eclectic furnishings, many antiques, fireplaces, baby grand piano. Huge rooms. Up to five bedrooms available. Private and shared baths. Suite available. This majestic home is located minutes from Yale and the downtown. Congenial hostess. $40 doubles. $25–$30 singles.

Guilford: In historic town sits this 18th-century restored colonial, furnished mostly in French antiques. The large twin-bedded double room has its own private bath, large closet, fireplace, and separate entrance. A showplace. Set on almost two acres. Off-street parking. Short drive to the town beach. Guests can enjoy a cocktail or tea in their own private downstairs sitting room. Close to antique shops, three museums, nature walking trail, and fine restaurants. A 33-foot sailboat is available for daily charter by avid sailor host. Two doubles. $40 and $45.

RATES
Singles $25–$30. Doubles $40–$50. A few higher.

Deposit requested. Ten percent discount on stays of one week or more.
Cancellation policy: Deposit refunded minus 20 percent service charge for all cancellations.

NUTMEG BED & BREAKFAST
MAXINE KATES
222 GIRARD AVENUE
HARTFORD, CT 06105

PHONE: 203/236-6698
Live Monday–Friday 9–5. Answering machine at other times.
OPEN: Year round.

ACCOMMODATIONS
B&Bs
Hosted private residences: 130.   B&B inns: 9.
Plus
A few unhosted furnished homes and apartments.
Both hosted and unhosted homes available by the month.

OTHER SERVICES: Pickup at airport, bus, and train station. Some hosts will prepare dinner for a fee.
Sightseeing tours available.

LOCATIONS   *Statewide—oceanfront, country, city homes.*

SETTINGS: From modest homes to elegant mansions, historic farmhouses, and country estates.

HOSTS: Social worker, architect, lawyer, artist, realtor, concert pianist, actress, doctors, farmers, antique dealer, educator. . . .

GUESTS COME FOR: Antiquing, foliage, theater, shoreline, skiing. For colleges including Yale, Trinity, Wesleyan, University of Connecticut. Private schools including Kent and Gunnery. Many are long-term guests as relocated business people, some of whom are house hunting.

BREAKFAST: Varies from help-yourself to an elaborate meal that could include souffles and homemade breads.

RESERVATIONS

Advance reservations preferred; in the summer and fall, they are necessary. If possible, last-minute reservations are made.
Groups: Maximum size is 10.
Also available through travel agents.

DIRECTORY (not required for reservations): $2 plus a $.39 business-sized self-addressed stamped envelope for the booklet. A two-page sample directory is sent without charge if you enclose a self-addressed stamped envelope (business-sized, please). *Samples* from the $55–$75 for two range:

Bloomfield: Second-floor twin-bedded room, private bath, antiques. Second-floor master bedroom suite, king-sized bed, private bath, fireplace. Second-floor twin-bedded room, private bath. Smokers O.K. Air conditioned. Pool. Located on 5.6 acres at the foot of Penwood State Forest, this house has a view of 70 miles of the Connecticut Valley, 200 varieties of daffodils in the spring, and 11 goats who cut the grass and answer to their names! This very impressive home is a favorite for long-term guests as well as overnight visitors. Convenient to Hartford, Farmington, and private schools.

Putnam: Two large double-bedded rooms, each with fireplace and private bath. No smokers, no resident pets. Spend the night with history in this beautifully restored pre-Revolutionary tavern. Relax in a Currier and Ives setting. Sleep in an antique-filled room and wake to a hearty country breakfast. Putnam is convenient to the Pomfret School, Providence, R.I., and Sturbridge Village.

RATES

Singles $35–$70. Doubles $40–$75. A few higher.
One-night surcharge: $5.
Weekly and monthly rates available.
Full payment in advance required.
Credit cards accepted: MasterCard and VISA.
Cancellation policy: If cancellation is received at least 48 hours before expected arrival date, refund is made less $10 service charge.

"Accommodations superb. The host treated us more like old friends than as paying guests."

—A guest from New Jersey

First-Timers Abound

"We offer a truly personalized service. I try to match hosts and guests with similar interests. . . . Among our first-timers were three lawyers who thought they would try something different from a hotel. They called after their first night just to say that they would never stay at a hotel again. They used this arrangement for three nights a week for six months, until the case ended. I am pretty sure they love B&B."

COVERED BRIDGE BED AND BREAKFAST

RAE EASTMAN
WEST CORNWALL, CT 06796

PHONE: 203/672-6052
Live Monday–Friday, 9–6. Answering machine at other times.
OPEN: Year round.

ACCOMMODATIONS
B&Bs
Hosted private residences: 37.   B&B inns: 3.
Most have private baths.

LOCATIONS   *In the northwest corner of Connecticut—Kent, Sharon, Cornwall, Norfolk, New Milford, Washington Depot, Lakeville, Essex.*
In the Berkshires of Massachusetts—Stockbridge, Sheffield, and Williamstown.
In the Berkshires, just over the border into New York—Pine Plains and Canaan.
In Vermont: Shaftsbury.

SETTINGS: Most are rural or in villages. They are primarily restored colonials. A few are "just plain home." One is a modern solar residence and one is a farm.

HOSTS: Concert musicians, retired businessman, newspaper editor, realtor, actress, lady chef. . . .

GUESTS COME FOR: Fall foliage. Scenic views. White-water canoeing. Appalachian Trail. Picturesque New England villages.

Dance performances at Jacob's Pillow. Theater. Tanglewood. Antiques. Car racing at Lime Rock. Cross-country and downhill skiing. Lakes. Schools: Hotchkiss, Kent, Salisbury, Marvelwood.

BREAKFAST: Varies according to host. Could be quite simple or elaborate.

RESERVATIONS
Three weeks in advance preferred. If arrangements can be made, will accept last minute.
Minimum stay: A few hosts require two nights on Tanglewood and summer weekends.

DIRECTORY (not required for reservations): $3. (Inquiries are answered with an abbreviated list with one-line descriptions and codes.) *Samples*:

> Cornwall, CT: Set in the center of this tiny New England village, this home was once a parsonage. It still looks like one from the outside, old and settled, from its deep wrap-around porch to its dormer windows. The inside, however, is full of surprises, starting with the indoor swimming pool in a striking setting. Next to it is terraced greenhouse, filled with plants. At breakfast, guests sit at one end of a great kitchen, overlooking both. Paintings fill the walls of the beautifully decorated rooms. One small dog is residence. Restrictions: Two-night minimum preferred. Summer months only. Rooms: One double, one double with twins; both use guest bath down a short flight of stairs. Rates per night: $45 double, two nights or more; $55 one night; $40 single.

> New Milford, CT: Vistas for viewing, woods for walking, hills for cross-country skiing, streams for fishing, flower gardens, a tennis court, and a pool are some of the attractions of this sprawling estate three miles outside of New Milford. Inside, a large, ground-floor bed-sitting room on ground floor furnished with antiques has its own entrance from the private deck just outside the door. Sunny is the best way to describe the charming upstairs twin-bedded room. Hostess, once a professional chef, will serve dinner by prior arrangement. Restrictions: Smoking outside only. Two-night minimum preferred. Available from June 15. Rooms: Twins share headboard, can turn into king-sized bed. Private bath. Twin-bedded room shares bath with

hostess. Rates: $60 downstairs double, two nights or more. $70 one night, $45 shared bath.

RATES

Singles $35–$50. Doubles $35–$70. A few are higher.

One-night surcharge: $5–$10 in a few places. Some weekly and monthly rates can be arranged.

Full payment required in advance.

Cancellation policy: Refund made if notice received at least 48 hours before expected arrival time; one night's lodging forfeited after that.

Rae says: "I worry! Am I making the right match? To this end, I interview hosts carefully, have a reasonable length chat with travelers, suggest area attractions, calculate mileage, map trip routes. Shouldn't! (Very time-consuming.) Can't help myself."

How successful is she? Here are some notes from hosts to Rae: "I owe you a thank you! Those guests were top notch and charming. . . . " "We had the most wonderful time. Send us more!"

Throughout Connecticut there are additional B&Bs represented by Pineapple Hospitality, page 156.

Delaware

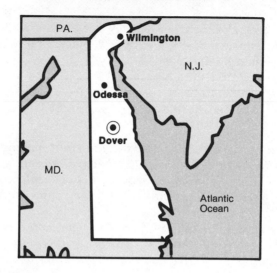

BED & BREAKFAST OF DELAWARE

BARBARA ROGERS
1804 BREEN LANE
WILMINGTON, DE 19810

PHONE: 306/475-0340
Live Monday–Friday, 3–7 p.m., and usually Saturday 9–6 and
Sunday 1–6. Answering machine at other times.
OPEN: Year round.

ACCOMMODATIONS
B&Bs
Hosted private residences: 28.
Most have air conditioning and private baths.
Plus
One unhosted private residence for overnight or weekend lodging.
Short-term housing, (up to two months), hosted and unhosted.

LOCATIONS   *Delaware: Wilmington and Odessa.*
Pennsylvania: Chadds Ford.
Maryland: Elkton.

SETTINGS: Wide range, from simple to luxurious.

HOSTS: Doctors, educators, museum curators, business executives, lawyers, health care executive, architect, river pilot. . . .

GUESTS COME FOR: Business, schools, and "just passing through." Many tourists come to see historic sites, Longwood Gardens, Winterthur Museum, New Castle, Hagley Museum and Brandywine River Museum, Nemours Mansion.

BREAKFAST: Depending on host's schedule, it can vary from help-yourself to an elaborate meal.

DIRECTORY: None available, but inquiries are answered with a page that has a few descriptions. *Samples:*

> Northern Delaware. City location. Elegant townhouse in Rockford Park area; two guest bedrooms and two guest baths. Lovely antiques. Double $40.

> Chadds Ford, Pennsylvania: Two hundred fifty—year-old home, on several acres of land. Near Winterthur and Longwood Gardens. Two guest bedrooms, both with double bed and fireplace. Two guest baths, living room, dining room, kitchen (self-serve breakfast). Patio and swimming pool. Double $52-$62.

RESERVATIONS
Advance reservations preferred. If possible, last-minute reservations accepted.

RATES
Singles $25–$40. Doubles $35–$60.
One-night surcharge: $5.
Weekly and monthly rates available.
Deposit required: Varies according to accommodation.
Cancellation policy: Full refund less a $5 handling charge is made.

For Wilmington, you could also contact Bed & Breakfast of Philadelphia, page 269.
Bed and Breakfast of Chester County, page 274, has a few in the Chesapeake Bay area of Delaware.

District of Columbia

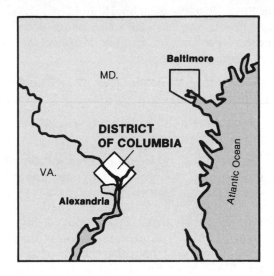

B&B GUESTS COME FOR: The nation's capital. All the major tourist and cultural attractions in Washington. Many come for universities, conferences, relocation, and government business.

THE BED AND BREAKFAST LEAGUE, LTD.
MILLIE GROOBEY
3639 VAN NESS STREET, NW
WASHINGTON, DC 20008

PHONE: 202/363-7767
Monday–Thursday 9–5, Friday 9–1.
OPEN: Year round. Closed all federal holidays and Christmas–New Year's.

ACCOMMODATIONS
B&Bs
Hosted private residences: 175.   B&B inns: 30.
Almost all have air conditioning and private baths.
Plus
Some unhosted private residences for overnight or weekend lodging.
Unhosted short-term (up to six months) housing also available.

LOCATIONS   *Many homes are in Washington, D.C., and its
suburbs.
Others are in communities across the country. A few are in
the U.S. Virgin Islands. The League's nationwide list of
represented hosts constantly changes. At press time the wide
spread included B&Bs in 25 states with, for example, one in
Wyoming, a dozen in Massachusetts, about 15 in Florida,
and four in Michigan. Send business-sized self-addressed
stamped envelope for a "basic list" that will give you an idea
of the locations beyond Washington, D.C.*

SETTINGS: From clean-and-attractive to elegant, new to historic.
Washington accommodations are in apartment buildings, townhouses, homes with large yards, and small inns. Some hosts offer
free parking. Most are located within an easy walk of public transportation, both subway and bus.

HOSTS: Cooking school instructor, Capitol Hill staff, lobbyists,
artists, doctors, lawyers, retired military personnel, homemakers. . . .

BREAKFAST: Most are continental; some full.

RESERVATIONS
Two weeks in advance recommended. If possible, last-minute arrangements are made. In high-demand areas, a month's advance
notice is necessary.
Two-night minimum stay required.

RATES
Guest membership fee: $30 per year covers all booking fees.
Booking fee (charged to nonmembers): $10 for each reservation.
Singles $35–$75. Doubles $40–$85. A few higher.
Deposit required: $25.
Credit cards: MasterCard, VISA, AMEX accepted for entire fee.
Cancellation policy: $25 deposit is nonrefundable. Remainder of
reservation charges refundable if cancellation made more than one
week before scheduled arrival date. If cancellation is made within
one week of arrival, one night's lodging is charged plus booking
fee.

BED 'N' BREAKFAST LTD. OF WASHINGTON, D.C.

JACQUELINE REED
P.O. BOX 12011
WASHINGTON, D.C. 20005

PHONE: 202/328-3510
Live Monday–Friday 10–5. Answering machine at other times.
OPEN: Year round.

Accommodations
B&Bs
Hosted private residences: 80.
Almost all have air conditioning. A few have telephones in rooms.
Plus
A few unhosted private residences for overnight or weekend lodging.
Some unhosted apartments by the month.

LOCATIONS *Most are located in downtown Washington, D.C., and are convenient to either bus or subway.*

SETTINGS: Accommodations range from budget to luxury. Some are in historic homes and some are very luxurious.

HOSTS: Lawyers, published author, social worker, naval commander, realtor, artist, caterer, school administrator, government workers. . . .

GUESTS COME FOR: "Among our guests are many associated with international organizations located in Washington such as the Peace Corps and International Voluntary Service."

BREAKFAST: All serve continental.

RESERVATIONS
One month in advance preferred but last minute may be possible.
Groups: Maximum size is 25.
Also available through travel agents.

DIRECTORY: None available, but inquiries are answered with a few detailed descriptions. A full page is used for each home. *Sample* of one located at Logan Circle:

> The House: A 100-year-old Victorian mansion of 18 rooms and 6 baths, built by John Shipman as his personal residence. The house has been carefully and extensively re-

stored by its present owners, who have added exterior landscaping, gardens, terrace, and fountains to the original townhouse. Features include original wood paneling, stained glass, chandeliers, Victorian-style lattice porch, and art-nouveau and Victorian antiques and decoration.

Unique features: Central air conditioning, heating with area controls, color televisions in each room, player piano, laundry facilities available.

Location: Seven blocks to Metro, 10 blocks to the White House.

Languages: English and French.

Your hosts: He is a former Fulbright Fellow and law clerk to Supreme Court Justice Tom Clark and is currently a senior partner of a prominent Washington law firm. He has also served with the Department of State. His wife has studied interior design and is a graduate of a professional pastry course taught by the White House pastry chef.

Rates: Single $30–$40 plus D.C. hotel tax. Double is a total of $25.25 per person. Secured parking space $3 per day.

RATES
Singles $30–$55. Doubles $40–$65.
Surcharge for one night: $5.
Deposit required: $40.
Credit cards accepted: VISA, MasterCard, and AMEX; no charge for deposit, 6 percent for entire fee.
Cancellation policy: $15 service fee if received within 72 hours of reserved date(s). One day's charge if no advance notice given. Taxes returned on a last-minute cancellation.

More than the Loan of an Umbrella

"A young couple was staying in one of our unhosted apartments. While checking the mail in the lobby, the woman locked herself out. I wasn't able to get the key until the next day. I was able to put them in another apartment for the night, but they had plans to go out to dinner. We solved the coat and shoe problem. (I loaned her mine.) Just recently they wrote from Connecticut that they are going to have a baby and I am to be an honorary aunt."

SWEET DREAMS & TOAST INC.
ELLIE CHASTAIN
P.O. BOX 4835-0035
WASHINGTON, D.C. 20008

PHONE: 202/483-9191
Live 11–5, Monday–Friday. Answering machine at other times.
OPEN: Year round, but office is closed December 17–January 6.

ACCOMMODATIONS
B&Bs
Hosted private residences: 90.
All have air conditioning.

OTHER SERVICES: Foreign guests are sometimes given additional opportunities to meet local residents. Answers to inquiries include information about D.C. travel and tourist information telephone numbers. (Requests for special attractions brochures accommodated.)

LOCATIONS *District of Columbia: Georgetown, Dupont Circle, Capitol Hill and general northwest area of city.*
Virginia: Alexandria, Arlington, McLean.
Maryland: Annapolis, Bethesda, Chevy Chase, and Silver Spring.

SETTINGS: Range from restored Victorian on Capitol Hill to elegant townhouse in northwest Washington.

HOSTS: Professional potter, retired Air Force colonel, government employees, writer, psychologists, professor, retired antique dealer . . . . "We have an Annual Open House for hosts so that they can meet other hosts in area. It is a wonderful way for them to meet others who are doing the same thing."

BREAKFAST: Most serve continental. Usually juice or fruit, toast or muffins or croissant or bagel, and coffee and tea.

RESERVATIONS
Advance notice preferred. Last-minute reservations may be possible, but they are not encouraged.
Minimum stay requirement: Two nights.

RATES
Singles $35–$55 plus tax. Doubles $50–$65 plus tax.

Credit cards accepted: VISA and MasterCard
Cancellation policy: Full refund less $10 service charge on cancellations made at least seven days before arrival date. $25 if less than seven days. Cancellations made with less than 24 hours notice charged one night's lodging.

How Do Guests Choose Their Location?

"After a caller and I had an extensive phone conversation about four different homes, each in a different location, he remarked, 'I forgot to ask the most important question of all. What ice cream stores are closest to each home?' He chose the home that was closest to his favorite ice cream."

Because of the good public transportation available from Alexandria, Virginia, it is one of the over-the-border communities that is an option for D.C. visitors. Most of the B&B hosts in Alexandria are represented by Princely Bed & Breakfast, page 324.

Florida

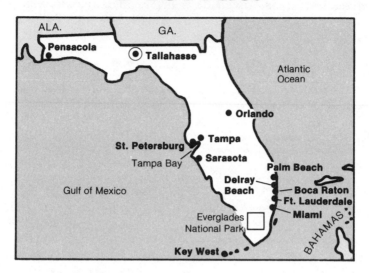

BED & BREAKFAST CO.

MARCELLA SCHAIBLE
P.O. BOX 262
SOUTH MIAMI, FL 33243

PHONE: 305/661-3270
   Monday–Friday, 9–5. Answering service at other times.
OPEN: Year round

ACCOMMODATIONS
B&Bs
Hosted private residences: 75.
Most have air conditioning and private baths. Some have pools.
Plus
Some short-term (up to one month) hosted housing.

OTHER SERVICES: Discount tickets to area attractions. Arrangements can be made with some hosts for a tour of the city or rides to special areas or events.

LOCATIONS *Spread over much of Florida, including the Florida Keys and Key West; Miami, Ft. Lauderdale, and Palm Beach areas; Jupiter; Melbourne; Palm Coast; Orlando, Gainesville, Naples, Tampa, and the Panhandle.*

SETTINGS: Range from modest to quite luxurious. On waterways, islands, and Keys, on the ocean and Gulf of Mexico, on a yacht, or a separate cottage.

HOSTS: Attorney, retail store owner, college professor, airline pilot, harbor pilot, engineer, publisher, real estate developer . . . . Among multilingual host families, the major second language is French, German, or Spanish.

GUESTS COME FOR: Everglades National Park. John Pennekamp State Park. Palm Beach areas. Local attractions in Keys, Miami, Ft. Lauderdale, Palm Beach areas, Orlando attractions, and the Panhandle region of Florida.

BREAKFAST: All serve continental.

RESERVATIONS
Two weeks in advance preferred. If possible, last-minute reservations are accepted.
Also available through travel agents.

DIRECTORY: A sampler of about 15 available homes is sent on request. (Please enclose a business-sized self-addressed stamped envelope.) *Samples:*

> Coconut Grove Area: The ultimate in comfort and luxury in this Mediterranean-style villa in an exclusive estate area. A large balcony off one bedroom overlooks the garden, pool, and the bay. Walk to the village along a banyan-canopied highway; dine, browse, shop, and explore this unique community on the Biscayne Bay.

> Ft. Lauderdale: Three bedrooms and baths available in this spacious contemporary home. Landscaped grounds and pool; on the waterway. Hosts enjoy tennis and square dancing. Convenient to public transportation. Nonsmokers preferred.

RATES
May 1–December 15: Singles $20–$38. Doubles $24–$44.
December 15–April 30: Singles $28–$54. Doubles $32–$70.
Deposit required: $25.
Surcharge: $5 per night for less than three nights.
Some monthly rates are available.
Cancellation policy: Full refund minus $5 administrative charge if cancellation is at least one week before expected arrival date.

> *"We enjoy matching guest and host according to their interests and/or occupation."*

FLORIDA & ENGLAND BED & BREAKFAST

CAROL J. HART
119 ROSEWOOD DRIVE, BOX 12
PALM HARBOR, FL 33563

PHONE: 813/784-5118
  Monday–Friday, 8–6.
OPEN: Year round.

ACCOMMODATIONS
B&Bs
Hosted private residences: 56.   B&B inn: 1.
All have air conditioning and private baths.
Some are accessible to handicapped.
Plus
Some unhosted private residences for overnight or weekend lodging.

OTHER SERVICES: Car rentals.

LOCATIONS   *Spread throughout the state. Located in Sarasota, Bradenton, Venice, St. Petersburg, Clearwater, Largo, Palm Harbor, Tarpon Springs, Orlando, Sanford. Most are within a 10-mile radius of center city. Almost all are near public transportation and Florida attractions.*

SETTINGS: About half are typical Florida type and half are luxurious in tropical settings with pools and on waterways.

GUESTS COME FOR: A vacation. Business. Conferences.

BREAKFAST: Varies from help-yourself to an elaborate meal.

RESERVATIONS
Minimum stay of two nights required.
At least one week in advance preferred. If arrangements can be made, will accept last-minute reservations.
Also available through travel agents.

DIRECTORY (not required for reservations): $3. Includes a map of Florida with the more than 20 communities that have B&Bs represented by Carol. *Samples*:

> #1. Former schoolteachers, now retired, enjoy a refreshing swim in their pool with B&B guests. Their Host Home is in Dunedin, not far from the Gulf of Mexico beaches, golf courses, shopping malls, etc. Their guest rooms consist of

one room with twin beds, adjoining bathroom, and a sitting room. A full American breakfast is served. Rates are: $25 single, $35 double per night.

#2. Join the hosts for a game of golf. Located in a resort with swimming, golf, and tennis available for guests. The Host Home is located on a lovely lake surrounded with two golf-course greens. Country club restaurant is open to guests for lunches and dinners. Two bikes available (his and hers) for rides in the beautiful park nearby. A full American breakfast is served. Rates are $25 single, $35 double per night. King-sized bed, adjoining bath. Mini-tours offered by the hosts. (Location is Palm Harbor.) Non-smokers preferred.

RATES
Singles $25–$35. Doubles $28–$60.
Minimum stay required: Two nights.
Deposit required is 20 percent of total cost.
Cancellation policy: Full refund for cancellation notice given two weeks in advance.

BED AND BREAKFAST OF THE FLORIDA KEYS, INC.
JOAN E. HOPP
5 MAN-O-WAR DRIVE, P.O. BOX 1373
MARATHON, FL 33050

PHONE: 305/743-4118
October 15–June 30, 8–5 daily.
During summer months: 201/223-5979, 7:30–10 a.m.

ACCOMMODATIONS
B&Bs
Hosted private residences: 30.
Almost all have air conditioning.

LOCATIONS *Along the entire length of the Florida Keys, from Key Largo to Key West. Hosts are also in Palm Beach County along Florida's East Coast.*

SETTINGS: Many are on the ocean, bay, and canal fronts, as the Keys are surrounded by water.

HOSTS: All have hosted for over three years.

GUESTS COME FOR: A vacation. "The average temperature year round is 72. Fifty miles in either direction takes you to Key West or Key Largo."

BREAKFAST: All serve a full meal.

RESERVATIONS
Minimum stay of two days required.
Advance reservations preferred. If possible, last-minute reservations may be made.
Groups: Maximum size is 16.
Also available through travel agents.

DIRECTORY: No charge for two-page directory that has brief descriptions of all listings. *Samples*:

> Marathon #1 Oceanview rooms (three) private entrances, and baths; all rooms have air conditioning, bahama fans, T.V.; and the hostess serves you a full breakfast which often includes her banana bread—made with bananas from their banana trees. $38 per night double occupancy. There is also (for an extra fee) a boat available for your fishing enjoyment. It may be tarpon fishing, dolphin fishing, king fishing, or bottom fishing depending on time of the year and what fish are running.
> Palm Beach #35. Room with queen-sized bed, also private sitting room, private bath. This home located between the intercoastal and the ocean, therefore a one-block walk to the beach. Five minutes to Worth Avenue. $75 double occupancy includes breakfast.

RATES
Singles $25–$35. Doubles $28–$75.
Some weekly rates available.
Deposit required: At least one night's lodging.
Cancellation policy: Deposit is refunded less a $5 service fee if cancellation is made at least one week in advance.

> *"One time I erred in sending out a confirmation for a Keys host. All our addresses down here go by mile markers. I sent guest to the wrong marker, which turned out to be a junkyard with the initials B&B. Fortunately, they had hosts' name and phone number (and a sense of humor), so all ended well."*

TROPICAL ISLES BED & BREAKFAST—PLUS

URSULA MUCCI
P.O. BOX 490382
KEY BISCAYNE, FL 33149

PHONE: 305/361-2937
Live after 7 p.m. Answering machine at other times.
OPEN: Year round.

ACCOMMODATIONS
B&Bs
Hosted private residences: 15.
All have air conditioning and most have private baths. Most have pools. All are close to the beach.
Plus
Unhosted short-term housing available for a minimum of two months.

OTHER SERVICES: Complimentary discount tickets for many attractions. The "Plus" in the name is a package arrangement that includes exercise classes, tours, and activities.
Se habla espanol.
Wir sprechen deutsch.

LOCATIONS *On Key Biscayne, in Miami, and all the way down to Key West.*

SETTINGS: From modern to luxurious. "Tropical settings on a lovely island."

HOSTS: Bank consultant, engineer, professor of music, decorator, doctor, former ski lodge owners, retired printer . . . .

GUESTS COME FOR: Relocation. University of Miami and Rosenstile University of Marine Sciences on Key Biscayne. Conferences. A vacation—area offers eight-mile beach, tennis, golf, seaquarium, Planet-Ocean Bill Baggs State Park, shopping centers, biking trails, fishing.

BREAKFAST: Varies from simple to elaborate according to host.

RESERVATIONS
From December 1 to April 30, they should be made four to six

weeks in advance. If arrangements can be made, will accept last-minute reservations.
Minimum stay of two nights required.

RATES
Singles $45–$65. Doubles $55–$100.
Weekly and monthly rates available.
Deposit required is 15 percent of total charge.
Cancellation policy: If cancellation notice received 14 days before expected arrival date, 80 percent of deposit is refunded; 7 days, 60 percent; 2 days, 50 percent.

> *Because Ursula's husband was in the diplomatic service, she has traveled and entertained extensively. When her own family recently had a reunion in Switzerland, her sister arranged for lodging in B&Bs; it was so successful that Ursula was inspired to host in the United States. She expanded the concept by establishing a reservation service with friends as her original hosts. Now she has gone one step further, as a certified fitness instructor with a strong interest in a healthy lifestyle and preventing osteoporosis, by adding a package arrangement with several variations of fitness programs, including one where you stay at her B&Bs.*

A&A BED & BREAKFAST OF FLORIDA, INC.
BRUNHILDE FEHNER
P.O.BOX 1316C
WINTER PARK, FL 32790

PHONE: 305/628-3233
  Monday–Thursday 9–6. Answering service at other times.
  TELEX: 523570 GRAFIMEX-MAIT.
OPEN: Year round.

ACCOMMODATIONS
B&Bs
Hosted private residences: 50.
All have air conditioning and private baths.
Plus
Some unhosted private residences for overnight or weekend lodging.
Some short-term (by the week or month) unhosted housing available.

OTHER SERVICES: Car rentals. Pickup at airport, bus, and train.

LOCATIONS *Winter Park, Orlando, Atlamonte Springs, Maitland, Longwood. Near Disneyland, Epcot, Space Center, Sea World, Cypress Gardens, Busch Gardens, Daytona Speedway, and beaches.*

SETTINGS: All are rather luxurious.

HOSTS: Realtor, dentist, engineers, insurance, ex-mayor. . . . They are personally visited by Brunhilde Fehner four times a year.

GUESTS COME FOR: Disney World, Epcot, Space Center, Sea World, Cypress Gardens, Busch Gardens, Daytona Speedway, beaches. For conferences, for business reasons, to visit relatives in the hospital, and for schools—University of Central Florida and Rollins College.

BREAKFAST: Complimentary full breakfast.

RESERVATIONS
Minimum stay of two nights required.
Advance reservations generally preferred, but necessary in February for Daytona race weekend.

DIRECTORY: None available, but a sampler is sent in answer to inquiries. (Please enclose a self-addressed stamped envelope.) *Sample:*

Winter Park—Inviting contemporary two-story home with a nostalgic touch, on quiet cul-de-sac close to downtown Winter Park with its justly famous Park Avenue shops. Two spacious bedrooms upstairs for our guests. Paddle fan in each room, but we have A/C too! One queen bedroom, one twin, private bath. Wake up to an incredible view outside your window! Carefully tended flower beds, lush lawn that slopes to a picturesque lake. Relax and work on your Florida tan, row around the lake, fish for a bass, or hop in the screen-enclosed swimming pool. Breakfast in a well-appointed dining room or poolside. Enjoy a bike ride or stroll down an old brick street. Convenient to all the "Worlds."

RATES
Singles $25–35. Doubles $40–$50. A few are $60.

One-night surcharge: $5.
Weekly and monthly rates available.
Deposit required: $25.
Cancellation policy: If cancellation notice is received 72 hours before expected arrival date, deposit, minus a $7 service charge, refunded.

A Chance to Meet

Many B&B reservation services speak of missing the opportunity to visit with the travelers they have made arrangements for. If you are in one of Brunhilde's host homes for more than two nights, she makes it a point to meet you!

More Than a Room

"You have such a lovely home and you made us feel so welcome. We hope we can visit you again. The peas were delicious in our stir-fry. We'll have to try growing some. I am enclosing my recipe for broccoli (or cauliflower) soup. We talked about it. (We prefer the broccoli.) Thank you again. . . ."

—A&A Bed & Breakfast guests

B&B SUNCOAST ACCOMMODATIONS
DANIE BERNARD
8690 GULF BOULEVARD
ST. PETE BEACH, FL 33706

PHONE: 813/360-1753
   Live 9 a.m.–9 p.m. daily.
OPEN: Year round.

ACCOMMODATIONS
B&Bs
Hosted private residences: 50.   B&B inns: 10.
Most are on or near water and have air conditioning.
Some have heated pools.
Plus
A few unhosted private residences.
Hosted short-term (a month) housing.
Unhosted housing (for a year or longer).

OTHER SERVICES: Airport and bus pickup can be arranged (for a fee). Discount tickets to attractions. Guided local tours. Babysitting. Laundry and kitchen privileges.

LOCATIONS *St. Pete Beach, Delray Beach, Orlando, Ft. Myers, Naples, Sarasota, St. Petersburg, Tampa, New Port, Richey, and Tarpon Springs.*

SETTINGS: Most are standard rooms with a bath. Some are luxurious. A few are historic.

HOSTS: "Most hosts are semiretired. All are interesting and dedicated to the guest's comfort and vacation enjoyment."

GUESTS COME FOR: Beaches. Salvador Dali Museum, Busch Gardens, Sunken Gardens, Ringling Museum, conferences, high-tech-related business, house hunting. Schools: Stetson Law School, University of Southern Florida, Tampa College, Eckerd. VA Hospitals.

BREAKFAST: Most serve continental. Others are full and/or self-serve.

RESERVATIONS
Minimum stay of two days required.
At least two weeks in advance preferred. If arrangements can be made, will accept last-minute reservations. (In February, March and April—the busiest months—a room near the water is seldom available on a last-minute basis.)
Also available through travel agents.

RATES
Singles $30–$50. Doubles $40–$75.
Weekly and monthly rates available.
Deposit required is 30 percent of total.
Cancellation policy: $20 service charge if less than 72 hours notice; otherwise $10.

"All inquiries accompanied by a self-addressed stamped envelope are answered."

TALLAHASSEE BED AND BREAKFAST, INC.
MARTHA G. THOMAS
3023 WINDY HILL LANE
TALLAHASSEE, FL 32308

PHONE: 904/421-5220
   Monday–Friday, 9–5. At other times: 904/385-3768.

ACCOMMODATIONS
B&Bs
Hosted private residences: 10.
All have air conditioning and private baths.

OTHER SERVICES: Airport pickup.

LOCATIONS   *All located in the capital of Florida, in the panhandle area near the Gulf of Mexico.*

SETTINGS: They range from modest to luxurious. Some are historic.

HOSTS: Teachers, retired military, university professors, administrators, builder, artist. . . .

GUESTS COME FOR: A vacation. Conferences. Visits with college students. Football games. Relocation. Job and house hunting.

BREAKFAST: Varies from simple to an elaborate meal.

RESERVATIONS
Two weeks in advance preferred. Will accept last-minute reservations.
Groups: Maximum size is six.

RATES
Singles $30–$50. Doubles $40–$65.
Deposit required: One night's lodging.
Cancellation policy: Full refund minus $10 made if notice received at least 48 hours before reserved date(s).

Georgia

ATLANTA HOSPITALITY

ERNA BRYANT
2472 LAUDERDALE DRIVE N.E.
ATLANTA, GA 30345

PHONE: 404/493-1930
   Live Monday–Friday 9–9. At other times: 404/325-2370.
OPEN: Year round.

ACCOMMODATIONS
B&Bs
Hosted private residences: 40.
All have air conditioning and most are near public transportation.
Plus
Some unhosted private residences for overnight or weekend lodging.
Short-term (up to six months) housing, hosted and unhosted.

OTHER SERVICES: Pickup at airport, bus, and train. Laundry and parking are available at or near most homes.

LOCATIONS *Most are within a 10-mile radius of center city. Quiet residential neighborhoods; many are on a bus line or near a rapid transit station.*

HOSTS: College professor, retired school teachers, homemaker, IRS personnel, entrepreneurs, bookkeeper. . . .

SETTINGS: "Rooms are simply furnished, in private homes, condominiums, and apartments."

GUESTS COME FOR: Many reasons, including schools—Georgia Tech, Emory University, Georgia State. "A lot of young women who wish a safe secure environment while job hunting." Vacationers.

BREAKFAST: Most serve continental. Full breakfast available upon request.

RESERVATIONS
Two weeks in advance preferred. If possible, last-minute reservations accommodated.
Groups: Maximum size is 50.

RATES
Membership (good for one year): $10.
Singles $20–$30. Doubles $30–$45.
Weekly and monthly rates available.
Deposit required: First night's lodging.
Cancellation policy: If full payment is made and reservations are not kept, the payment can apply to reservations anytime within the next 12 months.

BED & BREAKFAST ATLANTA
MADALYNE EPLAN AND PAULA GRIS
1801 PIEDMONT AVE. NE, SUITE 208
ATLANTA, GA 30324

PHONE: 404/875-0525
Live Monday–Friday, 9–12, 2–5. Answering machine at other times.
OPEN: Year round, except weekends and major holidays.

ACCOMMODATIONS
B&Bs
Hosted private residences: 75.   B&B inns: 5.
All have air conditioning and private baths. Some have pools and jacuzzis. Some homes are accessible to handicapped.
Plus
Hosted and unhosted short-term (up to three months) housing.

LOCATIONS *Most are within an eight-mile radius of center city (Atlanta). Many are in desirable close-up neighborhoods (some historic). Others are in lovely suburban communities: Sandy Springs, Dunwoody, Roswell, Decatur, Stone Mountain, Marietta, Kennesaw, Tucker, Alpharetta. Placements accessible to good public transportation can be made.*
Also: A few select getaway resort settings out of Atlanta in the mountains, at a lake, or near a beach.

SETTINGS: Contemporary condo. Simple ranch style. Elegant Victorian. Guest house in the woods. B&B homes may be near restaurants, shops, and museums, or in areas where the nearest neighbor can't be seen.

HOSTS: Several doctors, educators, scientists, interior designers, realtors, attorneys, business people, airline flight attendants, travel agents, nurses, contractors—"all interesting, of course!"

GUESTS COME FOR: Conferences. Schools—about a dozen including Emory, Georgia Tech, Martin Luther King Center, and Center for Disease Control. For business reasons, GA World Congress Center—marts or regional corporate offices.

BREAKFAST: Varies from simple to elaborate. Could include freshly baked breads, pancakes, fancy egg dishes, often accompanied by grits.

DIRECTORY: None available, but brochure sent in answer to inquiries includes a few descriptions. *Sample:*

This turn-of-the-century Victorian house encourages walking—to Colony Square, Cultural Arts Center, and restaurants. The host couple will direct you to all points of interest and recreation, or you may stay right "at home" to relax on the beautiful porch or swim in the pool in back. A park is located just across the street. The bedroom, with its queen-sized bed and sitting area (sofa bed), adjoins a small modern bath. The host couple, a retired nurse and a corporate executive, are both talented participants in the arts.

RESERVATIONS
Advance reservations of two to four weeks strongly preferred, but last-minute reservations may be possible. Each confirmation is accompanied by a personal note.

Groups: Up to 12 can be placed at several houses in the same area or at one inn.

Also available through travel agents.

RATES

Singles $24–$52. Doubles $28–$60. A few are higher.

One-night surcharge: $4.

Deposit required: $20 per room.

Cancellation policy: Reservation deposit is refundable only if accommodations prove to be unacceptable or if Bed & Breakfast Atlanta is unable to confirm placement.

A Typical Guest Report

"We were truly delighted with both our house and hostess. Have decided that is the only way to play tourist. Your city is beautiful and your Marta [transportation] system is great. . . . It was so nice to know that when we were done for the day we had a nice comfortable and quiet home to go to. Staying with someone who knows the area and what to do sure made it easy to be a tourist . . . would definitely do it again."

The Discovery of a Traveling Business Man

"The hosts were a delight. Previously on business trips I have found my [traditional] accommodations a dismal experience. Figuring to change this I was determined to find a more hospitable place to stay. I found it in your hosts' home. Thanks."

BED & BREAKFAST HIDEAWAY HOMES

ELMA WEIL-ETTMAN AND BETTY CALDWELL
DIAL STAR ROUTE BOX 76
BLUE RIDGE, GA 30513

PHONE: 404/632-2411 or 3669
   Live Monday–Friday 9–9. Answering machine or service at other times.
OPEN: Year round.

ACCOMMODATIONS
B&BS
Hosted private residences: Seven—and the list is growing. "B&B is catching on in this undiscovered area."

Plus

Short-term unhosted housing (for up to one month):
Antique furnishings blend with functional; provincial arts and crafts accent the decor. Homes are electrically heated and also have native stone fireplaces. All linens are furnished and kitchens are modern.

OTHER SERVICES: Guests arrive by private auto or chartered buses. (There is no public transportation in this region.) There are nearby airfields for small private planes. Ground transportation within 30 miles can be arranged.

LOCATIONS *Remotely located in sparsely settled area of Appalachian Mountains. The region, which encompasses a small part of North Carolina, Tennessee, and Georgia, is called Copper Basin. It is two hours north of Atlanta, 1½ hours east of Chattanooga, TN, and 2½ hours southeast of Knoxville, TN.*

SETTINGS: Gracious year-round mountain homes. They are located on or near rivers, streams, white waters, or lakes and all have a wide expanse of vistas.

HOSTS: Urban sociologist, realtor, civic worker, business woman, retired military. . . .

GUESTS COME FOR: Quiet weekends, family reunions, group gatherings, corporate meetings. White-water rafting, minerals, Appalachian folklore, mining museums, antiques, crafts. Appalachian and folk dancing, music, story telling, Cherokee Indian heritage. "Some of the most beautiful wild country to be found. The Jacks and Conasauga Rivers in the Cohutta Wilderness are known (but not too well known) for native trout." The Appalachian Trail has its southern terminus at nearby Springer Mountain as does the Benton MacKaye Trail now being cut through the forest.

BREAKFAST: Varies. Most offer a large country breakfast at guests' request.

RESERVATIONS

One week in advance preferred. If arrangements can be made, will accept last-minute reservations.
Groups: Maximum size is 40. Can be booked into three houses that are close to each other on the Toccoa River.
Also available through travel agents.

RATES
Singles $30. Doubles $35–$45. Seventh night is free.
Some family and group rates available.
One-night surcharge: $10.
Deposit required is 20 percent of total.
Cancellation policy: Deposit, less $5 service fee, is refunded if cancellation is made one week in advance.

Hideaway Is Being Discovered

"A couple of weary travelers from Texas found us in town doing community service at the Blue Ridge, Georgia Visitors Center. They asked for an alternative to the local motels for the night. We suggested a house along the scenic wild Toccoa River. They liked it so much that they stayed three days—and now send their friends.

"A young female executive from California called for a Saturday night placement in a North Georgia mountain bed and breakfast. She was flying into Atlanta for an IBM seminar the following week and planned to rent a car and see some of the surrounding countryside. We placed her in the lovely country home of a retired Atlanta lady executive. She enjoyed her stay in the mountains so much that she arranged to return on Friday night following her meeting in the city to spend another night with her mountain hostess."

QUAIL COUNTRY BED & BREAKFAST, LTD.
MERCER WATT AND KATHY LANIGAN
1104 OLD MONTICELLO ROAD
THOMASVILLE, GA 31792

PHONE: 912/226-7218 or 226-6882
(Call almost anytime.)
OPEN: Year round.

ACCOMMODATIONS
B&Bs
Hosted private residences: 12.
All have air conditioning and private baths.
Plus
Some unhosted private residences for overnight or weekend lodging.
Unhosted short-term (up to three or four months) housing.

LOCATIONS *All in the Thomasville, Georgia, area.*

SETTINGS: Range from a country estate to a neoclassical house in historic district, from a guest house with pool to a new, beautifully furnished condominium.

HOSTS Radiologist, antique car enthusiast, retired school teachers, nurse, banker, veterinarian, dance teacher, restauranteur, surgeon.

GUESTS COME FOR: Corporate training, conferences, house hunting, or just passing through. And for a vacation: In the late nineteenth century, Thomasville was a favorite winter resort for Northern tourists and industrialists, who were attracted by its mild climate and fresh pine-scented air. Current attractions include historic restorations, plantation tours, Pebble Hill Plantation Museum, the April Rose Festival, and hunting preserves.

BREAKFAST: Varies from help-yourself to an elaborate meal.

DIRECTORY: Sent without charge. *Samples:*

> Delightful 100-year-old restored Salt Box–style cottage on 20 acres of wooded land. Ten-minute drive from town. Relax on the deck overlooking a stocked pond and try your luck! Loft bedroom with half-bath upstairs, full bath downstairs. Continental breakfast. $30 single; $35 doubles.

> Quaint Williamsburg-style guest house with pool. Twin beds, private bath, dressing room, and full kitchen. Eighteenth-century garden. Children welcome. $40 single, $50 double.

RESERVATIONS
Advance reservations preferred. If arrangements can be made, will accept last-minute reservations.
Groups: Up to 30 can be booked into various locations in town. Also available through travel agents.

RATES
Singles $30–$40. Doubles $40–$50.
One-night surcharge: $5.
Weekly and monthly rates available.
Deposit required: $25.

Cancellation policy: Refund, minus a $7 processing fee, if cancellation made one week in advance.

SAVANNAH HISTORIC INNS AND GUEST HOUSES
SUSAN EARL
1900 LINCOLN STREET
SAVANNAH, GA 31401

PHONE: 912/233-7666
  Monday–Saturday 9–9, Sunday 1–7.
OPEN: Year round except Thanksgiving, Christmas Eve and Day, New Year's Eve and Day.

ACCOMMODATIONS
B&Bs
Guest houses: Eight.   B&B inns: Two.
Most have private baths. All have air conditioning, and antique and period decor and furnishings.
Plus
Hosted short-term (up to several months) accommodations.

LOCATIONS   *All are within a two-mile landmark historic district in downtown Savannah.*

SETTINGS: Some elegant garden suites and carriage houses of private homes; some have private guest entrances. The inns have from 7 to 26 rooms; one also has garden apartments and carriage houses. "Settings allow for a great deal of privacy. Owners live in separate quarters in the houses."

HOSTS: City budget director, professional couple, attorney....

GUESTS COME FOR: The largest landmark historic district in the country with its restored homes, streets, and squares, museums, shops and restaurants. Beaches, boating, fishing. For business. Some are en route to Orlando, Epcot, and Miami.

BREAKFAST: Most are continental. Many are help-yourself from stocked refrigerator. One inn serves a full breakfast; one provides a help-yourself arrangement in the parlor.

RESERVATIONS

Advance reservations preferred. If arrangements can be made, will accept last-minute reservations.

Groups: Maximum number is 20.

Also available through travel agents.

DIRECTORY: A page of descriptions sent on request without charge. *Sample:*

> Located in the loveliest of downtown neighborhoods, a carriage house, built in 1850, can accommodate one to four guests. Overlooking the courtyard of the Georgian townhouse to which it belongs, the carriage house has one bedroom (double bed) with ceiling fan, spacious living room with fireplace and double sleeper sofa, equipped kitchen, full bath. Furnished with antiques and family pieces. Complimentary wine and use of bicycles. Featured on Savannah Tour of Homes and Gardens. Owners are a young business executive, his wife, and two children. $65 double occupancy. Children under 12 free.

RATES

Singles $30–$98. Doubles $38–$115. A few are higher. Some weekly and monthly rates available.

Deposit required: One night's lodging fee.

Credit cards accepted: MasterCard, VISA, and AMEX.

Hawaii

B&B GUESTS COME FOR: Scenic wonders, volcanos, waterfalls, swimming, jogging, windsurfing, boating, walks for miles on the beach away from tourist areas—yet within half-hour drive to Waikiki . . . a vacation.

A special note about transportation: Oahu has good bus service but there is no public transportation on outer islands.

BED & BREAKFAST HAWAII

EVIE WARNER AND AL DAVIS
BOX 449
KAPAA, HI 96746

PHONE: 808/822-7771
   Live Monday–Friday 8:30–4:30, Saturday 9–3. Answering machine at other times.
OPEN: Year round.

ACCOMMODATIONS
B&Bs
Hosted private residences: 100.
Some are condos. Almost all have private baths. Some have pools.

116

OTHER SERVICES: Car rentals, theater tickets, and tour arrangements. Reduced rates on helicopter rides.

LOCATIONS *On all the islands of the state of Hawaii. Homes are situated throughout—on the ocean and in areas that are near cool rain forests.*

SETTINGS: Could be an extra room in a family home, in an apartment with a separate entrance, or in a cottage on the host's property.

HOSTS: Artists, social workers, realtor, lawyer, doctors, school teachers, musicians, designers, pilots. . . .

BREAKFAST: All continental.

RESERVATIONS
Many hosts require a two-night stay.
Advance reservations preferred but last-minute arrangements may be possible.
Also available through travel agents.

DIRECTORY (not required for reservations): $10. Maps included in the booklet. (A directory is included with a membership.) *Samples*:

Kauai, Poipu (K22A) This large plantation-style home is just two blocks from Poipu Beach Park and one block from Brenneckes bodysurfing beach. The home is on a full acre with plumeria, macadamia nuts, palms, and other tropical plants. Complete with large screened-in veranda for outside sitting and a large living room with color TV, game tables, and Betamax for guest use. Several bedrooms, each with a private bath. Hosts serve breakfast in dining room each morning. Queen or twin beds. $40 double, $5 extra per child. $60 two couples traveling together.

Honolulu (#0–2) Situated in the hills of Honolulu with an expansive view of the ocean is a one-bedroom apartment. Completely separate from the main house, it has its own barbecue and patio, large plate-glass windows, small kitchen area, and total privacy. It is just five minutes from Waikiki, right on the bus line for those who don't want to drive all the time. You'll enjoy the quiet charm of this studio. King bed and double sofa bed. $30 single, $35 double, $10 each additional person. Two-night minimum.

RATES
Membership fee: $10, good for one year.
Singles $20–$35. Doubles $35–$65.
One-night surcharge: $5.
Some weekly and monthly rates available.
Deposit required is 20 percent of total charge.
Cancellation policy: Deposit returned (less $10) if cancellation received one week before expected arrival date.

What's So Special about Us?

"We have a very personalized service and answer every request within one or two days. Rather than considering B&B as a big business, we intend to provide a low-key, more intimate way for people to visit Hawaii."

GO NATIVE .. HAWAII
FRED DIAMOND
P.O. BOX 13115
LANSING, MI 48901

PHONE: 517/349-9598
Covered 24 hours a day by an answering machine. Travelers may call collect and expect a call-back with one or two hours.

Travelers already in Hawaii should contact:
KEN WOOD
130 PUHILL STREET
HILO, HI 96720

PHONE: 808/961-2080

ACCOMMODATIONS
B&Bs
Hosted private residences: 60. B&B inns: 4.
Almost all have private baths.
Some are accessible to handicapped.
Plus
Some unhosted private residences for overnight or weekend lodging.
House rentals on a weekly or monthly basis.

OTHER SERVICES: Car rentals. Pickup at airport. Some hosts act as tour guides and provide transportation.

LOCATIONS *Throughout each of the Hawaiian islands. Public transportation is limited on all except Oahu.*

SETTINGS: Range from simple to quite luxurious.

HOSTS: Realtor, artists, archeologist, retired language teacher, professional clown, anthropologist, practical nurse, marketing manager. . . .

BREAKFAST: Most serve continental.

RESERVATIONS
Minimum stay required: Two nights.
Maximum stay: Flexible, but usually should not exceed one week at any one time "as our hosts like a break between bookings and do not accept semipermanent guests."
Advance notice: Thirty days preferred. If arrangements can be made, will accept last-minute reservations.
Groups: Maximum size is 10.
Also available through travel agents.

DIRECTORY (not required for reservations): Sent without charge on request. *Sample descriptions:*

Maui. Serene mountain retreat on slopes of Haleakala Crater. Hospitable hosts. Home is of Oriental design. Country living at its best. Easy access to all Maui attractions. One bedroom with twin beds, full bath, private entrance. $35 single, $40 double.

Oahu. Lovely home overlooking Chinaman's Hat and ocean on one side and Koolau mountains on the other. Pool. Peaceful. Master bedroom, Japanese bath, TV, kitchen privileges. $35 single/double.

RATES
Singles $25–$40. Doubles $30–$50. A few are higher.
Deposit required is 50 percent of total charge.
Cancellation policy: If notice received at least 30 days before expected arrival date, full refund; between 10 and 29 days, 50 percent; less than 10 days, none.

Fred began the business in Hawaii when he was associated with the travel industry there. He now coordinates the service from the main office in Michigan. Ken continues with the interviewing of new hosts and takes care of bookings desired by travelers who are already in Hawaii.

After three years of matching hosts and guests, they find that B&B guests travel to experience something new and different from that found at home. "They are generally flexible and anticipate the experience to be one like calling on old friends." To that end, Fred and Ken observe that capricious itinerary changes during the course of a visit can be extremely disruptive, particularly when you consider that hosts make special provisions for receiving guests much as they would in welcoming old friends.

PACIFIC-HAWAII BED & BREAKFAST

DORIS E. EPP
19 KAI NANI PLACE
KAILUA, OAHU, HI 96734

PHONE: 808/262-6026 or 263-4848
   Live Monday–Saturday 9–7. Answering machine at most other times.
OPEN: Year round.

ACCOMMODATIONS
B&Bs
Hosted private residences: 150.
Almost all have private baths.
Plus
Some unhosted homes available for vacationers.

OTHER SERVICES: Some hosts can provide airport pickup; some offer private island or yacht tours.

LOCATIONS *Many throughout the island of Oahu; some are on other islands too. Many in Kailua on or close to an "uncrowded untouristy beautiful sandy swimming beach" are about a 15-minute drive to Honolulu or a half hour's drive from Waikiki.*

SETTINGS: About 25 percent are rather luxurious. Wide range includes room and bath in private home from $20 per couple to yacht for two guest at $125.

BREAKFAST: All serve continental—"light, health-oriented meal with Hawaiian fruit."

RESERVATIONS
Some hosts require a three-day minimum.
Advance reservations preferred. Will accept last-minute requests.
Groups: Maximum size is 10.
Also available through travel agents.

DIRECTORY (not required for reservations): $2. Maps included. *Sample*:

Two rooms (sleeps four to five guests), private bath, in ocean-front home, separate entrance, patio, color TV, refrigerator, small sink, some cooking utensils and appliances. On long stretch of sandy swimming beach. $65 per night.
One bedroom, private bath, oceanfront home, separate entrance, refrigerator, TV. $25 couple.

RATES
Singles $20–$40; a few lower and a few higher.
Doubles $20–$125 (on yacht).
One-night surcharge: $10 at some B&Bs.
Deposit required is 50 percent of total charge.
Cancellation policy: If cancelled within five days prior to arrival, one night's fee is charged. (Balance of deposit returned to guests.)

Idaho

Many B&Bs in Idaho are represented by Northwest Bed & Breakfast, page 264.

Illinois

BED & BREAKFAST/CHICAGO, INC.

MARY SHAW
POB 14088
CHICAGO, IL 60614-0088

PHONE: 312/951-0085
  Live Monday–Friday 10–2. Answering machine at other times.
OPEN: Year round, but shortened hours midwinter.

ACCOMMODATIONS
B&Bs
Hosted private residences: 65.
Most have air conditioning and private baths.
Plus
Unhosted private residences for overnight or weekend lodging.
Hosted and unhosted short-term (up to six months) housing.

LOCATIONS *Most are close to or in the downtown Chicago area. Others are along the North Shore. Some vacation homes are in Indiana and Michigan along the shore of Lake Michigan.*

SETTINGS: High-rise apartments, 1890s townhouses, Victorian homes, country estates, lakeside retreats. About 70 percent are luxurious. Many are in historic areas. City residences tend to be smaller accommodations.

HOSTS: TV reporter, loads of bankers, art director at advertising agency, several writers, artists, librarian, realtor, several school teachers, a flight attendant. . . .

GUESTS COME FOR: Vacations, sightseeing, conferences, for business reasons, academia including Northwestern University and University of Chicago.

BREAKFAST: Most city hosts are not usually present.
About 75 percent of hosts serve continental.

RESERVATIONS
Minimum stay of two nights required in the city, one night in suburbs.
Advance notice preferred. If arrangements can be made, will accept last-minute reservations.

DIRECTORY: None available, but a sheet with about 20 descriptions accompanies all answers to inquiries. *Samples*:

> 50a. Chicago: Downtown. If you desire a spectacular view of Chicago from the 42nd floor, overlooking State Street, the Loop, Chicago yacht basin, and Illinois Center, stay in this delightful one-bedroom apartment. It is not hosted; however, breakfast is in the refrigerator. Balcony off both the living room and the bedroom. Within walking distance of the Loop and shopping on Michigan Avenue. . . . Parking available. Air conditioned. Twin beds in the bedroom; double hide-a-bed in the living room. TV. Single $65. Double $75. Three $85. Four $95.

> 48. This chauffeurs' garage built in 1926 has been converted into an architecturally interesting modern environment with an open, contemporary feeling, skylights, and a connecting bridge on the second level. It was designed and remodeled by its present owner, who is in public relations. It has antiques, Oriental rugs, plants, and a beautiful garden. Private baths. Single $40, twin or double $50.

RATES
Singles $30–$50. Doubles $45–$60.
One-night surcharge: $10.

Weekly and monthly rates available.

Deposit required: $15.

Credit cards accepted: MasterCard and VISA and extra 5 percent to charge.

Cancellation policy: Full amount, minus $5 handling charge, refunded if notice received 48 hours before expected arrival date.

Do you have a question? When writing to a bed and breakfast reservation service, please enclose a business-sized self-addressed stamped envelope (SASE).

Indiana

AMISH ACRES INC.
DEBORAH SCHMUCKER
1600 WEST MARKET STREET
NAPPANEE, IN 46550

PHONE: 219/773-4188
Live 9–5 April–November, daily; December–March, Monday–Friday. Answering machine at other times.
OPEN: Year round.

ACCOMMODATIONS
B&Bs
Hosted private residences: 20.

LOCATIONS *All in northern Indiana, about a 35-minute drive south from South Bend and about a half-hour drive from Elkhart. All within a 16-mile radius of Nappanee. Most are within a 10-minute drive of Amish Acres, a restored historic farm.*

SETTINGS: All are in rural surroundings. One is an historic home. Most are farmhouses, "genuine country homes typical of what you see in the countryside."

HOSTS: Most are farmers. "They represent the settlers in this area. Many are Mennonite or Amish families. Some are Old Order German Baptist homes. A few are residents who own television sets and radios."

GUESTS COME FOR: Amish Acres. Notre Dame football games. Seasonal festivals such as the annual apple and blueberry celebrations.

BREAKFAST: At least continental, but most offer a family farm breakfast.

RESERVATIONS
Advance arrangements preferred, but last-minute reservations are accepted.

DIRECTORY: Being prepared when this book was going to press. It will include descriptions of homes and some pictures. Inquire about availability and price.

RATES

Singles: $28. Doubles: $38. Additional person in same room, $10. Deposit required: For reservations made much in advance or for a busy season, $15.

By Popular Demand

Amish Acres, a restored Amish farm, was owned and home-steaded by one family for over 100 years. In 1968 the property was bought and restored as a place where visitors can learn about the Amish way of life. Tours are given in the Amish home on the grounds. Buggy rides are available. The dining room features Amish country cooking. After many visitors asked about B&B possibilities, Amish Acres started the new and entirely separate service of screening homes and placing travelers as paying overnight guests with area families.

Some additional Indiana B&Bs are available through reservation services in other states.

Elkhart has a B&B represented by Betsy Ross Bed & Breakfast of Michigan, page 194.

Some along the shore of Lake Michigan are represented by Bed & Breakfast/Chicago, page 123.

Three in southern Indiana have been selected by Kentucky Homes Bed & Breakfast, page 134.

Iowa

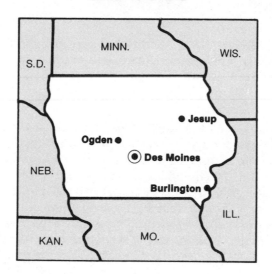

BED & BREAKFAST IN IOWA, LTD.

WILMA L. BLOOM

P.O. BOX 430

PRESTON, IA 52069

PHONE: 319/689-4222

Live at least Monday–Friday, 7–noon. Answering machine at other times.

OPEN: Year round. Closed December 20–February 1.

ACCOMMODATIONS

B&Bs

Hosted private residences: 25.

Most have air conditioning.

One in Des Moines is accessible to handicapped.

LOCATIONS *Throughout the state. Most are within a 10-mile radius of the centers of towns.*

SETTINGS: Most host homes are in relatively small towns or on farms. Some homes have historic significance.

HOSTS: Nurse, farmer, interior decorator, retired military, pilot, antique collectors, realtor, and housewives too. . . . Some hosts who live in towns have farm ownership connections also.

GUESTS COME FOR: A vacation. A visit on a farm. Fishing. Water-skiing, boating, snowmobiling and ice skating. Limestone bluffs and Indian history. Hunting. Conferences. Colleges. Business. Just passing through.

BREAKFAST: Most serve a full Iowa breakfast that could include homemade rolls or bread, Iowa meats, and home-raised garden vegetables.

RESERVATIONS
Advance reservations preferred. If arrangements can be made, will accept last-minute reservations.

DIRECTORY: $1. *Sample descriptions*:

Southeast Quarter: Burlington. A beautiful home of 1854 architecture in Heritage Hill, with spacious rooms filled with antique furnishings. Near the Mississippi, where the Delta Queen and the Mississippi Belle dock. Steamboat Days in June. Three rooms.

Northeast Quarter: Jesup. Sheltered earth home on 1,500-acre diversified modern farm; near a Frank Lloyd Wright home, 10 miles to Amish settlement. One room for up to four persons.

Northwest Quarter: Ogden. Three-generation family farm; home renovated and well decorated. Hunters welcome for turkey, pheasant, etc. Near Mamie Eisenhower birthplace. Two rooms available.

RATES
Singles $25–$50. Doubles $30–$60.
Deposit required (if time permits): $20.
Cancellation policy: Full refund if cancelled one week or more prior to date of reservation; otherwise refund minus $5 handling charge.

The community-oriented Blooms are native Iowans, have lived in several parts of the state, and have had careers in hog farming, writing, real estate, and teaching. Now, through this B&B service, they feel they are "in a position to show farm and small-town family life in Iowa in as many ways as it would be possible to assemble. There have been guests who have come to a home expecting to stay a night or two and have stayed as much as a week, after being caught up in the activity of a farming operation and the life with animals, pets, and ponds on the property."

Kansas

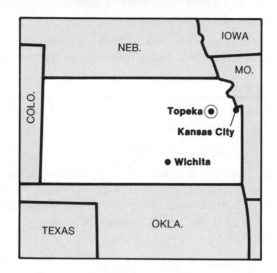

KANSAS CITY BED & BREAKFAST

DIANE C. KUHN
P.O. BOX 14781
LENEXA, KS 66215

PHONE: 913/268-4214
  Monday–Friday 9–5, May–August;
  5–9 p.m. September through May.
OPEN: Year round.

ACCOMMODATIONS
B&Bs
Hosted private residences: 23.   One B&B inn.
Almost all have air conditioning and private baths. One has a pool, and one has a hot tub.
Plus
Hosted short-term (up to six weeks) housing.

OTHER SERVICES: Pickup at airport, bus, and train.

LOCATIONS *All but two (Warrensburg, MO, and Modoc, KS) are within 10 miles of the greater Kansas City area. Some are near public transportation.*

SETTINGS: "Some are luxurious. Some are just plain. All are clean, comfortable, and attractive."

HOSTS: Nurse, builder, teacher, magazine editors, writer, farmer, retired policeman, professor, cooking instructor. . . .

GUESTS COME FOR: Medical meetings ("We seem to host many doctors"). Vacations: Worlds of Fun, Oceans of Fun, Royals Stadium, Truman Library, Crown Center, Country Club Plaza. University of Missouri at Kansas City, American Royal.

BREAKFAST: All full. Could include Belgian waffles, homemade breads, quiches, or omelets.

RESERVATIONS
Advance reservations of at least one week preferred. If arrangements can be made, will accept last-minute reservations.
Groups: Maximum size is eight.
Also available through travel agents.

DIRECTORY: Sent without charge to those who send a business-sized self-addressed stamped envelope. *Sample*:

> Kansas City, MO, #BO33. In historic Hyde Park, this shirt waist-style home was built by the Cowherd Brothers Construction Company in 1900. Today's owners have renovated the home by adapting the large, open floor plan to their personal style and taste. Hosts are collectors of American folk art and are active in renovation of historic Kansas City neighborhoods. Guest quarters with complete privacy on third floor include bedroom, bath, living room, dining room, and kitchenette. Full breakfast. $40 double. $35 Single. $5 per child.

RATES
Singles $30–$50. Doubles $30–$85.
Some weekly and monthly rates available.
Deposit required is 20 percent of total charge.
Cancellation policy: Full refund, minus $2 handling fee, if notice received 48 hours before expected arrival date.

> *"We had never tried B&B before and we were delighted . . . a charming hostess. We loved having the whole second floor to ourselves. Breakfast was not only delicious, but beautifully presented. And, when Chris needed time to study on Sunday, our gracious hostess let him spread his things out on her dining room table—and kept a pot of coffee hot and ready. Thank you!"*
>
> *—Kansas City Bed & Breakfast guests*

◇ ◇ ◇

Kentucky

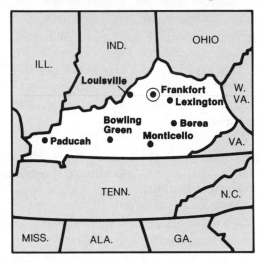

BLUEGRASS BED & BREAKFAST
BETSY AND DICK PRATT
ROUTE 1, BOX 263
VERSAILLES, KY 40383

PHONE: 606/873-3208
  Monday–Friday 8–5.
OPEN: Year round except December 15–January 6.

ACCOMMODATIONS
B&Bs
Hosted private residences: 18.
Almost all have air conditioning and private baths.
Plus
Some short-term hosted housing arrangements.

LOCATIONS *All are within 15-mile radius of city of Lexington, Kentucky in the "Bluegrass," the area with more than 350 thoroughbred horse farms that supply most of the horses running on American race tracks. The area is rich in old houses, estatelike farms, points of historic interest, and classic architecture.*

SETTINGS: Range from stone house built in 1792, before Kentucky became a separate state, to modern townhouse filled with American antiques and Chinese art.

HOSTS: Retired professor/engineering, stockbroker, travel agent, farmer, horse breeder, professor of art, retired oil company executive. . . .

GUESTS COME FOR: A vacation: Boating, swimming, horseback riding, camping, fishing, hiking. Scenic country roads bordered by parklike horse farms, big old historic homes, well-marked points of interest such as battlefields, early settlements, Indian villages, Daniel Boone's trail, and the famous Kentucky Horse Park. Schools: University of Kentucky, Center College, Transylvania College.

BREAKFAST: Varies from simple to elaborate meal according to host.

RESERVATIONS
At least 10 days in advance preferred. If arrangements can be made, will accept last-minute reservations.
Minimum stay of three nights required for special events only.

DIRECTORY: A house list is sent on request without charge. *Samples*:

> In the country. Welcome Hall. Built in 1792, when Kentucky was still the westernmost segment of Virginia, this handsome stone house and its grounds are a prime example of that period's self-sufficient country estate. Now devoted to blooded horses as well as general farming, it provides a unique experience for its guests. A brick-floored summerhouse set in the midst of an extensive walled garden provides a pleasant retreat for reading or conversation. One room available with twin beds and private bath ($60).

> In town. Versailles. An experience you'll never forget. This is a newly decorated suite—living room, bedroom, and bath—in a stately old Victorian brick home so large that it has a hallway 60 feet long, 10 wide, with a 12-foot ceiling. The suite boasts a fireplace, queen-sized brass bed, and a claw-footed tub deep enough to swim in. The suite is on the first floor and has a private entrance ($60).

RATES
Range: $36–$60.

Weekly and monthly rates available.

Deposit required is 25 percent of first night's fee.

Cancellation policy: All but $10 refunded if notice received 48 hours before expected arrival date.

> *"We bought a farm eight years ago and set about restoring the old house. Having stayed in B&Bs ourselves, we decided to take in a few guests. We found the cost of advertising more than the income from a single B&B, so we started a reservation service with unique, high-quality locations of unusual interest. We maintain a close, personal relationship with our hosts/hostesses."*

KENTUCKY HOMES BED & BREAKFAST

JO D. BOONE AND LILLIAN B. MARSHALL
1431 ST. JAMES CT.
LOUISVILLE, KY 40208

PHONE: 502/635-7341 or 452-6629
  Live Monday–Friday, 8–12, 2–5. Answering machines at other times.
OPEN: Year round; closed major holidays.

ACCOMMODATIONS
B&Bs
Hosted private residences: 75.
Almost all have air conditioning. Most have private baths.
Plus
A few hosted and unhosted short-term housing possibilities.

OTHER SERVICES: Specially marked map with B&Bs in a requested area and list of day trips possible from each location. The custom-drawn circle encompasses a 25-mile radius and includes vacation information and help in planning bicycling trips.

LOCATIONS *In Kentucky: Ashland, Bardstown, Bowling Green, Frankfort, Hodgenville, Lexington, Monticello, Nicholasville, Owensboro, Paducah, Sonora, Winchester, and Georgetown. Some homes are on farms near larger cities and interstates.*

*On the way in and out of Kentucky on major routes: Three
in southern Indiana and one in northern Tennessee.
There are B&Bs near all the scenic attractions, including
Mammoth Cave, Land-Between-the-Lakes, Daniel Boone's
first Kentucky Fort, Lincoln Country, and Bybee Pottery in
the low Cumberland Mountains.*

SETTINGS: Most are rather luxurious. Some are historic homes.

HOSTS: Doctors, lawyer, accountant, psychiatrist, university professors, insurance executives, dentists, veterinarian, realtors, city
planners, architects.... "Their flexibility and generosity is incredible. One hostess (at $48/night) serves country ham–cham-
pagne breakfast on the patio beside a freshwater lake. One host,
lest vacationers miss seeing, for example, the last home of George
Rogers Clark—Locust Grove—will drive them miles in his car to
see it."

GUESTS COME FOR: Business reasons. For schools: University of
Louisville, Spalding, Bellarmine, Eastern Kentucky University,
Western Kentucky University, Berea College. For attractions in
Louisville: Kentucky Derby, Actors Theater, Performing Arts
Center, horse racing. In Lexington: horse farms, Keeneland for
racing. In Frankfort: the state capitol.

BREAKFAST: Full breakfast at all B&Bs. If a host must leave
early, everything is laid out for guests to help themselves. Menu
could include hot biscuits, homemade jams, sausage, casseroles,
omelets, muffins.

RESERVATIONS
Advance reservations required. Allow time for exchange of mail so
that deposit is received at least a week in advance. Groups: 18–20
can be accommodated within one block in Old Louisville neighborhood, 10 minutes from downtown.

RATES
Singles $29–$39. Double $38–$44. A few higher.
Please note that rates more than double during Kentucky Derby
events week.
Weekly and monthly rates available.
Deposit required: $25.

*Jo is in real estate. Lillian is a cookbook author. Together
they run the B&B reservation service. "We worry if guests*

are late arriving, care if they are allergic to feather pillows, and want them to enjoy, enjoy!

"Among our most memorable guests is a California woman who celebrated her 65th birthday by buying one of those plane tickets on which you can go everywhere once. She called us to say she would be in town for Derby Weekend (when our rates are highest) and could spend $15 on a night's lodging. We explained that we don't have what are called "cheap sleeps," but that we would try to help her. We placed her with a dear friend who is not a B&B member, for a nominal rate. . . . On the plane trip here with other Californians she heard for the first time that one had to have a ticket for the Derby and that you almost had to inherit one at that. Undaunted, she insisted she would buy a ticket at the gate. A man in the group who heard this dialogue walked up to her and placed a box-seat ticket in her hand. His friend hadn't been able to come. Her charmed life held through six months of travel; she sent us postals from every eastern city of the United States."

Louisiana

B&B GUESTS COME FOR: A vacation, conferences, business, and universities. Attractions include inland seaports, small towns, historic sites, nature trails, salt and freshwater fishing, and Acadian French culture. New Orleans is known for its French Quarter, Garden District, Super Dome, the Super Bowl and Sugar Bowl, Mardi Gras and Spring Fiesta, in addition to jazz, food, museums, Audubon Park Zoological Gardens, and antique shops.

LOUISIANA HOSPITALITY SERVICES

MELISSA D. FOLKS
P.O. BOX 80717
BATON ROUGE, LA 70898

PHONE: 504/769-0366
   Monday–Saturday, 9–6.
OPEN: Year round except January 1, Easter weekend, July 4, Labor Day weekend, Thanksgiving, Christmas Eve and Day.

ACCOMMODATIONS
B&Bs
Hosted private residences: 16.   B&B inns: 10.
All have air conditioning and almost all have private baths.

Plus
Some unhosted private residences for overnight or weekend lodging.

OTHER SERVICES: Itinerary planning for attractions in the area and sometimes en route. Bookings made at other B&Bs throughout the country with other reservation services, or with inns that are in guidebooks from Melissa's library. Fees charged for these services.

LOCATIONS *Spread throughout rural and urban areas of Louisiana, Mississippi, Arkansas, and Alabama.*

SETTINGS: All are historic homes (built before 1930).

HOSTS: Retired dental hygienist, retired business man, school teacher, antique dealer, business woman, architect, retired military, housewife. . . . "All selected because of the commitment to 'the art of innkeeping.' "

BREAKFAST: Varies according to host.

DIRECTORY (not required for reservations): $2. *Sample*:

Shreveport HC-FFP-Al—This elegantly restored home (circa 1900), located in the Highland Historical Restoration district, offers spacious rooms with king-sized beds and private baths. Enjoy the coffee served from a sterling silver service. Here you are conveniently located to the central business district, medical center, airport, and I-20. Louisiana Downs Race Track is only minutes away. Breakfast is included. Deluxe range ($50–$69). $55 minimum deposit.

RESERVATIONS
Minimum stay required at some locations and during special events such as Natchitoches Christmas Festival.
Advance reservations of at least two weeks required. ($10 service charge if arrangements are made with less than two weeks' notice.)
No last-minute reservations accepted.
Groups: Maximum size is 10.

RATES
Singles $40–$100. Doubles $45–$110.
Deposit is required but varies as stated in directory.
Some hosts accept VISA, MasterCard, and AMEX.
Cancellation policy: $10.00 surcharge in all cases. Full refund less

$10.00 when more than seven days' notice is given. No refund if less than seven days' notice.

NEW ORLEANS BED & BREAKFAST/BED AND BREAKFAST OF LOUISIANA AND TOURS
SARAH-MARGARET BROWN
P.O. BOX 8163
NEW ORLEANS, LA 70182

PHONE: 504/949-6705 and 949-4570
   Monday–Friday 8 a.m.–9 p.m.
OPEN: Year round except Christmas and New Year's.

ACCOMMODATIONS
B&Bs
Hosted private residences: 50.   B&B inns: 5.
Almost all have air conditioning and private baths.
Plus
Some unhosted private residences (some are rooming houses) for overnight or weekend lodging.
Some hosted and unhosted short-term housing also available.

OTHER SERVICES: Car rentals. Tours of swamps and bayous and of Acadian country with its unique music and food.

LOCATIONS   *Throughout Louisiana and Mississippi. Most B&Bs in New Orleans are near good public transportation.*

SETTINGS: A wide range—from simple rooms and apartments appropriate for backpackers, to historic homes and luxurious plantations. Some camps and homes in Cajun country.

HOSTS: Retired teachers, interior decorators, architects, tour guides. . . .

BREAKFAST: Continental. Most plantations serve a full country breakfast.

RESERVATIONS
Minimum stay of five days required at Mardi Gras and Sugar Bowl times.

If arrangements can be made, will accept last-minute reservations. Groups: Maximum size is 30 depending on sleeping arrangements. Also available through travel agents.

DIRECTORY (not required for reservations): $7.50. Spiral-bound book includes some photos and sketches with descriptions. *Samples*:

> Lower Garden District: An absolutely beautiful restored town house, circa 1858, glittering with crystal chandeliers, priceless antiques. All rooms have private baths, telephones, TV, individually controlled air conditioning and heat. Complimentary cocktails in the double parlors or on the brick patio. Breakfast in the dining room. The Magazine Street bus lines takes you directly to Canal Street, French Quarter, Audubon Park Zoological Gardens. $50–$75.

> Uptown: In the Carrollton area, in a comfortable turn-of-the-century home furnished in antiques, a relaxed and friendly hostess offers three bedrooms, double beds, shared bath, at $35 a night, single occupancy, $40/double occupancy. Near bus line. Swimming pool also.

RATES
Singles $20–$100. Doubles $25–$125.
Some weekly and monthly rates available.
Deposit required: 20 percent or one night's lodging.
Credit cards accepted: MasterCard and VISA for deposits.
Cancellation policy: Full refund minus $10 service charge.

SOUTHERN COMFORT BED & BREAKFAST RESERVATION
SUSAN MORRIS AND HELEN HEATH
2856 HUNDRED OAKS
BATON ROUGE, LA 70808

PHONE: 504/346-1928 or 928-9815 daily 8–8.
OPEN: Year round.

ACCOMMODATIONS
B&Bs
Hosted private residences: 26.   B&B inns: 9.
All have air conditioning and most have private baths. Several have pools.

OTHER SERVICES: "For a booking fee of $15 we will make reservations almost anywhere outside of our membership for one trip. For a $25 membership fee we will provide this service to the traveler for an entire year. This covers private homes and inns in this country, Canada, Europe, and the British Isles. This is done through other reservation services and, in a few cases, with individual hosts."

Car rentals: Special auto rental arrangements are available in many areas of Louisiana. Eight categories of vehicles with special rates (seven days for price of five) for weekly rental. MasterCard, VISA, AMEX, Diners Club cards accepted.

LOCATIONS *Throughout Louisiana.*
In Mississippi, B&Bs are located from the Gulf Coast up the river to Vicksburg.
Rural and urban locations in both states.

SETTINGS: More than 75 percent are 50–150 year old homes and many are on the National Register of Historic Homes.

HOSTS: Registered nurse, homemaker, retired teachers, businesswomen, school teacher, retired banker (a woman), retired army officers and wives, a writer, a restaurant owner. . . .

BREAKFAST: Varies from simple to elaborate. Could include: shrimp/egg casserole; cane syrup French toast; biscuits and other hot breads; cheese grits; raisin bran refrigerator muffins; homemade preserves such as fig; toast with strawberry butter; eggs Benedict.

RESERVATIONS
At least two weeks in advance preferred. If arrangements can be made, will accept last-minute reservations.
Groups: Can book up to 200 in Baton Rouge; 6–25 in other areas. Also available through travel agents.

DIRECTORY (not required for reservations): $2. *Samples*:

Louisiana, Sulphur: Twelve miles from Lake Charles on I-10 and U.S. 90. Minutes away from Delta Downs Track at Vinton, the Creole Nature Trail, Brimstone Museum, beaches, parks, and golf courses. #LS1 Turn-of-the-century country inn with wraparound porch complete with swings for relaxing. Three bedrooms, one has private bath, two share a bath. Country atmosphere and hospitality. Refreshments on arrival, Creole "wake up" coffee, full breakfast. Lunch or dinner with Creole dishes on request $15. $48 weekdays, $58 weekends. $275 for entire house for weekend.

Mississippi, Natchez: The name is synonymous with gracious living of a bygone day when "cotton was king" and more than half the millionaires in the infant United States lived here. On U.S. 61. This mansion (built 1818 and now on the National Register of Historic Places) was once the home of a famous general who was also Governor of Mississippi and a U.S. Senator. You will see many of his personal belongings (that have been returned here by his descendants) as well as numerous Civil War mementos. Bask in early 19th-century elegance combined with air conditioning and TV. Full breakfast and tour of house and spacious grounds. Rates in garden cottages and mansion are $70, $80, and $90 single; $75, $85, $95 double; $20 for each additional person in a room.

RATES

Singles $25–$100. Doubles $32–$150.

(Rates for rooms on a plantation mansion are $50–$150 a day and cover room, breakfast, tour of house, sometimes flowers and champagne in the room, and a welcoming drink.)

Some weekly and monthly rates available.

Deposit required is 50 percent of estimated charges.

Credit cards accepted with 5 percent surcharge: MasterCard and VISA.

Cancellation policy: Refund, less $12.50 service charge, made if cancellation notice is received at least 72 hours before stated arrival time.

What's the Role of a Reservation Service?

"We enjoy taking a special interest in our travelers and their reasons for making the trip, what they might enjoy doing or seeing, helping them plan the trip. Many people from other sections of the country have no idea of the distances between cities and towns in this area and we try to give them information about this."

Proof: A letter from a Californian—" . . . We have become partial to the bed-and-breakfast method of lodging, since it has given us irreplaceable experiences and has allowed us to meet some fascinating people. . . . We were initially surprised and slightly dismayed when we located Lorman in our atlas, since it is not exactly in the neighborhood of Baton Rouge. We now thank our stars that we trusted your judgment because you clearly knew what you were doing. In the midst of various high points to our trip— excellent weather, the Natchez Pilgrimage, the outstanding cuisine of New Orleans—our B&B experience through you stands out above them all. . . . After all the remarkable [organized] tours around Natchez, none surpassed the tour our hostess gave us in her home . . . our museum of a bedroom. . . . Since we enjoyed their company so much, I was sorry to part company that evening. . . . Our breakfast was a veritable feast: delicious, elegant, abundant . . . uniquely honored by our good fortune. . . ."

Small World Department

"We booked a reservation for a family from Arizona with one of our Baton Rouge hostesses. The hostess's neighbor dropped in the next morning when the guests were eating breakfast. The visiting wife and the neighbor took one look at each other and fell into each other's arms. They had gone to high school together in Illinois some years ago, and neither had the faintest idea the other would be in Baton Rouge!"

A husband and wife traveled to his mother's childhood home area and spent two whole days on the rural highways and byways looking for possible cousins and other relatives, with no success. The last night in the area they discovered their B&B host was one of the long lost cousins!

BED & BREAKFAST, INC.
HAZELL BOYCE
1236 DECATUR STREET
NEW ORLEANS, LA 70116

PHONE: 504/525-4640
   Daily.
OPEN: Year round.

ACCOMMODATIONS
B&Bs
Hosted private residences: 30.   One B&B inn.
All have air conditioning. About half have private baths.
Almost all have easy access to public transportation.
Plus
One unhosted private home available for overnight, weekend, or monthly lodging.
Hosted and unhosted short-term (up to several months) housing.

OTHER SERVICES: Dinner available by advance arrangement at some houses. Some hosts will give city tours and book guests into other tours—and restaurants too.

LOCATIONS   *Most are in Metropolitan New Orleans. All are within 20 minutes of downtown, the French Quarter, convention facilities. Many are convenient to public transportation that services those three areas.*

SETTINGS: Many are in or close to historic neighborhoods.

HOSTS: Professors, interior decorators, licensed tour guides, retired oil company executives, preservationists. . . .

BREAKFAST: Most serve continental. Full available at some for an extra charge.

RESERVATIONS
Last-minute reservations accepted.
Groups: Maximum size is 50.
Also available through travel agents.

DIRECTORY: A sampler of listings sent without charge. *Samples*:

Restored 19th-Century Home. Architect–interior decorator couple warmly welcome guests into their home. Detailed millwork and finely etched glass are combined with all the modern conveniences. The historic streetcar, just 1½ blocks away, arrives at the French Quarter in 15 minutes. Continental breakfast. Guest bedrooms and suites $40 up single, $50 up double, $10 up each additional guest.

Algiers Point Home. Proudly designated as a New Orleans Historic Landmark. A quiet three-block walk to the free ferry and guests savor a brief romantic ride across the

Mississippi River, landing at the edge of the French Quarter. (Nearby bridge for cars). Swimming pool. Separate suite available with bedroom, living room (sofa bed), kitchen with continental breakfast makings. $30 single, $10 each additional guest.

RATES
Singles $25–$65. Doubles $35–$75. A few higher.
Some weekly and monthly rates available.

A New Way to Spread the Word

"A major newspaper printed the wrong phone number for my service. The very lovely lady whose number was listed instead of mine had never heard of B&B. She said, 'You sure must be tired of serving all those people breakfast!' When I explained B&B, she was fascinated and joined the thousands who agree that it was the only way to go."

Because B&Bs are all different, tell the service what you want. Think ahead of time about your needs. For a little help, turn to page 1.

Maine

B&B GUESTS COME FOR: Vacations. Stops going to and coming from Canada. Conferences. House hunting. Business reasons. Attractions include the rugged shoreline, inland lakes and ponds, Acadia National Park, Bar Harbor, offshore islands, sports and recreational activities, schools including Bowdoin College, Colby College, University of Maine, and Bates College.

BED & BREAKFAST DOWN EAST, LTD.

SALLY B. GODFREY
BOX 547, MACOMBER MILL ROAD
EASTBROOK, ME 04634

PHONE: 207/565-3517
 Live Monday–Saturday 8–8. Answering machine at other times.
OPEN: Year round. Closed Thanksgiving Day and Christmas Day.

ACCOMMODATIONS
B&Bs
Hosted private residences: 78.   B&B inns: 7.
One sailing yacht.

Plus
A few unhosted private residences for overnights, weekends, or by the week.

OTHER SERVICES: Some hosts pick up at airport, bus, and train. Car rentals can be arranged in Bar Harbor area. Boat charters can be arranged in some areas.

LOCATIONS   *From one end of the (very big) state to the other. Many along the coast; some in villages, cities, rural areas; on islands; on lakes and ponds; near ski areas and state and national parks.*

SETTINGS: The range is vast—some "just plain," some luxurious, historic, rural, oceanfront, a cottage, a camp. One is on a 46-foot coasting brigantine.

HOSTS: Several foreign service officers, teachers, college professors, lawyer, retired banker, nurse, several artists, farmers, several craftspeople, musician, writer, geologist, sea captain, retired military. . . .

BREAKFAST: Varies according to host from simple to elaborate meal. Could include toad-in-a-hole, walnut pancakes, homemade croissants, great assortments of home-baked breads, pastries, preserves, home-grown fruits. "Most hosts are present for breakfast and report that it is one of the most enjoyable parts of the B&B experience."

RESERVATIONS
Two weeks in advance preferred. In busy areas—Bar Harbor, for instance—a month ahead of time is recommended. If arrangements can be made, will accept last-minute reservations.
Minimum stay: A couple of homes request two nights.
Groups: Equipped to handle groups of 10–12 people in some locations.
Also available through travel agents.

DIRECTORY (not required for reservations): $3. A clear, easy-to-follow booklet that has its own regionalized map of Maine. *Sample:*

Bar Harbor: #165. One of Bar Harbor's wonderful old "cottages." Oceanfront turn-of-the-century shingle-style estate on four acres abutting Acadia National Park land. Lovely secluded setting within walking distance . . . screened porch, private beach. Large sitting rooms and dining room, all with fireplaces. Host couple are self-employed. He is a former baker. They enjoy tennis, chess, hiking, cooking, gardening, and travel. There are three guest rooms, two with fireplaces. All have ocean views. One has private full bath; the other two share a bath.

Resident pets: None.   Guest pets: No.

Resident smokers: None.   Guest smokers: Prefer not.

Breakfast: continental. Homemade croissants, Danish, fresh fruit or juice, freshly ground coffee, tea, hot or cold cereal.

Rates: $45–$65. Folding bed available $10.

Special features: Interesting old house, quiet, yet close to all Bar Harbor activities.

RATES

Singles $25–$45. Doubles $35–$50. A few higher: $60–$75. One suite is $125.

One-night surcharge: Several hosts have a $2–$3 fee. Some weekly and monthly rates available.

Deposit required: $20 per night per room.

Credit cards: AMEX, VISA, and MasterCard accepted.

Cancellation policy: If notice received at least 48 hours before expected arrival date, a $10 processing fee will be deducted from your deposit and the balance refunded.

Dear Bernice . . .

I take great pride in offering personal service. It's always interesting to help people find that perfect spot for their Maine stay. What fun to match architectural buffs with a couple who have restored a fine old home! Or to help plan an island-hopping honeymoon or suggest side trips, museums, or other points of interest for folks planning a vacation around their hobbies or special interests. The challenge of matching guests with appropriate hosts, or heading them in a direction they might otherwise not have known about, is satisfying. I find the business a joy—with never a dull moment. And—I've learned more about Maine history, architecture, geography, and natural history than I ever would have otherwise.

One couple (a nurse with her post-stroke, partially disabled doctor husband) arranged to come to Maine from Florida. They stayed with two wonderful ladies—retired teachers who are sisters. The older (age 80) sister took the couple under her wing and spent four days taking them (in her own car) all over Mount Desert Island to show them the park, Cadillac Mountain, Jackson Lab. They all had a splendid time—and still correspond. . . .

Also interesting are the wishful-thinking stories I hear from people who call or write from all over the country—even South America—telling me how much they want to move to Maine and find a place to buy so they can run a B&B. I'm no slouch in the daydreaming, building-castles-in-the-air department myself, so can daydream right along with them—though I try to impress on them the wisdom of being practical. Old houses (which most of them are looking for), at least the ones that can be "bought right", often need vast amounts of money—and good strong backs—to bring them back to life, to say nothing of the time, enthusiasm, and energy needed to be full-time hosts or innkeepers.

Well, had better get out to tend my sap buckets. It's running like mad today and I'm coming down with a full-blown case of spring fever. Temperature about 55 degrees (95 in greenhouse), lots of black ice on pond. If wind keeps up all afternoon, we'll have ice out before sundown. Ospreys are back already!

—Sally

BED & BREAKFAST OF MAINE
PEG TIERNEY
32 COLONIAL VILLAGE
FALMOUTH, ME 04105

PHONE: 207/781-4528
Live hours: Nights and weekends. Answering machine at other times.
OPEN: Year round except for two (unscheduled) out-of-season weeks.

ACCOMMODATIONS
B&Bs
Hosted private residences: 60.
Plus
A few apartments annexed to the main house.
One boathouse outfitted as an apartment for a family.

("Our historic Maine residences tend to have rambling ells and outbuildings that our hosts put to use.")

LOCATIONS *Spread throughout the entire state. They are in summer resorts and off the beaten path, spanning over 300 miles north to south, 150 miles east to west. Enormous variety offered.*

SETTINGS: In coastal villages, country towns, close to mountains or lakes or urban locations. The majority, but not all, are historic homes.

HOSTS: Retired social worker, artist, caterer, realtor, lawyer, craftspeople, historians, and many midlife career changers. . . .

BREAKFAST: Varies from simple to elaborate. Could be zucchini-and-walnut pancakes, creamed chipped beef, freshly baked popovers, quiche, fresh fruit topped with lemon yogurt.

RESERVATIONS
Two weeks in advance preferred.
Minimum stay is two nights on weekends during July and August in popular areas.
Last-minute reservations accepted (but not at night for tonight please).
Also available through travel agents.

DIRECTORY (not required for reservations): $1. *Samples:*

Kennebunkport: "Bufflehead Cove B&B" is named for the small diving ducks that inhabit this area. Nestled under the trees on the shore of a tidal river that empties into the sea a few miles away, this Dutch Colonial home overlooks the port village. There are sun decks on all levels, so guests may enjoy the sun or hide from it, as they choose. Your host is a commercial fisherman and your hostess enjoys reading, jogging, theater, and speaking Spanish. The area brims with activities for all ages. Guest parking stickers are available for sandy beach. Resident dog. Several guest rooms with private bath. $55 double. Shared baths $40–$55 double. Single room $25. These rates plus two-night minimum booking on weekends apply during July and August. Other months, they are reduced by $5. Hearty breakfast served.

Damariscotta: "1794 House" is tucked behind a traditional picket fence on a pie-shaped lot only minutes to town. Rent a canoe, eat lobsters, photograph the famous Pemaquid Lighthouse. Your host speaks German, studied in Switzerland, has a doctorate in counseling, and might even challenge a guest to a game of chess. Hostess is an excellent cook, and when time allows she writes poetry. A hearty breakfast is offered. Second floor has a twin-bedded room plus a single room with a shared bath. $35 double. $25 single. A party of three would be $50. Also a first-floor daytime sitting room with a sleep-sofa that converts to a bedroom at night. Private lavatory off this room. Wood stove for chilly times. $38 double.

RATES
Singles $25–$50. Doubles $30–$70.
One-night surcharge of $2–$10 at a few.
Some weekly and monthly rates available.
Deposit required: $25.
Credit cards: VISA and MasterCard accepted for deposit and/or entire fee.
Cancellation policy: Full refund less $10 service charge if made three days before expected arrival date.

"Many of the nicest accommodations are off the beaten path. Our reservation service gives people access to these marvelous places—and hosts!"

Several additional B&Bs throughout Maine are represented by Pineapple Hospitality, page 156.

Maryland

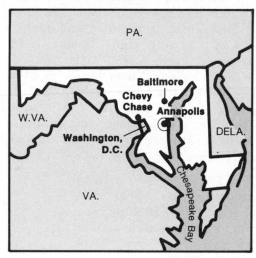

THE TRAVELLER IN MARYLAND

CECILY SHARP-WHITEHILL
33 WEST STREET
ANNAPOLIS, MD 21401

PHONE: 301/269-6232 or 261-2233
  Live 9–5, Monday–Thursday, 9–noon Friday.
OPEN: Year round except federal holidays, Friday and Monday of
  Thanksgiving, Easter Monday, and Good Friday.

ACCOMMODATIONS
B&Bs
Hosted private residences: 90.   B&B inns: 16.
Most have air conditioning and private baths. Some B&Bs are on
yachts, sailboats, and houseboats.
Plus
Some unhosted private residences, cottages and apartments.
Hosted and unhosted short-term housing.

OTHER SERVICES: British tours. Write for brochure that describes stays in traditional pubs, thatched taverns, historic inns,
and manor houses.

LOCATIONS   *Spread throughout Maryland in rural, suburban, urban, and waterfront areas.*

SETTINGS: On land and sea.

HOSTS: Docents at historic homes, collectors of Oriental art, sailors, educators, athletic coach, antiques collectors, retired foreign service personnel, gentleman farmer, minister, gift shop owners. . . .

GUESTS COME FOR: The Chesapeake Bay, the history and waterfronts of Annapolis and Baltimore, battlefields, conferences. Schools—Johns Hopkins University, U.S. Naval Academy, St. John's College, Annapolis and Chesapeake Sailing Schools.

BREAKFAST: Most serve continental. Could include blueberry muffins and raspberry pancakes, bacon, bread and homemade preserves.

RESERVATIONS
At least 24 hours in advance required. The Traveller in Britain tours require 72 hours' notice.

DIRECTORY: None available, but written inquiries are answered with a list of communities that have B&Bs represented by The Traveller in Maryland, "a service that takes requests and confirms reservations most expediently by phone."

RATES
Singles $33–$50. Doubles $33–$65. A few are higher. Weekly and monthly rates available.
Deposit required: $25 for each location. $50 for more than three nights at one place.
Reservation service charge: $3 for a $25 or $50 deposit; $4 for $75 or $100 deposit.
Credit cards accepted: VISA, MasterCard, AMEX for deposit only.
Cancellation policy: Deposit refunded minus $10 if cancellation received at least 10 days before expected arrival date.

We sampled a wide assortment, staying with lifelong residents and newcomers, in simple clean homes with knowledgeable natives, on a magnificent waterfront estate, and in a restored inn. The perspective of the various hosts helped us to feel part of the Eastern Shore.

—The author

AMANDA'S BED & BREAKFAST, LTD.
BETSY GRATER
1428 PARK AVENUE
BALTIMORE, MD 21217

PHONE: 301/383-1274.
OPEN: Year round.

ACCOMMODATIONS
B&Bs
Hosted private residences: 87.   B&B inns: 14.
Almost all have air conditioning and private baths.
Some listings are accessible to handicapped.
Plus
Some unhosted private residences for overnight or weekend lodging as well as short-term hosted and unhosted housing.

OTHER SERVICES: Car rental information, dinner reservations, tickets for ball games, theater tickets, tours of city, and information about shopping and attractions. Information about this B&B reservation service is available in braille. Some hosts who are retired nurses often request guests with special needs.

LOCATIONS   *Most are within 15- to 20-mile radius of Baltimore. All have good public transportation connections. Many hosts live in inner harbor area. Others are near the shore, in hunt country, or in the mountains of Western Maryland.*
In Maryland: Annapolis, Baltimore, Bel Air, Betterton, Chestertown, Crisfield, Columbia, Darnestown, Easton, Frederick, Glen Arm, Gibson Island, Harwood, Phoenix, Princess Anne, Oakland, Oxford, St. Michaels, Snow Hill, Solomons Island, Westminster, and White Hall.
In Delaware: Wilmington.
In Pennsylvania: York Glen Rock, Philadelphia, Pittsburgh.
In New Jersey: Avon by the Bay.
In Virginia: Virginia Beach.

SETTINGS: From comfortable to rather luxurious homes in beautiful areas. Some B&Bs are on sailboats and yachts in Baltimore's inner harbor and in Annapolis. Some are in townhouses in historic areas that overlook the harbor. Some are in carriage houses. Some of the inns are historic.

HOSTS: Doctors, teachers, lawyers, engineers, realtors, composers, writers, retired nurses, accountants, mental health staffers, business women, photographers, bird watchers, sea captain, artist, florist, and professional innkeepers. . . .

GUESTS COME FOR: A vacation. Conferences. Schools: Johns Hopkins University, U.S. Naval Academy, St. John's College, Annapolis. In Baltimore: The newly developed inner harbor area, The National Aquarium, Maryland Science Center and Planetarium, Mechanic Theater (Live) Baltimore Opera.

BREAKFAST: Varies from help-yourself to an elaborate meal. Most serve a full breakfast.

RESERVATIONS
At least a week in advance preferred. If arrangements can be made, will accept last-minute reservations.
Groups: Maximum size is 15.
Also available through travel agents.

RATES
Singles $30–$45. Doubles $40–$75.
Weekly and monthly rates available.
Deposit required: $25.
Cancellation policy: If a minimum of 48 hours' notice is given, refund minus a $10 service charge is made.

Many Guests Are Special

"We are happy to send our brochure and make reservations by mail. However, after talking to prospective guests, we sometimes spend hours on a placement, especially for those with special needs."

In addition to the Maryland based B&B reservation services described above, there are B&Bs in Maryland also available through Sweet Dreams & Toast, Inc., page 94, Bed & Breakfast of Delaware, page 88, and Bed and Breakfast of Chester County, page 274.

Massachusetts

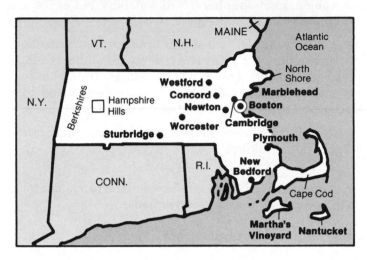

Bed and breakfast is so popular in Massachusetts, that just when it seems that every region of the state must have B&B representation by at least one reservation service, another service emerges. Still, advance reservations are strongly recommended for high season in resort areas or in downtown Boston. After Pineapple Hospitality, the following listings are arranged, as much as possible, from east (Cape Cod) to west (Berkshires).

PINEAPPLE HOSPITALITY, INC.

JOAN A. BROWNHILL
384 RODNEY FRENCH BLVD.
NEW BEDFORD, MA 02744

PHONE: 617/990-1696
   Monday–Friday 9–5.
OPEN: Year round except Christmas, New Year's, and July 4th.

ACCOMMODATIONS
B&Bs
Hosted private residences: 142.   B&B inns: 20.
Some listings are accessible to handicapped.
Plus
Some unhosted private residences for overnight or weekend lodging.

OTHER SERVICES: Some hosts will pick up at airport, bus, or train. Motor van or bicycle tours of Cape Cod. Private cruises of Cape Cod area including Buzzards Bay and Martha's Vineyard. Considerable information about New England sites with helpful details about the proximity of major attractions in the relatively compact region.

LOCATIONS *Although most of the homes are in Massachusetts, Pineapple has enough in the other five New England states to offer a popular "New England Experience" arrangement, a taste of various settings and lifestyles in all six states.*

SETTINGS: Historic houses in fishing seaports, oceanfront Cape Cod cottages, lakefront houses, restored farmhouses, rustic Maine lodges; on Rhode Island's coastline or in the mountains of Vermont and New Hampshire. One B&B is on a 41-foot Morgan sailboat on Cape Cod.

HOSTS: Physician and world lecturer, artist, captain of charter cruises, professor, teacher, engineer, state legislator, railroad retiree. . . .

GUESTS COME FOR: All or a small part of New England.

BREAKFAST: Varies from help-yourself to an elaborate meal.

RESERVATIONS
Two weeks in advance preferred; more for "New England Experience." If arrangements can be made, will accept last-minute reservations.
Groups: Up to 30 or 35 can be booked if several homes can be used. "Some of my inns can take that many under one roof."
Also available through travel agents.

DIRECTORY (not required for reservations): $4.50 includes postage and current supplement. *Samples:*

Massachusetts (southeast). New Bedford. Your hosts: He—computer teacher; she—administrative assistant, social service agency. Interests: historic preservation, antiques, and computers. Their house is an 1857 Greek Revival, gray with green trim, located in the historic area. Original owners were descendants of those who came on the Mayflower. Near city waterfront, 10 minutes from beach.

Guests may conveniently walk to all historic sites. [Codes in directory indicate that one bath is private, one shared, one room on ground floor, one upstairs; hosts' pet is indoors, guests' pet allowed, children allowed.] D $35. S. $27. Two rooms: one double bed in each. One room with two bunk beds.

Rhode Island (west of Newport). Narragansett. Hosts: He—sales. She—kindergarten teacher. Interests: gardening, jogging, skiing, bicycling, basketry, and quilting. Their home is on a quiet residential street three blocks from the ocean and the town beach. Twenty minutes to Newport. Discount bridge tokens available. Fifteen minutes from URI main campus at Kingston; 10 minutes from Narragansett Bay Campus. Fifteen minutes from ferry to Block Island. This Victorian home was built in 1896 and is on the National Historic Register. It is 2 1/2 stories, hip-roofed and natural-shingled, and has a Tuscan-columned veranda which offers guests relaxation in the white wicker chairs while sipping a complimentary glass of wine. Fresh flowers and hard candies await guests in the four bright, cheery bedrooms. Guests awaken to the smell of freshly baked homemade breads, served with fresh fruit from 8–9 a.m. On weekends special foods are usually added, such as Rhode Island Johnny Cakes or oven-baked pancakes. Plenty of parking. Some private, some shared baths. Bedrooms on second floor. Host has indoor pet. Nonsmokers preferred. Rates: $37–$49.

RATES
Singles $27–$52. Doubles $32–$65. A few are higher on Nantucket and Martha's Vineyard islands.
One-night surcharge: $3. Surcharge for each reservation in New England states other than Massachusetts.
Deposit required: $7 per night per room. Some hosts require larger deposits.
Credit cards accepted by some inns.
Cancellation policy: If notice received after confirmation of reservation, deposit minus $7 service charge refunded for a one-night stay, minus $14 for two nights or longer.

Joan noticed that her city, once known as the whaling capital of the world and now the largest fishing port on the east coast, had 200,000 visitors a year who were just passing through because they had no place to stay. With that situation in mind, she started her New Bedford–based reservation service in 1980; since then she has expanded to include some hosts in every New England state.

"These hosts have a [Cape Cod] location that dreams are made of, songs are written for, and artists try to capture. They bring out the best in their guests, great conversation around the breakfast table, very helpful information for first-time visitors. Every detail was considered. They go the extra mile."

—Guests from Minnesota

◇ ◇ ◇

CAPE COD

B&B GUESTS COME FOR: Cape Cod National Seashore, sand dunes, beaches, fishing excursions, whale watching, harbor cruises, clambakes, ferry rides to islands, bicycle trails, fresh seafood, Woods Hole Institute, museums, art galleries, New England charm, and the slower pace and relaxed atmosphere of winding roads and quaint villages.

BED AND BREAKFAST CAPE COD

JOYCE AND CLARK DIEHL
BOX 341
WEST HYANNISPORT, MA 02672

PHONE: 617/775-2772
  Live Monday–Friday, 8:30–4. Answering machine at other times.
OPEN: Year round.

ACCOMMODATIONS
B&Bs
Hosted private residences: 45.   B&B inns: 12.
More than half have private baths.
Plus
Hosted short-term housing.

OTHER SERVICES: Some hosts pick up at airport, bus, or train. ("If plans include any touring, we would advise the use of a car. Public transportation on Cape Cod is not extensive.")

LOCATIONS *All of Cape Cod and the islands of Martha's Vineyard and Nantucket.*

SETTINGS: All are less than 15 minutes' drive from the ocean. Some are on the ocean, on ponds or lakes, or in woodsy settings. Many are traditional Cape Cod homes. Others are quite contemporary. (Over 20 of the listings were built in the 18th or 19th centuries. One—with period furnishings—was built in the 17th century.)

HOSTS: Professors, engineers, teachers, antique dealers, artists, journalists, retirees, a dentist, and a college president. . . .

BREAKFAST: About half serve continental and half serve full. Some feature native cranberry and blueberry products, preserves, stuffed hot croissants, eggs Benedict, individual zucchini breads, farm fresh eggs, strawberries, and even champagne.

RESERVATIONS
Advance reservations preferred. When possible, last-minute accepted.
Two-night minimum required on weekends and holidays, and by many hosts for July and August.
Groups can be accommodated with advance notice.

DIRECTORY: None available. "We send descriptions that are tailored to guests' specific needs." *Samples:*

Sandwich (#43) The old-fashioned charm of a country-style home greets you in a 150-year-old inn on the main street of Cape Cod's oldest town. Delightful shops, museums, and restaurants are only steps away, and you may enjoy your breakfast overlooking the pool set in the quiet, flower-decked back yard. Queen, doubles, twins; shared bath. $35–$45.

Truro (#9) A pastoral outpost near the tip of the Cape is truly a city dweller's escape. Amidst a rolling green lawn, lilacs, and wisteria, sits a 200-year-old house which has two guest rooms, a double and two twins, separated by a full bath. The hostess is an artist who shows regularly in New York. $32 single, $44 double.

RATES

Booking Fee: $5 per reservation.

Singles $28–$45. Doubles $36–$85.

One-night surcharge: $5.

Deposit required is 25 percent of total charge.

Cancellation policy: Refunds given if notice is received seven days before expected arrival date.

> *"Due to the personal contact with our hosts, we had the best of all possible vacations. They directed us to the whale watch, a Portuguese bakery, and a wonderful restaurant. And one of the hosts phoned around, after our long day on the island, to find one that was open . . . made the vacation one I'd like to repeat."*
>
> *—Guests from Pennsylvania*

HOUSE GUESTS, CAPE COD

ELLIE COYLE GREENBERG

BOX 8-AR

DENNIS, MA 02638

PHONE: 617/398-0787

May–September, 10–7 daily. October, November, March, April, Monday–Friday, 10–7. Answering machine at other times.

OPEN: Year round.

ACCOMMODATIONS

B&Bs

Hosted private residences: 80.   B&B inns and guesthouses: 6.

Plus

Some hosted and unhosted efficiencies by the week.

OTHER SERVICES: Pickup from bus.

LOCATIONS   *All are on Cape Cod and the islands of Martha's Vineyard and Nantucket.*

SETTINGS: In villages, on the waterfront, and in the country.

HOSTS: Real estate agent, retired chemist, artists, gourmet cook from California, retired teachers. . . .

161

BREAKFAST: Varies. About half serve continental; half serve a full meal.

RESERVATIONS
Minimum stay required: Two nights on weekends, July through Labor Day. Last-minute reservations accepted.

DIRECTORY (not required for reservations): $3. *Sample:*

> Osterville (Wianno): Summer greenery almost hides this big and beautiful home at the end of a private lane. Relax in the quiet of the woods around their pool . . . and guests are invited on a private cruise through inland bays on the hosts' boat. You'll want to be there on the weekends for this! Osterville has wonderful, exclusive shops with unique clothing and crafts. You'll be eight minutes from golf, the same to Hyannis for dining and dancing, or a trip to Nantucket. There are two upstairs connecting bedrooms; one can be used as a sitting room. Private bath. Choice of breakfast. Then walk to a nearby sandy beach for a lazy day. Our guests return here again and again, for these hosts know how to treat you like royalty! For nonsmokers only, sorry.

RATES
Singles $28–$32. Doubles $40–$56. A few are higher.
Cancellation policy: If notice is received at least two weeks before expected arrival date, refund minus $10 service charge is made.

Ellie includes ferry schedules and information about the bicyclists' Cape Cod Rail Trail with answers to inquiries.

ORLEANS BED & BREAKFAST ASSOCIATES
MARY CHAPMAN
P.O. BOX 1312
ORLEANS, MA 02653

PHONE: 617/255-3824
Daily 8–8. Answering machine at other times.
OPEN: Year round except Christmas week.

ACCOMMODATIONS
B&Bs
Hosted private residences: 46.   B&B inns: 3.
Most have private baths. Several have private beaches.

OTHER SERVICES: Referrals made to other B&B reservation service organizations.

Locations *The elbow area (still quite unspoiled) of Cape Cod, known as the Outer Cape: Harwich, Chatham, Brewster, Orleans, Eastham, Wellfleet, and Truro.*

SETTINGS: Great variety, from "hideaways" to "people places." Most houses are within one mile of ocean, bay, or Nantucket Sound. Several overlook salt marshes or conservation areas. Many are furnished with fine antiques.

HOSTS: Artists, librarians, social workers, realtors, advertising people, public relations consultant, musicians, engineers. . . .

BREAKFAST: Varies from continental to full. Could be home-baked breads of all kinds, muffins, French toast, eggs any style. Beautiful fresh fruit bowls.

RESERVATIONS
Minimum stay requirement: Two nights in season (June 15–September 15).
Advance reservations of two weeks preferred. If arrangements can be made, last-minute reservations accepted.
Groups: Small groups up to 12 can be accommodated at one of the small inns. Larger groups can be accommodated in homes close together.
Also available through travel agents.

DIRECTORY: Sent with answer to every inquiry—along with a personal note. *Samples:*

Orleans: Winterwell—A beautifully restored Cape Cod farmhouse. Stroll only .3 mile to Skaket Beach. Separate entrance to secluded first-floor guest room with double bed and twin bed. Full private bath. Charming living room for occasional reading or TV. Continental breakfast with fresh fruit and homemade breads served on enclosed porch overlooking large quiet yard. Close to town and bike path. Extra first-floor room with twin bed available for another family member ($20 additional). $45 double.

Brewster: Stonybrook—A pre-1776 restored colonial house with a storybook setting next to the old Grist Mill and

famous Stony Brook Herring Run. Private entrance to upstairs large bedroom with fireplace, double bed, private
bath, and sitting room. This suite has TV and air conditioning. Attractive sitting area outside overlooking the millpond. Breakfast is included but there is also a small, modern kitchenette. No smoking. $50 double.

RATES
Singles $30–$50. Doubles: $30–$50. A few higher.
One-night surcharge: $10.
Some weekly rates available September 15–June 15.
Deposit required: Full price of two nights.
Credit cards accepted: VISA, MasterCard, and AMEX for deposit
only.
Cancellation policy: Reservation deposits will be refunded, less a
$20 service charge, when notification is received seven days prior
to the arrival date. There is no refund with less than seven days'
notice.

*"Our reservation service is an association of independent
hosts, offering its guests a variety of accommodations with
diversity of style. Hosts meet regularly to share experiences,
role-play B&B situations with new members, discuss future
plans, and tour member homes. Each host is aware that a
guest's experience in his or her home reflects on the association as a whole.*

*"There are many rewarding moments. We made reser-
vations last year for two couples traveling together for the
first time, although they were friends of long standing. We
arranged for them to stay in a host home which had a beautiful guestroom in the main house and a very stunning
apartment over the garage. Well, within a half hour of their
arrival, the guests called us. Could they come over right
away? It was pouring rain, an utterly miserable day, and
within minutes four handsome, well-dressed people decked
out in yellow slickers came dripping into our living room.
They were so thrilled with their B&B that they wanted to
thank us before they even unpacked or went out to lunch."*

◇ ◇ ◇

BE OUR GUEST, BED & BREAKFAST, LTD.
DIANE AND DAVID GILLIS, MARY AND JAIME GILL
P.O. BOX 1333
PLYMOUTH, MA 02360

PHONE: 617/837-9867
Live 10–9 daily. Answering machine at other times.
OPEN: Year round.

ACCOMMODATIONS
B&Bs
Hosted private residences: 18$^+$ (depends on time of year).
One B&B inn.
Almost all have private baths. A few have pools.
Plus
Some unhosted short-term housing.

LOCATIONS *Many homes are located within walking distance of Plymouth Harbor. Others, also south of Boston, are 30–60 minutes' drive north to parts of Boston or southeast to Cape Cod.*

SETTINGS: The variety includes Victorians, oceanfront properties, homes on ponds, a mini-villa, a 250-year-old carriage house.

OTHER SERVICES: Information about car rentals, bus schedules, and local attractions.

HOSTS: Teachers, opera singer, insurance agents, retirees, nurse, filmmaker, sailor. . . .

GUESTS COME FOR: A vacation. Conferences. Business. Plimoth Plantation. Plymouth Rock, museums, and historic houses. Winery tour. Day trips to Boston and Cape Cod.

BREAKFAST: All offer "at least a very good continental." Some are full meals that could include blueberry pancakes or homemade breads.

RESERVATIONS
In May, July, and November, a two-night minimum stay required on long holiday weekends.
Advance reservations requested. Last-minute reservations accepted.
Groups: Maximum size is 20.

DIRECTORY: No charge for a one-page sheet that has brief description of each B&B. *Samples:*

> Plymouth (#106) Beautiful Dutch Colonial with decks offering ocean views off every room. One room with queen-size bed and private full bath. One room with double bed; one room with single bed. Private bath shared by these two rooms. $48–$52 double. $38 single.

> Scituate (#603) Mini-villa—master suite with king-size bed, sitting area with fireplace, and full bath. Balcony. Breakfast served on terrace. $59. Twin-size room extra charge.

RATES

Singles $32–$45. Doubles $40–$65.

Some weekly and monthly rates available.

Deposit required: $25, or 25 percent of total charge for longer stays.

Credit cards accepted: VISA, MasterCard, and AMEX for deposit or entire fee.

Cancellation policy: Full refund, less a $10 service charge, with a minimum of seven days' notice prior to arrival time.

> *"The location, the accommodations, the food, and the extraordinary hospitality . . . the hosts went beyond the call of duty in using their car to help us, in providing extra snacks, and in just being nice people. It is a fine service you offer."*
> —*Guests from Oregon*

> *"Under your wing, you have in my view, the best hostess, cook, and conversationalist in the country. . . . I am now a public relations agent for her and for you."*
> —*Guest from Massachusetts*

CHRISTIAN HOSPITALITY BED AND BREAKFAST

ANN KOPKE

BLACK FRIAR BROOK FARM

636 UNION STREET

DUXBURY, MA 02332

PHONE: 617/834-8528

Monday–Friday, 10–9. Answering service at other times.

OPEN: Year round.

ACCOMMODATIONS
B&Bs
Hosted private residences: 80.   B&B inns: 5.

OTHER SERVICES: Some hosts pick up at airport, bus, or train.

LOCATIONS   *Some in every New England state. Others are along the east coast, including Florida, Georgia, Maryland, New Jersey, New York, Pennsylvania, Rhode Island, South Carolina, Tennessee, and Virginia.*

HOSTS: Pastors, retired pastors, professional people, retired missionaries, teachers, business men and women. . . .
Fifty percent have hosted for over two years. All supply references when they apply; many are personally interviewed. "Our service is made up mainly of dedicated Christians who open their homes because they love people and feel they are offering a service. Though they appreciate the monetary recompense, they enjoy the fellowship of travelers."

BREAKFAST: Most serve a full breakfast.

RESERVATIONS
Advance reservations of two weeks preferred, to give time for receiving deposit and sending directions and some information about the hosts. Will accept last-minute reservations.
Also occasionally available through travel agencies.

DIRECTORY: $1 plus self-addressed stamped envelope. A list of locations with description of many of the homes. *Sample:*

Duxbury (southeast of Boston). Built in 1708. Authentic in spite of having been added on to, this home has hand-hewn gunstock beams and much of the charm of the original saltbox house. Two rooms in main house, double or single beds, private or shared bath. Private suite attached to main house with double and single bed and a second double bed upstairs. Full breakfast served. Ten minutes to Plymouth, one hour to Providence, 40 minutes to Boston. $35 for two in main house. Suite is $45.

New Hampshire: Northwood. Beautiful restored Federal home with several fireplaces on 50 acres of fields and woods, bordering Jenness Pond. Country, rural setting with quiet atmosphere. Recreational activities available include hiking, skiing, swimming, boating, and tennis. Hostess is a professor at the University of New Hampshire and an accomplished equestrian. She makes breads, homemade jams, and jellies from products in her own garden. Host has traveled to many countries, including iron curtain countries at their invitation, to promote a unique farming aid which he manufactures. $35/two.

RATES

Singles $20–$35. Doubles $30–$55.

Weekly and monthly rates available.

Deposit required: Total for one night plus 25 percent for remaining nights.

Cancellation policy: If notice received at least 72 hours in advance, refund sent minus $10 service charge.

◇ ◇ ◇

BOSTON AREA

B&B GUESTS COME FOR: Cultural attractions—theater, museums, music, dance. Sightseeing. Historic sites. Boston Marathon. Sporting events. Festivals. Faneuil Hall Marketplace. Harbor cruises. Whale watches. Conferences. Colleges and universities. Medical centers. Many come for business reasons, for relocating, and for house hunting.

A special hint about transportation: Parking facilities are limited. Traffic can be heavy. Streets are relatively narrow. If you must drive, it is recommended that you pay to leave your car in a garage and get around by some other means. Boston is a compact town and can be well covered on foot or by cab, bus (some are double-deckers), or subway. Many suburban locations are very convenient and close to downtown Boston and are near a transit stop. Cambridge is just across the Charles River; Harvard Square is only 2½ miles from Boston.

BED AND BREAKFAST AGENCY—BOSTON WATERFRONT, FANEUIL HALL, AND GREATER BOSTON

FERNE MINTZ
47 COMMERCIAL WHARF
BOSTON, MA 02110

PHONE: 617/720-3540
Live 9 a.m.–8 p.m. daily. Answering machine at other times.
OPEN: Year round.

ACCOMMODATIONS
B&Bs
Hosted private residences: 35.
Many have air conditioning.
Plus
Some unhosted private residences for overnight or weekend lodging.
Some hosted and unhosted short-term (up to one month) housing
also available.

OTHER SERVICES: Car rentals. Theater tickets. Trips on private
sailboat.

LOCATIONS *All are in downtown Boston, on or near the
harbor or in historic districts.*

SETTINGS: Some are waterfront condominiums. Some are historic
townhouses.

HOSTS: Business men and women, architect, psychologist, real
estate broker, computer specialist. . . .

BREAKFAST: All serve a full meal.

RESERVATIONS
If arrangements can be made, will accept last-minute reservations.
Also available through travel agents.

RATES
Singles $28–$55. Doubles $40–$70.
Some weekly and monthly rates available.
Deposit required: one-third of total charge.
Credit cards accepted: MasterCard, VISA, and AMEX.
Cancellation policy: Deposit is nonrefundable.

*Ferne has lived on Boston's waterfront for 20 years and feels
that it is very much a neighborhood. Before starting her*

reservation service in 1985, she was a host for 2 years. Last Christmas her beagle puppy (and Ferne) received 62 greeting cards from B&B guests.

BED & BREAKFAST A LA CAMBRIDGE & GREATER BOSTON BY RIVA POOR
73 KIRKLAND STREET
CAMBRIDGE, MA 02138

PHONE: 617/576-1492
Live 9–6, Monday–Friday in the warm months, and at least 5–6 daily during the cold months. Answering machine at other times.
OPEN: Year round except major holidays and December 16–31.

ACCOMMODATIONS
B&Bs
Hosted private residences: Over 100.
Many have air-conditioning.
Plus
Unhosted private residences for brief rentals.
Short-term hosted housing also available.
Long-term and share-a-home arrangements are also offered.

OTHER SERVICES: Some hosts pick up at airport, bus, and train.

LOCATIONS   *Most are in downtown Boston and Cambridge, near Harvard University and M.I.T. Others are in the major suburbs, north to Marblehead, northwest to Lexington and Billerica, southwest to Wellesley and Waltham, and south to Duxbury, Cape Cod, and Nantucket.*

HOSTS: Architects, physicians, designers, professors, executives, computer specialists, clergy, health administrators, psychiatrists and psychologists, authors, consultants, lecturers. . . .

BREAKFAST: All serve a full breakfast.

RESERVATIONS
None are accepted by mail.
Advance reservations not required. Last-minute reservations accepted. "We require a telephone conversation with each guest mak-

ing a reservation, to ascertain their needs and to make sure that there will be no misunderstanding or difficulty."

Groups: Almost any size can be booked by booking several large houses.

RATES

Guest membership fee of $6 for adult (18 or over) required annually. Singles $39–$65. Doubles $45–$75. A few are less and some are more.

Weekly and monthly rates available.

Deposit required: One-third of total cost. Nonrefundable.

Credit cards accepted: All major credit cards accepted for deposit (preferred) or entire fee. Credit card charges added to bill.

> *"We have had the pleasure of placing guests who have gone to their job or college interviews plumped up by our hosts— and won what they came for . . . hearing about thank-you notes written to Fanny, the beagle hound who has enlivened many a guest's visit . . . appreciating the guest whose husband thought the book she was reading was hers and packed the book in their suitcase. His wife Federal Expressed the book back to the host. . . ."*

BED & BREAKFAST ASSOCIATES BAY COLONY, LTD.

ARLINE KARDASIS AND MARILYN MITCHELL
P.O. BOX 166
BOSTON, MA 02157

PHONE: 617/449-5302
Live 10–5 Monday–Friday. Reduced hours in winter. Answering machine at other times.

OPEN: Year round. Closed mid-December through New Year's.

ACCOMMODATIONS
B&Bs
Hosted private residences: 90.   B&B inns: 5.
Many have air conditioning and private baths.
Plus
Some unhosted private residences, apartments, and suites for nightly, weekly, or monthly lodging.
Hosted and unhosted short-term (one month or more) housing.

OTHER SERVICES: Discount coupons for car rentals. Some homes offer kitchen privileges.

LOCATIONS *Forty-five communities represented, including Boston, Brookline, Cambridge. All urban locations and many suburban homes are near public transportation. Other locations are north, south, and west of Boston, and at the shore. A few are in other New England states.*

SETTINGS: City brownstones to seaside retreats. Many historic homes. Some are very luxurious.

HOSTS: Health care professionals, lawyers, realtors, teachers, librarians, caterers, artists, computer consultants, camp director, stress management consultant, Metropolitan Opera representative. . . .

GUESTS COME FOR: Boston attractions. In Plymouth: Historic Plymouth and beaches. North Shore: beaches, Plum Island National Wildlife Refuge, quaint villages, shopping. . . .

BREAKFAST: Most are continental. Some full and gourmet. If help-yourself, it's a nicely set table or tray when host must be at work.

RESERVATIONS
Advance notice of at least 48 hours is best, but last-minute reservations will be accepted when possible.
Minimum stay: Two nights preferred.
Groups: Maximum size is eight in one house. Large groups can be placed in several homes.
Also available through travel agents.

DIRECTORY (not required for reservations): $2. (Map of Massachusetts area covered is included.) *Samples:*

M810: Cambridge. This majestic home overlooks the Charles River at Harvard Square. Guests are surrounded by French and English heirlooms in two master suites. Each finely appointed guest room has a king-size bed, an elegantly furnished living room, along with a private bath. Full breakfast is served in the formal dining room or guests may have a continental breakfast in their room. Luxury like this cannot be duplicated. $85 (sgl or dbl).

M225: Boston. In the heart of Boston, adjacent to the stunning Copley Place complex, this brownstone is located one block from the Colonnade Hotel and across from the Prudential Center. Your hostess, a talented graphic artist, offers a lovely twin-bedded first-floor guest room, which shares her bath and includes a full breakfast for $45 sgl/ $55 dbl. Her second-floor apartment has recently been redone and provides complete privacy, double-bedded guest room plus two twin beds in living room, a kitchenette, and a private bath. $65 sgl/$80 dbl (plus $15 per additional person).

RATES

Singles $30–$55. Doubles $35–$85. A few higher in unhosted apartments. (Homes just outside the city in the "inner suburbs" to the north, west, or south have lower rates than those in the city.) One-night surcharge: $10.
Weekly and monthly rates available.
Deposit required is 30 percent of total.
Cancellation policy: $20 cancellation fee. Remainder of deposit refunded when 72 hours' notice of cancellation is provided.

"A former hostess in a distant suburban town had told us that she was hesitant to accept single men as guests. When she had gone a long while without any guests, we called to offer her (as her first guest) a single gentleman who was an executive from Sweden. Understanding her stated reluctance, we made it clear that she was certainly not obliged to accept. Well she did accept, and today they are married and living in Sweden."

"A well-traveled host couple were planning their next African safari and called us to let us know that they would be gone for a month that coming winter. Time passed and prospective guests called to book a weekend in Boston. In the course of conversation, they mentioned their interest in Africa. They stayed with this host couple and decided to join them on their safari. They spent 30 days and nights camping and trekking together. It was a joyful and spectacular experience for all."

BED AND BREAKFAST BROOKLINE/BOSTON

ANNE DIAMOND
BOX 732
BROOKLINE, MA 02146

PHONE: 617/277-2292
Live Monday–Saturday 9–4. Answering service at other times.
OPEN: Year round. Closed Christmas and New Year's.

ACCOMMODATIONS
B&Bs
Hosted private residences: 55.
Plus
Short-term (up to a few months) unhosted housing.

LOCATIONS *Within a 10-mile radius of downtown Boston in Brookline, Boston, Cambridge, Newton, Arlington, and Needham. Almost all are near public transportation.*
A few are a half hour north of Boston in Marblehead and others are on Cape Cod.

SETTINGS: Some are luxurious. A few are historic. Most are pleasant, attractive homes-away-from-home.

HOSTS: Biologist, caterer, librarian, psychiatrist, guidance counselor, baker, teacher, nurse, pianist, chaplain, chef, court stenographer. . . .

BREAKFAST: All hosts serve a full meal on weekends, when specialties could include quiches, cranberry pancakes, homemade muffins, or vegetable omelet. Hosts who work leave the makings of a help-yourself breakfast.

RESERVATIONS
Minimum stay requirement: Two nights.
Advance reservations preferred. If arrangements can be made, will accept last-minute reservations.
Groups: Maximum size is 10 or 12.
Also available through travel agents.

DIRECTORY (not required for reservations): $1 plus a business-sized self-addressed stamped envelope will bring you descriptions of most of the listings. *Samples:*

Beacon Hill Federal: The third floor of this four-story Federal house on Beacon Hill is a tiny private apartment. A bedroom with double bed, fireplace, view of Charles River, private bath, and kitchenette. Host, a baker, leaves refrigerator stocked with fresh baked goodies for cook-your-own breakfasts. $62 per night.

Brookline: Salisbury House. This classic turn-of-the-century Victorian house has very large rooms, lovely woodwork, nine fireplaces with unique antique mirrored mantels. The host's world travels include a lengthy stay in Spain. Spanish and French spoken. Your host is a member of the Museum of Fine Arts and is happy to share her extensive knowledge of Boston culture. The double brass bed and antique cradle reflect the family's interest in antiques ($44/36). A double ($48/36) on the top floor is adjacent to a full bath. Use of separate sitting room and large pool table in game room. Ample parking. One block for public transportation and one mile from Boston College. Children welcome. Smoking OK. Full breakfast.

RATES
Singles $38–$44. Doubles $44–$55. A few are higher.
One-night surcharge: $5.
Deposit required is 25 percent of total charge.
Credit cards accepted: MasterCard and VISA for deposit only.
Cancellation policy: If notice received at least 72 hours before expected arrival date, refund minus $10 service charge made. After that, deposit forfeited.

Guest from Virginia wrote: "The accommodations were charming, with a real sense of privacy. The location was excellent (great accessibility to sites and public transport) and the hostess made every effort to make us feel comfortable and provide us with delicious homemade style breakfasts. . . . Clearly one of the highlights of our visit. . . .

A New Hat

Anne, a new proprietor of this established reservation service, was a summer B&B host on the island of Nantucket. In the fall the mother of seven and grandmother of seven came to Boston to work for the service—and ended up buying the business!

175

BED & BREAKFAST IN MINUTEMAN COUNTRY

SALLY ELKIND, JUDY PALMER
8 CARRIAGE DRIVE
LEXINGTON, MA 02173

PHONE: 617/861-7063
Answering service at all times. Same-day call-backs.
OPEN: Year round.

ACCOMMODATIONS
B&Bs
Hosted private residences: 30.
Most have air conditioning and private baths.
Plus
Hosted short-term housing.

LOCATIONS *Lexington, Concord, Cambridge, Burlington, Waltham, Newton—all within easy driving or commuting distance of Route 128 and Boston.*

HOSTS: Pianist, scientist, artist, teacher, attorney, book editor, economist. . . .

BREAKFAST: Varies according to host.

RESERVATIONS
Advance reservations of at least one week preferred. Last-minute reservations accepted.
Also available through travel agencies.

DIRECTORY: A two-page sheet sent without charge in answer to inquiries. (Please enclose a business-sized self-addressed stamped envelope.) *Samples:*

Concord: Enjoy the countryside at Flintlock Farm, a New England cape situated on 20 acres just minutes away from downtown historic Concord. The spacious private bedroom suite has a separate entrance and deck overlooking fishing pond (equipped with canoe for your use) and spring-fed, sandy-bottomed swimming pond. Host is a Concord firefighter. Hostess will play organ for you with a little encouragement. Resident cat. No smokers, please.

Lexington: The Red Apple Inn. An authentically constructed colonial home, 30 years in the building. The colors, textiles, handcrafted furniture, wide pine floors, and braided rugs all add to the warm, cozy atmosphere. Hosts are willing and eager to help plan sightseeing in Lexington and Concord as well as day trips to the north country in Maine and New Hampshire and south to Cape Cod. Crib available.

RATES
Singles $35–$40. Doubles $40–$50.
Monthly rates available.
Deposit required: One night's lodging.
Cancellation policy: Full refund if cancellation received at least 48 hours before expected arrival date.

> *"I am hired by an engineering firm which provides my services to clients all over the country. One very important thing a person needs is peace of mind and relaxation, something not found in bars and motels. . . . I was happily provided with a comfortable large room and private bath in the most delightful couple's home. . . . Some of the most interesting evenings I have ever spent were enjoyed with both my hosts. In some respects it was even better than family get-togethers."*
> —*A Bed & Breakfast in Minuteman Country guest*

BOSTON BED & BREAKFAST
CYNTHIA SPINNER AND ELISABETH MONCREIFF
16 BALLARD STREET
NEWTON, MA 02159

PHONE: 617/332-4199
  Monday–Friday, 9–5. Answering machine at other times.
OPEN: Year round except for national holidays.

ACCOMMODATIONS
B&Bs for a specialized audience (please see below)
Hosted private residences: 100.
Plus
Some unhosted homes for overnight or weekend lodging.

LOCATIONS *Boston (Beacon Hill, Back Bay, Copley Square area), and nearby Newton, Brookline, and Cambridge.*

HOSTS: All professionals.

GUESTS COME FOR: All are professionals who come to the area for professional reasons.

BREAKFAST: All full. Usually served.

RESERVATIONS: Minimum stay requirement of two nights.

RATES
Singles $45. Doubles $60.
Deposit required: Full prepayment.
Credit cards accepted: VISA, MasterCard, AMEX for entire fee.
Cancellation policy: Refund all but $15 unless cancellation is made less than 48 hours before scheduled arrival time; in that case, one night's lodging fee is forfeited.

GREATER BOSTON HOSPITALITY
LAUREN A. SIMONELLI
P.O. BOX 1142
BROOKLINE, MA 02146

PHONE: 617/277-5430
   Answering service at all times. Calls returned same day.
OPEN: Year round.

ACCOMMODATIONS
B&Bs
Hosted private residences: 60.   B&B inns: 3.
Almost all have private baths.
Plus
Some unhosted private residences for overnight or weekend lodging.
Some short-term (up to a month) housing available.

LOCATIONS *Boston and nearby communities of Cambridge, Brookline, Newton, Needham, Somerville, Belmont, Winchester. (Plus Marblehead on the north shore and Duxbury on the south shore.) Most are within a 10-mile radius of downtown Boston. All are within walking distance of public transportation.*

SETTINGS: "All are lovely. Many are luxurious."

HOSTS: Retired chef, financier, banker, watercolorist, real estate broker, college administrator, writer, psychiatrists, union leader, corporation president. . . .

BREAKFAST: Most offer full breakfasts that could feature homemade peach preserves, hot chocolate, eggs Benedict, waffles with Vermont maple syrup, fresh strawberries in port wine, homemade blueberry coffee cake, scrambled eggs with smoked salmon and onions, homemade popovers, whole-wheat pancakes with lemon dressing, English muffins with cream cheese and bacon.

RESERVATIONS

Advance reservations preferred. Will accept last-minute reservations. Most reservations made in writing.
Groups: Maximum size is 30.
Also available through travel agents.

DIRECTORY: Sent on request without charge. *Sample description:*

Brookline #36: This unusual five-star B&B is a converted Georgian carriage house, formerly part of a larger estate, located on cul-de-sac in one of Brookline's finest areas. Set in among gracious older homes, this home offers a twin-bedded guest room with guests' bath and den with piano on a completely separate level. Glass doors open from your bedroom to a tree-enclosed terrace where breakfast is frequently served in summer. Many amenities. Rave reviews. Parking included, but minutes' walk to express car line to Boston. Your host and hostess are city oriented and very friendly. Adults only. $45 single, $52 double. A Brookline #36 guest from Tucson wrote: "All the extras provided did not go unnoticed and were especially appreciated. Peter said it best and I'm trying to recall his words; something like 'charming without gushing, attentive without hovering.' "

RATES

Singles $30–$45. Doubles $40–$55. A few higher.
One-night surcharge: $10.
Some weekly and monthly rates available.
Deposit required: At least one night's lodging.
Cancellation policy: If notice received at least 72 hours before expected arrival date, deposit returned less a $10.00 processing fee.

HOST HOMES OF BOSTON
MARCIA WHITTINGTON
P.O. BOX 117
NEWTON, MA 02168

PHONE: 617/244-1308
Live 8–9 a.m., 3–6 p.m. weekdays, 8–noon Saturdays. Answering machine at other times. Same-day response given to all messages. Requests for one-night reservations returned collect. TELEX: 136575
OPEN: Year round. Closed Sundays, major holidays, and one week in late January.

ACCOMMODATIONS
B&Bs
Hosted private residences: 40.   One B&B inn.
Plus
Some hosted short-term (one week to one month) housing subject to availability and compatibility.

OTHER SERVICES: Accommodations arranged for guests of large weddings and anniversary celebrations.

LOCATIONS   *Many are in Newton, a suburban community that is 5–10 miles west of Boston, near Route 128 and public transportation into Boston. Others are in Boston (Back Bay and waterfront) or in nearby Brookline, Cambridge, and Watertown; or north and west in Reading, Bedford, and Needham near Route 128/I-95. Some are in vacation areas— on the north shore in Marblehead and to the south on Cape Cod.*

SETTINGS: Residential areas of the city and suburbs.

HOSTS: Doctors, professors, engineers, editor, actress, media specialist, school teacher, host who renovates and restores old buildings, gourmet cooking teacher. . . .

BREAKFAST: Varies according to host's schedule. Most serve hearty continental weekdays and full on weekends with an emphasis on natural and fresh food.

RESERVATIONS
At least three days in advance requested. Will accept last-minute reservations, if arrangements possible, with credit-card security.

Minimum stay required: Two nights on weekends mid-May through mid-October. Many B&Bs are not available on Thanksgiving, Christmas, and New Year's.

Groups: Maximum size is 30 by using several homes in Newton, Brookline, or Needham.

DIRECTORY: Sent without charge in answer to inquiries. Please include a self-addressed stamped business-sized envelope. *Sample descriptions:*

> Newton, village of Waban: $37/S, $47/D. Cotswold House. Built in 1910, this enormous Cotswold saltbox, bright with bay windows, sits on a quiet road with mature trees and wooded paths, yet is only three blocks from the village center. Your host is a music aficionado with coveted Symphony seats and offers guests a spacious, gracious home-away-from-home. Accommodations: second-floor large twin-bedded room with connecting room with one twin bed. Third second-floor room with one twin bed. Guest bath serves these rooms. Resident golden retriever. Smokers accepted. Three blocks to public transportation.

> Boston/Charlestown. On Freedom Trail and harbor. $41 S, $51 D. Constitution Quarters 2. Five-star B&B on fifth floor of renovated Old Charlestown Navy Yard apartments in historic Boston area offers special blend of old/modern atmosphere with Continental/American lifestyle. Your hosts are French-born. Accommodations: Private twin guest room and bath with full view of skyline is separate from rest of this three-level apartment. Breakfast is served in hosts' second-level quarters, and rooftop terrace on third level offers fresh air and inspiring view of harbor and skyline. Cigarette smokers accepted. No resident pets. Street parking only. Location: Walk to Quincy Market/Faneuil Hall. Five-minute drive from Logan Airport.

RATES

Singles $37. Doubles $47. A few higher.

Deposit required: First night's fee.

Credit cards accepted: MasterCard, VISA, AMEX.

Cancellation policy: If notice is received by the office at least 72 hours before reservation date, refund minus a $10 service fee is made.

> *Marcia observes: ". . . With good matching, guests almost always get much more than expected, because the host is*

*happy and extends and bends more. . . . When guests walk
in the B&B door, they have paid in advance and are greeted
as welcome friends."*

*Guests write: ". . . I feel like a six-week-old kitten; my eyes
have been opened!" (a first-time B&B guest). ". . . Couldn't
ask for a nicer family or more congenial hosts—loved the
"purple room" and all the fresh flowers, fireplaces, pineapple bedposts, stairways, and molded ceilings—and meeting you all! Thanks for being so nice about my schedule
and transportation."*

MAYFLOWER BED & BREAKFAST, LTD.
BARBARA S. MERCER
P.O. BOX 172
BELMONT, MA 02178

PHONE: 617/484-0068
  Live hours: evenings. Answering machine at other times.
OPEN: Year round.

ACCOMMODATIONS
B&Bs
Hosted private residences: 15.
Almost all have air conditioning.
Plus
Some short-term (three to six weeks) hosted housing.

LOCATIONS *All within a 10-mile radius of Boston and
Cambridge. Most are in Belmont, near public transportation
as well as with direct access to Routes 2 and 128.*

SETTINGS: In established suburban community. "They are handsome and substantial, well-maintained and tastefully furnished."

HOSTS: Self-employed, writer for an in-house newspaper, communications consultant, physician and family. . . .

BREAKFAST: All continental. Most hosts not present for breakfast
during the week.

RESERVATIONS
Advance reservations preferred but will accept last-minute reservations.

RATES
Singles $40–$50. Doubles $50–$60.
One-night surcharge: 10 percent.
Weekly and monthly rates available.
Deposit required is 25 percent.
Cancellation policy: With 48 hours' notice, the full amount is refunded minus a $10 service charge.

NEW ENGLAND BED & BREAKFAST, INC.

JOHN AND MARGO GARDINER
1045 CENTRE STREET
NEWTON CENTRE, MA 02159

PHONE: 617/244-2112
Live Monday–Friday 9–5. Answering service: 498-9819 at other times.
OPEN: Year round.

ACCOMMODATIONS
B&Bs
Hosted private residences: 50.   B&B inns: 3.
Most have private baths.
Plus
Unhosted private residences
Hosted and unhosted short-term housing.

LOCATIONS *Greater Boston area, most within walking distance of public transportation. A few homes are in other New England areas.*

SETTINGS: "Our emphasis is on moderately priced accommodations near public transportation."

HOSTS: Retirees, a chef, architect, psychologist... "all nice people."

BREAKFAST: All serve continental except one retired chef in Maine.

RESERVATIONS

Advance notice preferred. If arrangements can be made, will accept last-minute reservations.

Also available through travel agents.

RATES

Singles $25–$36. Doubles $38–$45. A few are higher.

Weekly rates at a few.

Deposit required: First night's fee.

Cancellation policy: Refund less $10 service charge made if cancellation is received in writing five days before the expected arrival date.

UNIVERSITY BED AND BREAKFAST LTD.

RUTH SHAPIRO AND SARAH YULES

12 CHURCHILL STREET

BROOKLINE, MA 02146

PHONE: 617/738-1424

Live 9–5, Monday–Friday. At other times: answering machine.

OPEN: Year round.

ACCOMMODATIONS

B&Bs

Hosted private residences: 50.

Almost all have private baths.

Plus

Some unhosted private residences for overnight or weekend lodging.

Short-term (one to three months) hosted and unhosted housing.

LOCATIONS   *Most are within a 10-mile radius of downtown Boston and Harvard Square in Cambridge. Almost all are near public transportation. Some are within walking distance of area academic institutions and hospitals.*

GUESTS COME FOR: (Usually) schools and industry. They visit students or faculty at area universities and colleges, attend graduations, take seminars and courses, or attend meetings.

BREAKFAST: Most serve continental.

RESERVATIONS
Minimum stay of two nights preferred. One-week advance reservation and prepayment requested. Last-minute reservations are possible sometimes.

RATES
Singles $40. Doubles $55. A few are higher.
Some weekly and monthly rates available.
A deposit is required.
Cancellation policy: For a one-night reservation, no refund.
For others, refunds, less $10, if 48-hour notice given before expected arrival date.

BED & BREAKFAST MARBLEHEAD & NORTH SHORE
HELENA CHAMPION
54 AMHERST ROAD
BEVERLY, MA 01915

PHONE: 617/921-1336
Live Monday–Friday, 8 a.m. 10 p.m., weekends 8–5. Answering machine at other times.

ACCOMMODATIONS
B&Bs
Hosted private residences: 35.
Most are near bus transport to Boston; some are near the train (30–45-minute ride) to Boston.
About half have private baths and air conditioning.

LOCATIONS *All in communities along the north shore, including Marblehead, Salem, Beverly, Topsfield, Manchester, and Magnolia.*

SETTINGS: Some are historic and in designated historic areas. Others are in surrounding suburban neighborhoods. Many are close to beaches. Some are right on the ocean.

HOSTS: Antique dealer, interior decorator, theology professor, insurance broker, educator, real estate developer. . . .

GUESTS COME FOR: Sightseeing, museums, whale watching, day trips, relocation, visits with friends and relatives, shopping, Old

Town Marblehead, Salem National Historic Park, sailing, Race Week.

BREAKFAST: Most serve continental. Among those who offer a full breakfast is one who enjoys a menu that could include a souffle.

RESERVATIONS
Advance recommended, but will take last-minute calls.
Also available through travel agents.

RATES
Singles $36–$50. Doubles $42–$66.
Some weekly rates available.
Deposit required: First night's lodging.
Credit cards accepted: MasterCard and VISA for deposit only.
Cancellation policy: Deposit is refunded if cancellation received at least two days before expected arrival date.

◊ ◊ ◊

BEYOND METROPOLITAN BOSTON

THE BED & BREAKFAST FOLKS
MS. TIMMIE BASKIN
73 PROVIDENCE ROAD
WESTFORD, MA 01886

PHONE: 617/692-3232
Live (usually) 8–10 a.m. and 4–10 p.m. Answering machine at other times.
OPEN: Year round.

ACCOMMODATIONS
B&Bs
Hosted private residences: 11.
Plus
Hosted short-term (for months) housing; some with kitchen and laundry privileges.

OTHER SERVICES: Health club discount.

LOCATION *All near high-tech industries, historical communities, skiing, shopping outlets. Forty minutes northwest of Boston in Acton, Boxborough, Billerica, Burlington, Chelmsford, Dunstable, Groton, Harvard, Pepperell, and Westford.*
In New Hampshire: Nashua.

SETTINGS: Classic country New England.

GUESTS COME FOR: Business travel, mostly in high-tech industry. House hunting. Groton School. Apples. Maple sugaring. Cross-country skiing. Historic Concord and Lexington are a 20-minute drive. Lowell's National Historic Urban Park.

HOSTS: Retired, artist, lawyer, teacher, psychologist, florist, engineer. . . .

BREAKFAST: Most serve a full breakfast. Could include home-made breads and muffins, local cheese and syrup, and farm-fresh eggs.

RESERVATIONS
At least one week in advance preferred. If arrangements can be made, will accept last-minute reservations.
Groups: Maximum size is six in one home.

RATES
Singles $35–$40. Doubles $40–$55.
Monthly (corporate) rate available.
Deposit required: One night's lodging.
Credit cards accepted: MasterCard and VISA.
Cancellation policy: If notice is received 48 hours before expected arrival date, deposit less $10 returned. After then, deposit is forfeited.

FOLKSTONE BED & BREAKFAST
MARGOT FRENCH
P.O. BOX 131, STATION A
BOYLSTON, MA 01505

PHONE: 617/869-2687
Live at least Monday–Friday, 7–9 a.m. and 6–10 p.m.; 7–6 most weekends. Answering machine at other times.

OPEN: Year round, except for March, November, and a week in January.

ACCOMMODATIONS
B&Bs
Hosted private residences: Seven.
One (West Boylston) is accessible to handicapped.

OTHER SERVICES: Pickup at airport, bus, and train. Transportation can be arranged to the Medical Center that is close to most hosts.

LOCATIONS *Most are within 10 miles of Worcester. Barre is a 35-minute drive and Ashburnham is an hour's drive from downtown Worcester.*

SETTINGS: Range from "just plain" to country antique to beautifully appointed and luxurious. Five are suburban. Barre and Ashburnham are rural.

HOSTS: Doctors and their spouses, organist/music teacher, travel agency executive, physical therapist, farmers, business manager. . . . "Everyone has his own style of hosting, but they all seem to agree on the request for nonsmoking guests."

GUESTS COME FOR: College- and university-related activity—there are 10 schools in the area, including Assumption, Clark, Anna Maria, Holy Cross, University of Massachusetts Medical School, and Worcester Polytechnic Institute; also Worcester County and its museums, concerts, historic sites, hiking trails, and restaurants. It is a good central base for touring New England. Business, including high-tech, also brings travelers to the area.

BREAKFAST: All continental. Full breakfast is offered by some hosts as an option.

RESERVATIONS
Advance reservations requested, especially for summer and fall.
Last-minute reservations may be possible.
Groups: A couple of homes can accommodate up to eight people.

DIRECTORY: A flyer with descriptions is sent without charge on request. (Please send a business-sized, self-addressed, stamped envelope.) *Samples:*

Grafton: Located just 15 minutes from downtown Worcester, this Federal period home has been restored to its original grace. Four bedrooms are available as well as common rooms and a music room with a grand piano. Hostess is gourmet cook, collector of antiques, and creator of beautiful dried flower arrangements. $25 per person.

Ashburnham: A working farm, circa 1750, nestled in the upstate hills where guests enjoy walking the country lanes, a swim in the spring-fed pond with its sandy beach, and the breathtaking beauty of the surrounding hills and meadows. Winter offers cross-country skiing and ice skating at the door, and downhill skiing at Mt. Wachusett or Mt. Monadnock. Within a 45-minute drive to Cathedral in the Pines, Fitchburg Arts Museum, and Pickety Place Herb Farm and Restaurant in Mason, New Hampshire. Hostess can accommodate three guests, and serves the best homemade English muffins this side of the Atlantic. Single $30. Double $35.

RATES
Singles $25–$30. Doubles $30–$50. A few are higher.
Deposit required: One night's lodging.
Cancellation: If notice is received at least 24 hours before expected arrival date, one-half of deposit is refunded.

Massachusetts-based reservation services are arranged, as much as possible, from east (Cape Cod) to west (Berkshires).

◇ ◇ ◇

HAMPSHIRE HILLS BED & BREAKFAST ASSOCIATION
MARY MCCOLGAN, SECRETARY
P.O. BOX 307
WILLIAMSBURG, MA 01096

PHONE: 413/268-7925 or 634-5529
OPEN: Year round.

ACCOMMODATIONS
B&Bs
Hosted private residences: 16.

LOCATIONS *Located in eight rural hill towns of Western Massachusetts: Goshen, Williamsburg, Huntington, Cummington, Worthington, Chesterfield, Chester, Blandford.*

SETTINGS: Wide range including working farm, Greek Revival, and contemporary homes.

HOSTS: Former state legislator, retired minister, art professor, librarian, retired foreign service staffer. . . . They have formed their own association to "spread the word."

GUESTS COME FOR: The countryside. Five colleges and universities in Northampton and Amherst. Day trips to the Berkshires, just a little west.

BREAKFAST: Varies from continental to a full country or gourmet meal.

DIRECTORY: Please send a business-sized self-addressed stamped envelope for the brochure that includes attractions in each town. Name of host, address, phone, and directions included with each listing. *Sample:*

> Cumworth Farm is a 200-year-old-farmhouse offering five bedrooms and three bathrooms, and a choice of continental or American breakfast. The farm produces sheep, apples, vegetables, berries, and maple products. Opportunity for a farm vacation. Children welcome! $35 double, $25 single. Cots $10 extra.

RESERVATIONS
Made directly with each host.
Advance reservations preferred—and strongly recommended for commencement and fall foliage weeks. When possible, last-minute reservations accepted.

RATES
Singles $25–$30. Doubles $30–$40.

Hidden Treasures
Even Massachusetts natives, particularly those in the eastern part of the state, are unfamiliar with this wonderful territory filled with interesting hosts.
—The author

BERKSHIRE BED AND BREAKFAST

TERRY ROSS
P.O. BOX 211
WILLIAMSBURG, MA 01096

PHONE: 413/268-7244
Monday–Friday, 9–5. Answering machine at other times.
OPEN: Year round. Closed all federal holidays.

ACCOMMODATIONS
B&Bs
Hosted private residences: 58.   B&B inns: 4.
About half have private baths. A few have air conditioning, pools, tennis courts, trout streams, ponds, cross-country ski trails, and/or blueberry patches.
One listing is accessible to handicapped.
Plus
Some short-term (three months or more) housing available.

OTHER SERVICES: Car rentals arranged. Pickup at airport, bus, and train. Tours of the area that, depending on season, could include maple sugaring, square dancing, and restaurant reservations.

LOCATIONS   *In Massachusetts, all the area west of Worcester.*
Upstate New York, primarily Columbia County (Berlin, Cherry Plain, Stephentown, Lebanon Springs, Canaan).
In Vermont and New Hampshire along the Massachusetts border.

SETTINGS: Elegant country estates, National Register historical homes, hillside and mountainside places, a few split-entry ranch homes. All sorts of working farms—dairy, horse, strawberry, sheep—are represented. Most are in rural areas. Some in Pittsfield, Massachusetts, and in residential areas of Springfield, Massachusetts.

HOSTS: Retired social worker, artist, caterer, realtor, lawyer, doctors, writers, farmers. . . .

GUESTS COME FOR: New England with its country roads, scenic drives with rivers running along the highway, the architecture, antique shops. . . . Spring with its maple sugaring time; summer for Tanglewood and summer stock theater; fall's foliage; winter's

191

cross-country and downhill skiing. One guest wrote, ". . . Their maple syrup is A+. . . . They even supplied dogs for a morning walk."

BREAKFAST: Half serve continental (fresh fruit or juice, breads, jam, and hot coffee or tea) and half serve full breakfasts (could be eggs, bacon, French toast, homemade granola, omelets, freshly picked berries). All hosts are required to serve fresh baked goods, either their own or from a reputable bakery.

RESERVATIONS

Advance reservations of two weeks preferred. If arrangements can be made, will accept last-minute reservations.
Groups: Maximum size is 40.

DIRECTORY (not required for reservations): $3 includes information about and maps of the area, sketches and photos of the host homes. *Samples:*

> Great Barrington. #SC-1. Peace and quiet on this lovely 300-acre horse farm where everything works but the guest. Your hosts' lovingly maintained turn-of-the-century home was especially designed with summer visitors in mind, wraparound porches, views in every direction, and acres of lawn, woods, and fields. Host is Harvard-trained pediatrician specializing now in adolescent medicine. Hostess manages family farm and is a published poet. They serve a continental breakfast with homemade croissants, jams and jelly, coffee, tea, and juice. Three guest rooms, all furnished in antiques. Shared guest baths.

> Petersburg, NY, just over the Massachusetts border. #NY-1. Rolling hills, freshwater streams, and numerous ponds are waiting for you to explore at this mountainside retreat. Hike to spectacular view or pick-your-own in the wild blackberry, blueberry, and raspberry patches. Families welcome! Host couple from Switzerland. Multilingual (five languages). Two beautiful young daughters. Pony cart available for rides. Bedrooms furnished with wonderfully carved pieces brought from Europe. King-sized bed. Private bath. Full breakfast served.

RATES

Doubles $25–$125. $5 less for a single. $10 for additional person in room. Deposit required: $20 per room. Rates for extended stays (three weeks or more) negotiable.

Credit cards accepted: MasterCard and VISA accepted by the service only (not by inns).

Cancellation policy: If notified 10 days before expected arrival date, refund made minus $5 service fee.

Are Any of These Old (Restored) Houses Haunted?

"One guest insisted that one of our hosts' homes was haunted. On the second night of her stay, the guest, still secure in her belief, asked our hosts if they would like to have her read the Tarot cards for them. So there they were, all around the table, until late in the evening. About 11:00, the guest brings up the haunted house idea again. The hosts respond that they are sure that they would know if the house were haunted. Well, at that very moment every light in the house went out. The guest said, 'See, I told you!' (There had been an accident down the road and a light pole had been knocked down.)"

Private homes in the Berkshires are also available through Covered Bridge Bed and Breakfast, page 85.

Michigan

BETSY ROSS BED & BREAKFAST OF MICHIGAN

BERT HOWELL AND NORMA BUZAN
3057 BETSY ROSS DRIVE
BLOOMFIELD HILLS, MI 48013

PHONE: 313/647-1158 and 646-5357
Live Monday–Friday 9–5. Answering machine at other times.
OPEN: Year round. Closed December 20–January 5.

ACCOMMODATIONS
B&Bs
Hosted private residences: 50.   B&B inns. 55.

OTHER SERVICES: Car rentals. Pickup at airport, bus, train.
Theater tickets.

LOCATIONS *In about 50 communities throughout the state—and in Elkhart, Indiana.*

SETTINGS: Near the beach and ski areas. In Detroit and near Greenfield Village. Homes range from neat-and-attractive to rather luxurious.

HOSTS: Artists, business people, interior decorators. . . .

194

GUESTS COME FOR: The Great Lakes. Beaches. Greenfield Village. Detroit River and Renaissance Center. General Motors Technical Center. Business. Relocation. Conferences. Some just passing through.

BREAKFAST: "Our hosts fit their cooking to the palate of the guests."

RESERVATIONS
Ten days in advance preferred. If arrangements can be made, will accept last-minute reservations.
Also available through travel agents.

DIRECTORY (not required for reservations): Descriptions of all Betsy Ross B&Bs are included in Bert and Norma's *Bed & Breakfast in Michigan and Surrounding Areas* ($8.25).

RATES
Singles $25–$35. Doubles $40–$60. Children under 12, half price. Children using their own sleeping bags stay at a nominal fee. Seventh night free.
Weekly and monthly rates available.
Deposit required: $25.
Cancellation policy: Deposit refunded less $5 handling charge if cancellation received 48 hours before expected arrival date.

Watch the Midwest!

Norma is working with the Governor's Council to help with the development of bed and breakfast hospitality in Michigan. With the nationwide recognition of B&Bs, she sees this as a pretty exciting B&B time for the entire midwest.

FRANKENMUTH BED AND BREAKFAST RESERVATION AGENCY
BEVERLEY J. BENDER
337 TRINKLEIN STREET
FRANKENMUTH, MI 48734

PHONE: 517/652-8897 or 652-6747
Usually 9–8 daily. Answering machine at other times.
OPEN: Year round.

ACCOMMODATIONS
B&Bs
Hosted private residences: 10.
Most have air conditioning.

OTHER SERVICES: Pickup at airport or bus. One-hour tours of
Frankenmuth. Referrals, but not bookings, to B&Bs to the north in
Traverse and Freeland, and to the south in Schiawasse County.

LOCATIONS   *Most are in the center of Frankenmuth within
walking distance of tourist attractions. (Frankenmuth is two
miles long with businesses and attractions clustered on
Main Street.)*

HOSTS: Educators, baker, computer specialist, nurse, engineer,
world traveler, Frankenmuth natives, inventor. . . .

GUESTS COME FOR: This German community (the number one
tourist spot in Michigan), with its heritage that dates back to 1845.
Guided and self-guided tours of town. The fifth- and sixth-largest
restaurants in the country. Bavarian Festival in June (with over
200,000 attending), Volksflaufe walking and running race in July,
Polka Festival in August, maybe an Oktoberfest to come. Christmas shopping all year round at Bronner's Christmas Wonderland
with its one-acre showroom. Some come for business reasons, to
house-hunt, or just passing through.

BREAKFAST: All serve a continental "plus" (plus = fruit salad,
cheese and hard rolls, or hard-boiled eggs) breakfast.

RESERVATIONS
Advance arrangements generally preferred but necessary during
festivals.
If arrangements can be made, will accept last-minute reservations.
Whether you have made reservations before arriving in town or at
the last minute, all guests receive the name and address of host by
meeting Beverley in person first. You are given directions to the
home and a packet of tourist information.
Groups: Maximum size is 15.
Also available through travel agents.

RATES
Singles $20–$35. Doubles $30–$50.
Some weekly rates available.

Deposit required: $20 per room.

All payments are made to the agency before stays.

Cancellation policy: Deposit refunded minus a $5 service charge.

> *"Although Frankenmuth is a town of only 3,800 people, when we introduced the idea of bed and breakfast at a workshop sponsored by our county extension service, over 100 people came to see what was involved in welcoming travelers into a private home as paying guests. Our hosts love their role—and seem to appreciate the prepayment arrangement that frees them from any direct financial transaction with the guest."*

BED & BREAKFAST OF GRAND RAPIDS

JOYCE MAKINEN
344 COLLEGE S.E.
GRAND RAPIDS, MI 49503

PHONE: 616/451-4849 or 456-7121

Live Monday–Friday 9–9. Answering machine at other times.

OPEN: Year round except Christmas and New Year's.

ACCOMMODATIONS
B&Bs
Hosted private residences: seven.

OTHER SERVICES: Special tours arranged to museums, tea and tours at historic homes, escorted tours of historic homes combined with luncheon.

LOCATIONS   *All are in the Heritage Hill Historic District (1,500 historic properties), adjacent to downtown Grand Rapids. All houses are on local bus routes. Many are within walking distance of the downtown cultural and entertainment center and very close to expressways leading to northern, southern, and eastern parts of Michigan.*

SETTINGS: All are Victorian houses built between 1870 and 1910. One is on the National Register of Historic Places.

HOSTS: Lawyer, wallpaper hanger, educator. . . .

GUESTS COME FOR: The Gerald R. Ford Museum, Grand Rapids Art Museum. Two hospitals and two colleges in the area or bordering it. Business reasons.

BREAKFAST: All are continental.

RESERVATIONS
Three days in advance strongly preferred. Last-minute reservations are seldom possible.

RATES
Singles $30–$40. Doubles $50.
Deposit required: $20.
Cancellation policy: Deposit is refunded, minus $3 handling charge, if notice received 48 hours before expected arrival date.

CAPITAL BED & BREAKFAST
SUSAN SMITH
5150 COREY ROAD
WILLIAMSTON, MI 48895

PHONE: 517/468-3434
  Monday–Friday 9–5.
OPEN: Year round.

ACCOMMODATIONS
B&Bs
Hosted private residences: Six and growing.
Most have air conditioning and private baths.
Plus
Some short-term housing available.

OTHER SERVICES: Pickup at airport or bus. Gourmet meals available.

LOCATIONS *All in the Lansing and Williamston area.*

SETTINGS: Most are in the country, yet "close in." Most are furnished with antiques.

HOSTS: Antique dealer, sales engineer, teacher, retired realtor, retired school secretary. . . .

GUESTS COME FOR: Michigan State University. Museums. Golf and cross-country skiing. Antiquing in an area that bills itself as Antique Country.

BREAKFAST: All serve continental.

RESERVATIONS
Two weeks in advance preferred. "Early planning becomes part of the fun." If arrangements can be made, will accept last-minute reservations.

RATES
Singles $18–$25. Doubles $25–$35.
Deposit required: At least $10. One-quarter of total if more than one night.
Cancellation policy: Full refund minus $3 handling charge if notice received 48 hours before expected arrival date.

Along the shore of Lake Michigan there are B&B hosts represented by Bed & Breakfast/Chicago, page 123.

Minnesota

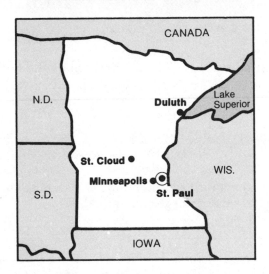

BED & BREAKFAST REGISTRY

MARY WINGET
P.O. BOX 80474
ST. PAUL, MN 55108

PHONE: 612/646-4238
Live Monday–Friday 9–5. Answering machine at other times. Call-backs made at Registry's expense.

OPEN: Year round. Closed December 20–January 5 and all holidays.

ACCOMMODATIONS
B&Bs
About 300 countrywide (see LOCATIONS listing.) Most are private homes. Some are inns. Most have air conditioning. Some are accessible to handicapped.
Plus
Some hosted and unhosted short-term (up to three months) housing available.

OTHER SERVICES: Some hosts offer pickup at transportation points. Theater tickets, area tours, use of bicycles or boats, child care, and additional meals may be arranged at some homes.

LOCATIONS *In 200 communities of 36 states and Puerto Rico. In Minnesota, 9 are in Minneapolis, 3 are in St. Paul, 11 are in Minneapolis–St. Paul suburbs.*
Other Minnesota locations: Afton, Albert Lea, Cokato, Dassel, Ely, Grand Marais, Lake Wilson, Marine-on-St. Croix, Melrose, Northfield, Pierz.

SETTINGS: Urban, suburban, rural, waterfront, and mountainside settings. Nationwide, they range from modest to luxurious. Several are historic. One is a houseboat.

HOSTS: Designer, clergy, salesmen, realtors, bankers, artists, architects, nurses, engineers, farmers, business people, writers, teachers, doctors, lawyers. . . .

BREAKFAST: Varies from simple to elaborate depending on host.

RESERVATIONS
Two weeks in advance preferred. If arrangements can be made, will accept last-minute reservations.
Groups: Some locations can handle up to 16 or 20.
Also available through travel agents.

DIRECTORY (not required for reservations): $9.50 includes postage. A spiral-bound 200-page book with full descriptions of B&Bs, some photos, and some sketches. *Sample:*

Minneapolis. I-94, I-35W, Lowry Hill East Area, 24th and Hennepin. Spacious 1890s neoclassical house has a highly embellished interior with the original dark oak woodwork, a fireplace in the living room, antique Victorian furnishings throughout, including the three guest rooms. The first guest room has a single bed and a double bed, the second two twin beds, and the third a double bed. Shared guest bath. Breakfast is served in the formal dining room or in the guest's room, as preferred. There is a third-floor sitting area for guests which has a refrigerator, coffee maker for snacks, and separate phone for guests' use. Resident poodle. The house is six blocks from the Guthrie Theater, the Walker Arts Center, and the Minneapolis lake district. It is on a direct bus line to downtown, and within walking distance of many cafes and fine restaurants. These very cordial hosts, whose interests take in running, antiques, travel, the arts, and cooking, help make this one of the most popular B&Bs in the area. Rates: $20–$25S; $35/D; $45/T.

RATES

Singles $20–$160. Doubles $25–$300. Most are at the lower end of the scale.

One-night surcharge: $5–$10. Many offer weekly rates. Deposit required: First night's fee plus $10 for each successive night.

Credit cards accepted: VISA and MasterCard.

Cancellation policy: If notice received at least seven days before expected arrival date, refund, minus $10, is made.

Deposit forfeited if seven days or less.

It's a Big Country

Mary screens some homes personally. Others are screened by representatives of Bed & Breakfast Registry or by other reservation services that work with the Registry in a cooperative arrangement.

Do you have a question? When writing to a bed and breakfast reservation service, please enclose a business-sized (#10) self-addressed stamped envelope (SASE).

Mississippi

LINCOLN, LTD. BED AND BREAKFAST
BARBARA LINCOLN HALL
P.O. BOX 3479
MERIDIAN, MS 39303

PHONE: 601/482-5483
Monday–Friday 8:30–4:30. Answering machine at other times.
Will always return calls for a reservation request.
OPEN: Year round.

ACCOMMODATIONS
B&Bs
Hosted private residences: 27.   B&B inns: 3.
All have air conditioning and private baths.

OTHER SERVICES: Car rentals. Pickup at airport or train by special arrangement. Tickets to Merrehope, Lively Arts Festival, Jimmie Rodgers Festival in Meridian, and other state festivals.

LOCATIONS   *Throughout Mississippi, from the Hills to the Plains to the Gulf Coast. Communities represented include Natchez, Vicksburg, Port Gibson, Lorman, Brookhaven, Jackson, Meridian, Columbus, Oxford, Holly Springs, Indianola.*

SETTINGS: All are rather luxurious. Many are historic.

HOSTS: Artist, lawyer, retired pharmacist and spouse, manufacturer's representative and spouse, decorator, insurance executive, retired military, young executives, mayor, retired university professor, bank president, newspaper editor. . . .

GUESTS COME FOR: A vacation. Business with local manufacturing plants. Merrehope (antebellum home), schools—Meridian Junior College; Mississippi State University, Meridian Branch; University of Mississippi–Oxford, Mississippi College for Women–Columbus; Millsaps College–Jackson. Festivals and pilgrimages. "We started appealing to tourists, but have found that corporate travelers sometimes welcome the change of an alternative lodging experience. Now we place executives who are being relocated to Meridian. This gives the person in the family sent ahead an opportunity to get to know someone in the community, other than coworkers, and allows a more relaxed and easier relocation adjustment."

BREAKFAST: All but one serve a full meal. They are typical Southern-style breakfasts and may include grits; some are quite elaborate.

RESERVATIONS
Advance reservations of one to two weeks preferred.
If possible, last-minute reservations are made.
Groups: Maximum size of 16 or 18 in most towns.
Also available through travel agents.

DIRECTORY (not required for reservations): $3. *Samples:*

> Pass Christian (on the Mississippi Coast) #27. Enjoy the unique opportunity of staying in a log home on 40 acres! Just 2½ miles north of I-10, 2½ miles from the beach. This home has a private bedroom and bath, a loft for families traveling with children, and a swimming pool for your pleasure. The hosts have lived in this area for over 36 years and will direct you to all the many and varied activities here. $45–$55. $10 additional for each person sharing the loft. Breakfast included.

> Vicksburg (On the Mississippi River at I-20. Civil War Battlefield and National Park. Spring and fall Battlefield Pilgrimages.) #29. An original Federal-style structure, this home combines history with every modern amenity, includ-

ing a hot tub and a swimming pool. Step back in time as you sleep in an antique-filled bedroom and enjoy a plantation-style breakfast in the formal dining room. $75–$110.

Meridian (I-59 at I-20. Settled in 1833. Lively arts festival in April and Jimmie Rodgers Festival the last week in May.) #14. Restored Victorian home filled with antiques and located on 10 wooded acres within the city limits. Hostess is a noted gourmet cook and will, on special arrangement, prepare dinner for an additional charge. Full breakfast included. $60–$65.

RATES

Singles $45–$90. Doubles $40–$100. A few higher. Weekly and monthly rates available.

Deposit required: One night's lodging.

Credit cards: VISA accepted for deposit. If full payment is made in advance, for entire fee.

Cancellation policy: Refund of deposit, less $10 service fee, if cancellation received one week before expected arrival date. If last-minute cancellation, a $25 fee is prorated with host.

Guests reported—"They made us feel like houseguests, not paying tourists." "A quite outstanding B&B experience. The accommodations were luxurious and the hospitality bounteous. Their beautiful home filled with treasures was fascinating ... also the surrounding woods and countryside ... very warmhearted and made us feel right at home ... very informed and interesting to talk to. Map to their house and directions were good."

The "Who" of the Service

When Barbara was in real estate, she loved matching people to houses. She has also been director of sales for a local hotel and convention center. After traveling B&B in Florida and England, she decided to open a bed and breakfast reservation service to match hosts and guests. "Our very first guest, in January of 1984, was a young advertising account executive who had come to town to sell me some advertising in a national publication. Having never stayed in a bed and breakfast, and not knowing what to expect, she decided to give it a try. Sold she was. Now she stays in a B&B at least one of her four weeknights on the road. Also, she has personally been my best advertiser and a positive advocate for bed and breakfast.

NATCHEZ PILGRIMAGE TOURS
CANAL STREET DEPOT, P.O. BOX 347
NATCHEZ, MS 39120

PHONE: 601/446-6631 or 800/647-6742
   Live 8:30–5:30 daily year round.
OPEN: Year round. Some B&Bs are seasonal.

ACCOMMODATIONS
B&Bs
Hosted private residences: 20.   B&B inns: 2.
All are air conditioned and have private guest baths.
Most are hosted by owners; a few have managers in residence.

LOCATIONS   *Most are in town. A couple are about six miles out.*

SETTINGS: Mansions, plantations, cottages (converted slave quarters), country inns. All are antebellum and furnished with antiques.

GUESTS COME FOR: Tours of the homes and area.

BREAKFAST: A few serve continental. Most serve a full Southern breakfast.

RESERVATIONS
Advance preferred and necessary (much in advance) for Pilgrimage sessions, the first two weeks of October and all of March and the first week of April.
If arrangements can be made, last-minute reservations accepted. Also available through travel agents.

DIRECTORY: Brochure with descriptions of each home sent without charge. *Sample:*

> D'evereux. Circa 1840. Pure Greek Revival. Original furnishings of builder John Elliott. Home of Mr. and Mrs. Jack Benson and family. One bedroom in main house. $90 double occupancy. Champagne continental breakfast. Tour of house. National Register.

RATES
$60–$100 for two. Single rates available. Some off-season (December–February) rates available. Some weekly rates may be available.

Deposit required for Pilgrimage sessions and requested for other times.

Natchez Pilgrimage Tours was established in 1932 as a private nonprofit organization to provide tours and help to maintain the properties that were built between 1790 and 1857. Five are historic landmarks and 30 are on the National Register. The B&Bs are all privately owned.

Throughout Mississippi there are additional B&Bs represented by Louisiana Hospitality Services, page 137, and by New Orleans Bed & Breakfast, page 139.
Along the river north as far as Vicksburg there are B&Bs selected by Southern Comfort Bed & Breakfast Reservation, page 140.

Missouri

OZARK MOUNTAIN COUNTRY BED & BREAKFAST SERVICE

KAY CAMERON AND LINDA JOHNSON
BOX 295
BRANSON, MO 65616

PHONE: 417/334-4720
  Live 5–10 p.m. daily. Answering machine at other times.
OPEN: Year round.

ACCOMMODATIONS
B&Bs
Hosted private residences: 20. B&B inns: 3.
Almost all are owner-occupied and have private baths and air conditioning.

LOCATIONS *Most homes are within a 30-mile radius of Branson and include the communities of Hollister, Kimberling City, Cape Fair, and Walnut Shade. One is 18 miles north of Springfield. One is 15 miles east of Springfield, and one on Lake of the Ozarks is 90 miles northeast of Springfield near Camdenton.*
  In Arkansas: Two homes, one in Eureka Springs and the other in Pindall (south of Harrison).

SETTINGS: Most are clean homes-away-from-home. A few are luxurious and a few are historic. All are in quiet lovely areas of the Ozarks, but still within a few minutes' drive of Silver Dollar City, White Water, and Mountain Music Shows.

HOSTS: Include school teachers, postmaster, college professors, physician, and retired business people.

BREAKFAST: Could be continental or an elaborate meal with funnel cakes and eggs Benedict.

RESERVATIONS: Advance reservations appreciated but last-minute reservations accepted. Can handle groups up to 10.

DIRECTORY: Send a self-addressed, stamped envelope for five pages of descriptions. *Sample:*

> OMC—Fisherman's Delight: Walk out front door each morning to your own private fishing dock! The covered dock offers a 5½-foot boat slip for guest use. Large boat can be secured to dock. Shopping, boat launch and rentals only half mile away. This lovely home, located on beautiful Lake Taneycomo, is in a secluded, peaceful area of Branson. It offers a private entrance to its guest area on lower level facing lake side. One bedroom with king-size bed, private full bath, sitting room with queen-size hide-a-bed, fireplace, refrigerator, and freezer. A/C, TV, ice, wheelchair access, $40 for two, $50 for four.

RATES
Singles $20–$30. Doubles $26–$40. A few higher.
Deposit required: $20.
Cancellation policy: Refund made if one week's notice given.

TRUMAN COUNTRY
BARBARA EARLEY
424 N. PLEASANT
INDEPENDENCE, MO 64050

PHONE: 816/254-6657
    Sunday–Friday after 5 p.m.
OPEN: Year round except Thanksgiving and Christmas.

ACCOMMODATIONS
B&Bs
Hosted private residences: Three—and growing.
One is accessible to handicapped.

OTHER SERVICES: Pickup at transportation points.

LOCATIONS   *In Independence and the Kansas City metro-politan area.*

GUESTS COME FOR: Truman Library and Museum, Truman Home, Fort Osage and Honey Farm, Vaile Mansion. . . .

BREAKFAST: Varies according to host.

RESERVATIONS
One week in advance preferred. If possible, last-minute reservations accepted.

DIRECTORY: A listing is sent on request without charge. *Sample:*

1850s Victorian home near the Harry Truman Home. Entirely furnished with Victorian antiques. (Hostess gives tours of her home.) Shuttle bus available in front of Truman Home. Historical sites within walking distance. No pets or smoking. Air conditioned. Full meal. Private bath. Cots available in summer for children over eight years at $5. $37.50 single. $40 double.

RATES
Singles $25–$40. Doubles $25–$40.

"We are a small service but what we have to offer is excellent."

BED & BREAKFAST OF ST. LOUIS/RIVER COUNTRY OF MISSOURI AND ILLINOIS INC.
MRS. MIKE WARNER
1 GRANDVIEW HEIGHTS
ST. LOUIS, MO 63131

PHONE: 314/965-4328
Live at least 10–2 Monday–Friday. Answering service 7–6 Monday–Friday, 7–noon Saturdays. Emergency or last-minute res-

ervations can often be accommodated (if Mike isn't at her son's soccer game then).

OPEN: Year round.

ACCOMMODATIONS
B&Bs
Hosted private residences: About 100.   B&B inns: 10.
Most have air conditioning and private baths.
Plus
Some unhosted private residences for overnight or weekend lodging. Some hosted and unhosted short-term housing and unhosted long-term also available.

OTHER SERVICES: Some hosts arrange for pickup at airport, bus, or train. Limousine service by prior arrangement.

LOCATIONS   *In addition to homes in the Central West End and Lafayette Square areas of St. Louis, there are hosts in 11 St. Louis County communities, in urban and suburban locations. In West County, near several hospitals, is a special experience at the DeSmet Jesuit Community. In River Country, in Missouri and Illinois, there are hosts in about 25 communities.*
Recently this service has expanded to Germany, with hosts on farms and in castles.

SETTINGS: High-ceilinged townhouses, romantic hideaways, a home that was once a restaurant, a farmhouse on a working farm, homes in wine areas. They range from baronial to a three-room cottage where you carry your own water.

HOSTS: Doctors, dentists, educators, world travelers, school head-master, bilingual (Italian speaking) woman married to a Chinese doctor, two mayors, retired Air Force colonel and wife. . . . Mike doesn't specialize in, but lists some hosts who are particularly good placements for visiting families.

GUESTS COME FOR: A vacation. Conferences. Relocation. Weddings. Just passing through. Business reasons.

BREAKFAST: Varies from help-yourself to an elaborate meal.

RESERVATIONS
Preferably made on the phone to provide a good match of hosts and guests. If arrangements can be made, will accept last-minute reservations.

Groups: Maximum size is 30.
Also available through travel agents.

DIRECTORY (not required for reservations): $4. Informative and attractive booklet that introduces you to each community, tells you where it is in relation to major roads, and describes the homes and hosts. *Sample:*

> Louisiana, Missouri: This historic riverboat town dating back to the early 1700s is named after King Louis of France. It is the home base for the oldest nursery in the United States, Stark Nursery. One of the few bridges crossing the Mississippi to the Illinois side is at the town's point. A marina offers stopovers for boaters. Parks offer swimming and tennis and many great areas to view the riverboats while sitting on park benches. This is a great area for the true history buff, with many antique shops and an array of antebellum and Victorian "gingerbread" houses. The River Festival in August is a fun time to visit the area. This small town is hospitable and very open to visitors. Location: 100 miles north of St. Louis, 43 miles south of Hannibal.
> It is a glorious B&B situated in a 20-room baronial house. The first floor of the home is paneled with cherrywood, decorated with old tapestries. Since a June 1983 article, this is a popular place. Make plans and place reservations ahead of time! Dinner reservations may be arranged at host's country club if private parties have not reserved the evening. Boaters may be picked up at the marina by prior arrangement.
> Bed: Guests stay in a large ivory-and-teak room. Private bath right off the bedroom.
> Breakfast: Croissants, cakes, sweet butter, homemade strawberry jam, coffee, and juice left at your door at a prearranged time. A leisurely breakfast is served either on the porch or in the bedroom.
> Rates: $45 for two per night.

RATES
Singles $20–$60. Doubles $30–$200. (Top rate includes a package arrangement with a five-course gourmet dinner.)
Deposit required is 20 percent of total charge.
Credit cards accepted: MasterCard, VISA, Diners Club, Carte Blanche for deposit or entire fee.

Cancellation policy: $20 handling charge for cancellations received at least one week before expected arrival date.
Total deposit forfeited on reservations cancelled six days or less before intended arrival.

One of the Most Active B&B Agencies in the Midwest

In the early days of bed and breakfast reservation services, Mike Warner accepted a New Yorker's challenge of "just who would want to come to Missouri." She not only developed a full list of active hosts—and as this book went to press she had close to 100 waiting to be interviewed and inspected—but she has championed the B&B concept with a slide-tape show that is a hit wherever she goes. The storefront location of her office is the first—and only one—of its kind in North America. Visitors have the opportunity to meet the enthusiastic reservation service owner, and learn about B&B in St. Louis—and far beyond.

River Country guests seem to be sophisticated travelers. They have led Mike to become involved in many different fields including restoration and history. Her experiences with people and a love for the bed and breakfast concept may soon be combined in a place of her own, perhaps in a very special city location or with her dream of a small country inn on a riverbank. Inquire!

Because B&Bs are all different, tell the service what you want. Think ahead of time about your needs. For a little help, turn to page 1.

Montana

WESTERN BED & BREAKFAST

SYLVA JONES
P.O. BOX 322
KALISPELL, MT 59901

PHONE: 406/257-4476
  Monday–Saturday 9–5.
OPEN: Year round.

ACCOMMODATIONS
B&Bs
Hosted private residences: 25.   B&B inns: 2.
Almost all have private baths.

OTHER SERVICES: Arrangements made for hunting, fishing, white water, and hiking trips, and for skiing and horseback riding.

LOCATIONS *Spread throughout the state in rural, suburban, and urban areas. Some are close to Glacier National Park and Yellowstone.*

HOSTS: Mostly retired ranchers and government employees. . . .

GUESTS COME FOR: Glacier National Park, Yellowstone National

Park, National Bison Range, Indian reservations, hiking, hunting, fishing, skiing on Big Mountain in Whitefish.

BREAKFAST: From simple to elaborate, according to host.

RESERVATIONS
Two weeks in advance preferred. If arrangements can be made, will accept last-minute reservations.

DIRECTORY (not required for reservations): About 20 descriptions are yours for a self-addressed stamped envelope. *Samples:*

> #101 Between Kalispell and Big Fork, yet close to Glacier Park, charming log home on small lake with gorgeous view from patio area. Fish for bass or perch or take a walk to the mountains. Comfortable bedroom has double bed and large closets. Shower bath plus your own separate sitting room with view of lake and mountains. Cheerful hosts are avid gardeners and birders. A full breakfast with homemade sweet rolls included. Single $25. Double $30.

> #112 Close to Missoula in Alberton. Rustic but cozy cabin. You can view elk or deer in the morning or evening; trout fishing or commercial white-water rafting nearby. Or unwind from a day of travel by hiking one of the many trails. Cabin has electricity but no running water. Shared bathroom/shower facilities available in main house next to cabin. Full or continental breakfast included of course. Resident dog and cat. Smoking permitted with great care. Alcoholic beverages in moderation. No pets. Single $20. Double $23.

RATES
Singles $18–$30. Doubles $22–$50. A few are higher.
Deposit required. $20.
Cancellation policy: Deposit less a $5 service fee will be refunded for cancellations received 72 hours before expected arrival date.

Sylva reminds us "Montana is (still) a rural state with a total population of 820,000."

Additional B&Bs in the western and southern parts of Montana are represented by Bed & Breakfast—Rocky Mountains, pages 76–77. A few B&Bs in the state are also available through Northwest Bed & Breakfast, page 264.

Nebraska

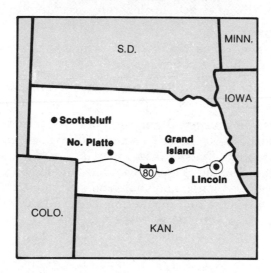

Bed and Breakfast of Nebraska

MARLENE VAN LENT
1464 28TH AVENUE
COLUMBUS, NE 68601

PHONE: 402/564-7591
  Live 5–10 p.m. daily. Answering machine at other times.
OPEN: Year round.

ACCOMMODATIONS
B&Bs
Hosted private residences: 15.
Almost all have air conditioning and private baths.
Plus
Some unhosted private residences for overnight or weekend lodging.

OTHER SERVICES: Some hosts pick up at airport, bus, and train.

LOCATIONS *Most are near Interstate 80, including South Sioux City, Omaha, Grand Island, Kearney, North Platte, Chadron, York, Columbus, Blair, Scottsbluff, Lincoln, Crawford.*

GUESTS COME FOR: Hunting. Fishing. Just passing through.

216

BREAKFAST: All hosts serve a full meal.

RESERVATIONS
Four or five days in advance preferred. If arrangements can be made, will accept last-minute reservations.

RATES
Singles $20–$30. Doubles $30–$40.
Family rates available.
Deposit required: $20.

Do you have a question? When writing to a bed and breakfast reservation service, please enclose a business-sized self-addressed stamped envelope (SASE).

New Hampshire

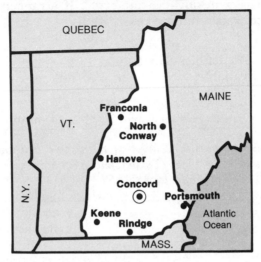

NEW HAMPSHIRE BED & BREAKFAST
MARTHA W. DORAIS
RFD 3, BOX 53
LACONIA, NH 03246

PHONE: 603/279-8348
Live Monday–Friday 10–6. Answering machine at other times.
OPEN: Year round.

ACCOMMODATIONS
B&Bs
Hosted private residences: 50.
Almost all have private baths.
Plus
Some short-term (one month maximum) hosted housing available.

LOCATIONS *Throughout New Hampshire.*

SETTINGS: A little bit of everything—mountain views, beachfronts, historic, farms—rural, suburban, and in towns.

HOSTS: Lawyer, teachers, realtor, doctors, musicians, architects, contractors, homemakers, garden designer, weaver, equestrian. . . .

GUESTS COME FOR: A vacation. House hunting. Passing through. Natural beauty, the mountains, ocean, lakes (365 of them), sports, tax-free shopping, and many colleges.

BREAKFAST: Most hosts serve a full breakfast. Possibilites include homemade muffins, fresh berries, real maple syrup, organic veggies, eggs and meat ("homegrown"), and some gourmet cooking.

RESERVATIONS
Minimum stay of two nights on holiday weekends.
Two weeks in advance preferred.
If arrangements can be made, will accept last-minute reservations.
Groups: Maximum size is 20.
Also available through travel agencies.

DIRECTORY (not required for reservations): $1. *Sample:*

Canaan (Dartmouth Region) #315. Only 15 miles from Dartmouth College in Hanover, this large 18th-century home on lovely historic street is surrounded by large fields, mountain view, and large shady trees. Walk to beach on small lake or cross-country ski from the back door. In the evening relax and enjoy the cool breezes and beautiful views from screened porch. Hostess enjoys cooking (try her delicious muffins), flowers, and herb gardening. Four guest rooms, both twin and double, private and shared full baths. Full breakfast served in dining room. Spacious living room for guests, TV, porch. Nonsmokers preferred. No facilities for young children. $30 single, $40 double.

RATES
Singles $20–$45. Doubles $30–$55.
Weekly and monthly rates available.
Deposit required is 20 percent of total plus tax.
Credit cards accepted: MasterCard and VISA.
Cancellation policy: Full refund, minus $5 service, made if notice is received at least one week before expected arrival date.

Throughout New Hampshire there are B&Bs represented by Pineapple Hospitality, page 156.
Along the southern border there are B&Bs represented by Berkshire Bed and Breakfast, page 191, and Covered Bridge Bed and Breakfast, page 85.

New Jersey

BED & BREAKFAST OF NEW JERSEY

ASTER MOULD
103 GODWIN AVENUE
MIDLAND PARK, NJ 07432

PHONE: 201/444-7409
  Live Monday–Friday 9–5; Saturday 9–12. Answering machine
  at other times.
OPEN: Year round.

ACCOMMODATIONS
B&Bs
Hosted private residences: 49.   B&B inns: 17.
Almost all have air conditioning and private baths.
A few are accessible to handicapped.
Plus
Some unhosted private residences for overnight or weekend lodging.
Many variations of arrangements. (Please see Directory, below.)

OTHER SERVICES: Car rentals. Pickup at airport, bus, and train
by most hosts. Much resource information about where to go, what
to do, and schedules.

LOCATIONS *Spread throughout the state in rural, subur-*
ban, and urban areas. Most are near some type of public
transportation and all are easily accessible by major routes.

SETTINGS: From very modest with a shared bath to extremely
luxurious complete with resort facilities. Some other possibilities
include a high-rise condominium overlooking the Manhattan sky-
line, a converted boat house (a "floating home"), a converted grist
mill, and an artist's studio built in 1889.

HOSTS: Corporate executives, realtors, speech therapist, doctors,
architect, teachers, engineers, medical assistant, personnel assistant, administrator, farmers, chemist, stock broker. . . .

GUESTS COME FOR: Business. Many private schools and colleges
including Rutgers, Princeton, and St. Peter's College. A vacation:
sports activities, arts, parks, historic sites, museums, cultural
centers, beaches, and boardwalks. House hunting. Atlantic City.
And some are just passing through.

BREAKFAST: Varies from simple to elaborate depending on host.
Could include freshly made bagels, puff pancakes, lots of gourmet
egg recipes. One host offers bacon, sausage, and farm-fresh eggs
from her own farm.

RESERVATIONS
At least two weeks in advance preferred. If arrangements can be
made, will accept last-minute reservations.
Minimum stay required: Some shore properties require at least a
two-night stay.
Groups: Up to 15 or 20 can be booked if much advance notice given.
Also available through travel agents.

DIRECTORY (not required for reservations): $1.50. It highlights
some of the accommodations for short-term and longer stays. Descriptions include listings of single rooms, suites, whole floors,
apartments, and entire homes and villas available. Because additional listings are added every week, not all listings are in the
directory. Many of the longer-term listings are also not in the
directory. *Sample:*

> River Edge: Discover the gracious atmosphere of living
> that prevails in this beautiful white colonial. A truly
> unique home, located just blocks from a main roadway and

recognizable by the old-fashioned sleigh on the front lawn. On the main floor, you will find a sitting room with double sofa bed, private bath, and TV. Upstairs are single and double rooms with a shared bath. Your friendly hosts will be delighted to provide you with all the comforts of their home. A continental breakfast (including freshly made bagels!) will be served in the bright, plant-filled kitchen solarium, and special diets are accommodated. Enjoy all of the special features of this home, such as central air conditioning and a piano that fills the house with music. Single $35. Double $48.

RATES

Singles $25–$55. Doubles $30–$90. Seventh night is usually free. For B&B inns that have a published rate, there is an additional one-time charge of $15.

Deposit required is 25 percent of total stay.

Cancellation policy: If reservation was made within one week of arrival date, refund minus a small service fee will be made as long as cancellation is received 48 hours before expected arrival date; otherwise at least a week's notice is required for refund due to cancellation.

"Even though we are growing rapidly, we still take a lot of care in determining the needs of the guest and matching them with one or two special hosts."

"We started appealing to tourists and then found there was a real need here in New Jersey for short-term housing, especially for transferees and corporations. Now some of our host homes do offer longer stays at special rates."

NORTHERN NEW JERSEY BED & BREAKFAST

AL BERGINS
11 SUNSET TRAIL
DENVILLE, NJ 07834

PHONE: 201/625-5129
Live many weekends and 4–9 p.m. Monday–Friday. Answering machine at other times.
OPEN: Year round.

ACCOMMODATIONS
B&Bs
Hosted private residences: 20.   One B&B inn.
Half have private baths. About half have air conditioning.
Plus
Hosted short-term (a month or more) housing.

LOCATIONS   *All in northern New Jersey, including Denville, Rockaway, Landing, Flemington, Mountain Lakes, Fairfield, Clifton, Verona, Cresskill, Livingston, Bloomingdale. Many are located within walking distance of bus or train service to Manhattan. Some are about a half hour's drive to Manhattan.*

SETTINGS: All are in residential areas within a few miles of the centers of towns. Some are on lakes and include swimming and boating privileges. All are quite comfortable. Some are luxurious.

HOSTS: Many teachers. Many experienced B&B travelers.

GUESTS COME FOR: Corporate travel. Weddings. Major exhibitions and shows. Some are just passing through.

BREAKFAST: Varies from continental to full according to host.

RESERVATIONS
Advance reservations required. Same-day B&B reservations are not accepted.

RATES
Singles $25–$30. Doubles $35–$40.
Deposit required: One night's lodging for reservations of one to seven days.
Cancellation policy: If notice received at least a week before expected arrival date, refund minus a service charge of $10 or $20 (depending on length of reservation). Less than seven days' notice, deposit is forfeited.

As a host, Al found that he couldn't accommodate all who wished to stay in his area, so he organized this service.

TOWN AND COUNTRY BED & BREAKFAST
ANITA IMPELLIZERI
P.O. BOX 301
LAMBERTVILLE, NJ 08530

PHONE: 609/397-8399
  Monday–Thursday 7–9 p.m.
OPEN: March through December.

ACCOMMODATIONS
B&Bs
Hosted private residences: 12.   B&B inns: 6.

OTHER SERVICES: Dinner reservations and theater reservations made on request. Car rental information provided but arrangements not made by service.

LOCATIONS   *In New Jersey in the Delaware River Valley and Hunterdon County (Lambertville and Flemington). In Pennsylvania's Bucks County: New Hope and surrounding communities.*

HOSTS: Artist, health food store owner, school teachers, retirees. . . .

GUESTS COME FOR: Restaurants. Craft and antique shops. Flea markets and country auctions. Hiking and cycling along the Delaware River Towpath or on country roads. Boating, tubing, fishing. Theater. A hot-air balloon ride. Historic sites. Factory outlets. Princeton University.

BREAKFAST: Varies according to host from simple to elaborate.

RESERVATIONS
All reservations are made on the phone.
One-night reservations available on weekends. Two-night minimum on weekends at most inns.
Advance reservations preferred but will accept last-minute reservations.
Groups: Arrangements can be made for several (6–12) couples.

RATES
Doubles $30–$130. (Single rates same as for double occupancy.)
Discount sometimes given for extended stays.
Deposit required: $30 per reservation.

Credit cards accepted: VISA and MasterCard for deposit only.
Cancellation policy: Reservation must be cancelled one week before
scheduled arrival date or guest forfeits deposit.

---

*Because B&Bs are all different, tell the service what you
want. Think ahead of time about your needs. For a little
help, turn to page 1.*

New Mexico

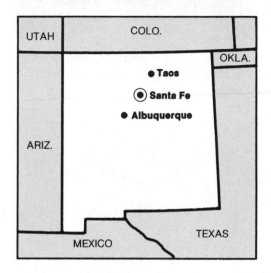

BED & BREAKFAST OF SANTA FE

STAR JONES
218 E. BUENA VISTA
SANTA FE, NM 87501

PHONE: 505/982-3332
Monday–Saturday, September–May 9–5. June–August 7–7. "If the answering machine is on during those hours, I may be at the post office, bank, or the copy machine office—or visiting my host families."

OPEN: Year round. Closed major holidays and Sundays.

ACCOMMODATIONS
B&Bs
Hosted private residences: 15.
Almost all have private baths. Many of the listings are accessible to handicapped.
Plus
Some unhosted individual guest houses on main house property (where hosts are in residence) and apartments.

OTHER SERVICES: Complimentary pickup at bus and train. Reservations made on shuttle from Albuquerque airport. Information sent on request includes car rental arrangements, restaurant lists, opera schedules.

LOCATIONS *All are within three-mile radius of inner city. Most within walking distance of historic plaza, museums, and restaurants.*

SETTINGS: Most are "Santa Fe–style" adobe with patios and southwestern decor.

HOSTS: College professor, school teachers, bank president, attorney, working artist, retired social worker, nurse, business executives. . . . "I would like travelers to know that we are four years old and we carefully select our accommodations." (Star rejects a high number of the potential hosts who call wanting to be listed.)

GUESTS COME FOR: Santa Fe summers with opera, chamber music concerts. Fall—aspencades, local fiestas, Indian Market. In winter there is skiing at local ski basin and famous farolito displays during Christmas week. Largest folk art collection in the world. Art galleries. Nearby are ancient cliff dwellings and modern pueblos, and the Los Alamos (birthplace of the atom bomb) museum.

BREAKFAST: Most are continental—croissants, fresh fruit, and hot beverage.

RESERVATIONS
Two weeks in advance preferred.
Last-minute reservations rarely made.
Groups: Maximum size: 60.

DIRECTORY: Please send a self-addressed stamped envelope to receive a list of accommodations available. *Sample:*

> #BC: Three separate accommodations in colorful spacious home of busy artist and builder. Two talking/singing birds reside! Guest house: double bed, full kitchen, private bath, outside entrance. $60 for facility. . . . Guest room with fireplace, full private bath, queen bed, sitting/lounging area. $55 for one or two. . . . Turret room! In separate living area of this large home. Bedroom with double bed is at top of charming stairway. Private bath and dressing room at foot of stairs in your own private wing of the house. $35 for one; $40 for two.

RATES

Singles $25–$65. Doubles $30–$65.

Weekly and monthly rates available off-season.

Deposit required is 20 percent plus tax.

Cancellation policy: Deposit refunded less $5 service fee if notified two weeks prior to first day of reservation. Half of deposit, less $5 service fee, if less than 14-day notice. No refunds for 48-hour or less notice. No refunds for cancelled reservations for Indian Market Week in August or for December 15–January 5.

> *Star writes: "So many of my calls are from people looking for an inn, not understanding or even knowing about host families on the list of a B&B reservation service. They are usually somewhat surprised and a little hesitant to commit to staying in a private home. Once they try it, they are delighted to have the personal contact and relaxed atmosphere they find. And we find that guests are very appreciative. Recently we heard from a repeat B&B couple who came back to Santa Fe this year to look for a house to buy. I introduced them to a local realtor and attorney who were able to help them. The couple is moving to Santa Fe this year. . . ."*

Some additional New Mexico B&Bs in Albuquerque, Santa Fe, and Los Alamos are represented by Bed & Breakfast— Rocky Mountains, pages 76–77.

New York

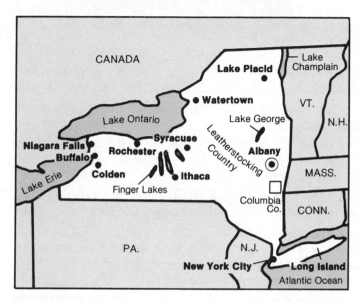

BED & BREAKFAST U.S.A., LTD.

BARBARA NOTARIUS
P.O. BOX 606
CROTON-ON-HUDSON, NY 10520

PHONE: 914/271-6228
Live Monday–Friday 9–4. Answering machine at other times.
OPEN: Year round.

ACCOMMODATIONS
B&Bs
Hosted private residences: 150 (in New York State). Some are accessible to handicapped.
Plus
Some unhosted private residences for overnight or weekend lodging. Some short-term (up to three months) hosted and unhosted housing. In Europe: Four hundred small (under 25 rooms) family-owned hotels.

LOCATIONS *Throughout New York State for B&B U.S.A. listings. Throughout United States and Great Britain (homes screened by local agencies and booked through B&B U.S.A.).*

SETTINGS: The wide range includes farmhouses, historic houses, townhouses, Georgians, colonials, and a 52-foot sailing yacht.

HOSTS: Archaeologists, teachers, physical therapist, veterinarian, psychiatrist. . . .

GUESTS COME FOR: New York State with its tourist attractions, cities, and countryside, conferences, colleges and universities, businesses, and passing through on the way.

BREAKFAST: All B&B U.S.A. hosts serve a full breakfast. Some feature specialities such as baked eggs or berry pancakes.

RESERVATIONS
Advance reservations preferred. If arrangements can be made, will accept last-minute reservations.
Also available through travel agents.

DIRECTORY (not required for reservations): $2. Information about each region is given, followed by descriptions of homes. *Sample:*

> #36 Croton-on-Hudson. A large riverview Victorian home with apple orchard and 35-foot in-ground pool. The home is furnished with many Victorian antiques and includes two pianos and two fireplaces. Host is a computer consultant. Hostess a psychologist. One six-year-old daughter. Accommodations include four guest rooms, three with double beds, one with two twin beds—all with antiques. Hostess enjoys serving elaborate breakfasts on the patio beside the pool in summer or in a 35-foot sun room which looks out on the Hudson River. Hostess can speak a little French. Host can understand Russian. Smokers are not welcome. Children of all ages are welcome. All baby equipment is available. Bicycles are also available. A French bulldog is also in residence. This home is convenient to Van Cortlandt Manor, Teatown Reservation, and the Croton Dam. It is accessible from NYC by Metro North train (50 min.). Cab from station $1.75. Rates: S $30–$35 daily $210 weekly, D $50 daily $240 weekly. Children over two $10 each per night. A 2½-room apartment is also available at $250 a week for two or three people.

RATES

Guest membership fee: $25 good for one year, or $15 per reservation.
Singles $25–$50. Doubles $30–$95. A few are higher.
Some weekly and monthly rates available.
Deposit required: Half of total charge.
Credit cards accepted: MasterCard and VISA with 3 percent use fee.
Cancellation policy: If notice received less than seven days before expected arrival date, one night's lodging and the reservation fee are charged.

> *"The family was a delight and made me welcome. For a woman traveling alone, B&B offers a safe feeling. Just great."*
>
> *—A Bed & Breakfast U.S.A. guest*

◊ ◊ ◊

NEW YORK CITY

THE B&B GROUP (NEW YORKERS AT HOME) INC.
FARLA ZAMMIT
301 EAST 60TH STREET
NEW YORK, NY 10022

PHONE: 212/838-7015
Live Monday–Friday 9–4. (Friday hours May 15–September 15, 8:30–11 a.m.) Answering service at other times.
OPEN: Year round except for a vacation time that is preannounced on all written communications from the B&B Group. Closed federal and state holidays.

ACCOMMODATIONS
B&Bs
Private residences: 244. Some are unhosted.
Almost all have air conditioning and about half have private baths.

LOCATIONS *All are in the borough of Manhattan. Additional summer listings are in the Hamptons, Long Island.*

SETTINGS: About 25 percent are "just nice places" and the rest are rather luxurious.

HOSTS: Banker, marketing consultant, actor, freelance writer, TV commercials actress, TV soap opera actress, editor of national magazine, psychologist, computer consultant, fashion stylist, hospital technician, dress designer, stewardess, corporate bond trader, gentleman farmer, account executive, teacher, real estate broker, financial advisor, literary agent, attorney, psychotherapist. . . .

BREAKFAST: All continental. Most hosts are not usually present for breakfast.

RESERVATIONS
Must be made three to four weeks in advance.
Minimum stay of two nights required.

DIRECTORY: Please send a self-addressed stamped envelope for a description of all available accommodations for the current period. *Sample:*

> #165 Marketing consultant (& her cat) offer bedrm/pvt full bth. Qn. sz trundle bed (can be 1 lge or 2 single beds) in 2 bdrm 2 bth apt. in luxury Park Ave. (95st) doorman elev bldg. 2 blks Central Park, excl transp. Museum Row $45 S $55 D.

RATES
Singles $40–$55. Doubles $55–$65. A few are higher.
Unhosted apartments: $65–$135.
Deposit required: $10 for each night of stay for singles and $15 each night for doubles. Full payment for unhosted apartments.
Credit card accepted: AMEX for deposit or entire fee.
Cancellations for B&Bs (hosted residences) received more than 10 days before arrival date are subject to a $25 cancellation charge. Cancellations for hosted B&Bs received less than 10 days before arrival date are subject to 1 night's lodging cost. Shortening of confirmed reservations dates allowed only before arrival date (with the addition of 1 night's lodging cost). There are no refunds or adjustments on or after arrival.

> *"My stay was most pleasant. . . . I felt free to come and go whenever I felt like it. The room was large and convenient. I liked the location: a few blocks from Greenwich Village. This of course is personal, but for somebody who first visits New York and rambles around the town and its museums all day, it is enjoyable to be in the neighborhood of the restaurants, cafes, jazz-inns, and off-Broadway theaters in the evening."*
>
> —*Guest from the Netherlands*

NEW WORLD BED & BREAKFAST, LTD.
JANICE IKOLA AND RAY SCHIFF
150 5TH AVENUE, SUITE 711
NEW YORK, NY 10011

PHONE: 212/675-5600 (New York State) or 1-800/443-3800 (out of state)
   Live Monday–Friday 10–4. Answering service at other times.
OPEN: Year round.

ACCOMMODATIONS
B&Bs
Hosted private residences: 120.
About half have private baths and almost all have air conditioning.
Plus
Many unhosted private residences for two nights or longer. Short-term (one to two months) unhosted housing occasionally available.

LOCATIONS *All are in Manhattan—in Midtown, Upper East Side, Upper West Side, Greenwich Village, a few in the business district or Wall Street area. All are within a $5 cab ride of the center of Manhattan, and have good access to public transportation.*

HOSTS: Actors, actresses, artists, musicians, lawyers, teachers, linguists, social workers, caterers, realtors, housewives, interior decorators, psychologists, fashion designer, stock broker. . . .

RESERVATIONS
Minimum stay of two days required.
Minimum one to two weeks in advance preferred but last-minute accommodations can usually be made. Reservations any time within 14 days of arrival date must be made on the phone rather than by mail.
Groups: Up to 10 can be placed in the same accommodation.

BREAKFAST: Most are continental and are seldom served. Hosts are not usually present at breakfast.

RATES
Singles $25–$65. Doubles $35–$75.
Weekly and monthly rates available.
Deposit required: In most cases, 25 percent of total cost.
Credit cards accepted: MasterCard and VISA.
Cancellation policy: "If they don't like it, we give a full refund. If

cancellation received very close to the scheduled reservation and the room isn't subsequently filled, sometimes one night is compensated to host or hostess. We are very reasonable."

"After location and price, callers ask about privacy, and if we sense they are better placed in an unhosted unit, we will attempt to stress this.

"One of our busiest hostesses is a budding fashion designer. She boasts a large studio and living quarters in which she offers three private rooms and three private baths for B&B guests. In the heart of the city, one is made to feel at home while observing a most creative lady. She has sold several of her custom-designed pieces of clothing to her guests. Both business folks and vacationers request her over and over again. Ironically enough, another dream of this hostess was to run an inn, and we are helping her fulfill this one."

—Janice and Ray

URBAN VENTURES
MARY MCAULAY, RENA RAPPAPORT, THERESA SWINK
P.O. BOX 426
NEW YORK, NY 10024

PHONE: 212/594-5650
Live Monday–Friday 8:45–5:15, Saturday 9–3. Answering machine at other times.
OPEN: Year round except July 4, Thanksgiving, Christmas, New Year's.

ACCOMMODATIONS
B&Bs
Hosted private residences: 350.
Most have air conditioning and private baths.
Plus
Two hundred unhosted apartments for overnight or weekend lodging.
Hosted and unhosted short-term (up to three months) housing.

OTHER SERVICES: Theater tickets.

LOCATIONS *All B&Bs are in New York City.*

SETTINGS: From penthouse apartments to student spare. In Brooklyn, century-old mansions.

HOSTS: Stage, screen, and radio producers and directors, actors, makeup experts. Caterers, advertising executives, fashion coordinators, doctors, active retirees. . . .

RESERVATIONS
Minimum stay of two nights required.
Advance reservations, in time for receipt of deposit, preferred. If arrangements can be made, will accept last-minute reservations. Groups: Up to 10 may be accommodated on the same block, but not in the same building.
Also available through travel agents.

BREAKFAST: Continental at all B&Bs. Hosts are not usually present.

DIRECTORY: None available, but inquiries answered with a neighborhood map of NYC that indicates locations of major attractions and a few sample listings. *Samples:*

#20009 Hummingbirds have been seen on patio outside your window. The Metropolitan Museum of Art is just down the block. Pvt. bath. $52/1; $58/2 on E83St.

Apt #6328 A small 1 bdrm apt in Chelsea in a nicely kept bldg. Once a home, this is the parlor floor with a non-wking fireplace. Dble futon $55 a night.

#2006 The epitome of East Side chic & elegance in this modern apt. w/architectural built-ins. A rm w/pvt bath is $65/2; $80/3 as a loft bed for a third person makes for super comfort. On E 66 St.

RATES
Singles $24–$55. Doubles $34–$80. A few are higher.
Deposit: One night's fee.
Some monthly rates available.
Credit cards: AMEX accepted for deposit, for entire fee, or to hold a reservation until check arrives.
Cancellation: A $15 booking fee charged if cancellation received up to three nights before arrival. One night's fee is forfeited if the cancellation is within three days of arrival.

"Dear Urban Ventures: Just a note to say that we had a wonderful (if cold!) week in New York. It was so comfort-

*able and homey in Mary Ann G's apartment. Warm and in
an interesting location. We walked everywhere. Thanks so
much for being in this business!"*
                          —*Mrs. J. W. from Encinitas, California*

◇ ◇ ◇

LONG ISLAND

B&B GUESTS COME FOR: The resort communities of the Hamptons with their beaches, swimming, golf, tennis, restaurants, and
nightlife. Summer theater. Honeymoons. Antiquing. Rural farming and fishing area of the North Fork. Pick-your-own vegetable
farms. Horse racing at Roosevelt Raceway. The off season has its
quiet appeal, which attracts city residents in search of a getaway.
Some come for relocation reasons, for the many colleges, or (in the
western Suffolk and Nassau Counties) for the commercial and industrial centers.

A REASONABLE ALTERNATIVE
KATHLEEN DEXTER
117 SPRING STREET
PORT JEFFERSON, NY 11777

PHONE: 516/928-4034
   Winter: Live Monday–Friday 9–1. Summer: Live Monday–Fri-
   day 10–4. Answering machine at other times.
OPEN: Year round.

ACCOMMODATIONS
B&Bs
Hosted private residences: About 60.
Most have private baths.
Plus
Unhosted private residences for a week, month or the season.

LOCATIONS *Most are on the north and south shores of
Nassau and Suffolk Counties. Some are near the industrial
areas.*

SETTINGS: Varied. From colonial to modern, from cottage to condominium.

HOSTS: Active and retired educators, advertising staffers, financial consultants, television personnel. . . .

BREAKFAST: Usually continental.

RESERVATIONS
Minimum stay requirement: Some hosts on eastern Long Island have a two-day minimum.
Groups: By using several homes, it is possible to book 15 or 20 wedding guests.
Also available through some travel agents.

DIRECTORY: None available, but brochure (please send a self-addressed stamped envelope) includes general descriptions of possibilities in several areas. *Sample:*

> If the North or South Fork appeals to you but living on a boat doesn't, you can choose to stay in one of our New England–style homes, some of which have the original "cooking" fireplaces. Comfortable homey accommodations will make your visit to this charming area a pleasure.

RATES
Singles $28–$60 in season, $24–$48 off season.
Doubles $32–$60 in season, $28–$48 off season.
A few in resort areas go up to $100 in summer.
Deposit required: $25.
Credit cards accepted: MasterCard and VISA.
Cancellation policy: Refund, less $10 service charge, if notice received at least 72 hours before expected arrival date.

ALTERNATE LODGING INC.
FRANCINE HAUXWELL
BOX 1782
EAST HAMPTON, NY 11937

PHONE: 516/324-9449
Live 9–6, Monday–Friday. Answering machine at other times.
OPEN: March 15–September 30.

ACCOMMODATIONS
B&Bs
Hosted private residences: 75.

LOCATIONS *Communities with B&Bs in this resort area are Westhampton Beach, Quogue, Hampton Bays, Southhampton, Watermill, Bridgehampton, Wainscott, Sag Harbor, East Hampton, Amagansett, and Montauk.*

SETTINGS: Homes with pools, private entrances, spacious gardens, large decks, courtyards, and tree houses.

HOSTS: Professors, writers, medical personnel, and theatrical people. . . .

BREAKFAST: All hosts serve a continental breakfast.

RESERVATIONS
One week in advance preferred. Last-minute reservations accepted with credit card.
Minimum stay requirement: Two nights. Exceptions: July 4 requires a four-night minimum and Labor Day a three-night minimum, in addition to a $5 per night surcharge.
Also available through travel agents.
Maximum size of groups that can be accommodated: Six.

RATES
Singles $30–$60. Doubles $45–$75. Seventh night is free.
Credit cards: MasterCard, VISA, and AMEX accepted for entire fee.
Deposit required: For a week or longer, 25 percent of total charge. Balance due before arrival.
Cancellation policy: In the event of cancellation, payment will be applied to any future reservation made within the next 12 months.

BED & BREAKFAST OF LONG ISLAND
NAOMI KAVEE
P.O. BOX 392
OLD WESTBURY, NY 11568

PHONE: 516/334-6231
Live Monday and Wednesday 8–9:30 a.m. and 4:30–6:30 p.m.

Tuesday, Wednesday, and Friday, 9:30 a.m.–1 p.m. and 9–10:30 p.m. Weekends usually 10–12 noon. Answering machine at other times.

OPEN: Year round.

ACCOMMODATIONS
B&Bs
Hosted private residences: 43.
Most have private baths.
Some accessible to handicapped.
Plus
Some unhosted private residences for weekend or weekly lodging. Hosted short-term (up to six months) housing available.

OTHER SERVICES: Some hosts offer laundry and limited kitchen privileges. Some offer use of bikes and rowboats.

LOCATIONS *Almost all are near public transportation. In Nassau County: Baldwin, Hempstead, Franklin Square, Garden City, Freeport, N. Babylon, Massapequa, Roslyn, Westbury, West Hempstead, Syosset, Sands Point, Port Washington. In Suffolk County: Amityville, Huntington, Amagansett, Hampton Bays, Eastport, Easthampton, Southampton, Quogue, Miller Place, Port Jefferson, Peconic, Westhampton Beach, Bridgehampton, Sag Harbor, Watermill, Montauk, and Fire Island.*

SETTINGS: From modest attractive homes to historic and luxurious homes.

HOSTS: Interior designer, attorney, retired military officer, retired banker, teacher, court stenographer, nurse, actor, social worker, woman paperhanger. . . .

BREAKFAST: Varies from help-yourself to a full meal.

RESERVATIONS
Minimum stay required: Two nights during summer in Hamptons. Two weeks in advance. If arrangements can be made, will accept last-minute reservations.

DIRECTORY: Please send a self-addressed stamped envelope for the descriptions of all listings. *Sample:*

Water Mill. At the end of country road, this stunning contemporary saltbox offers a choice of several rooms. Two double-bedded with semiprivate bath ($60). Also, king-sized-bedroom has private bath. $65. Midway between Sag Harbor bathing and ocean beach. Continental breakfast.

RATES
Singles $30–$40. Doubles $45–$85. A few are higher.
One-night surcharge: One-half daily rate in resort areas.
Weekly and monthly rates available.
Deposit required: One night's lodging fee.
Cancellation policy: If cancellation is received seven days before expected arrival date, complete refund less a $10 handling charge is made.

The Hesitant Beginner Host

"One of our newer hosts was apprehensive about hosting. She wanted to start off slowly, perhaps just single women, possibly a middle-aged couple, preferably no children, and no more than a two- or three-day stay. We called her several times but each time she felt she would be more comfortable with 'just a single woman'. Finally we called with reservations for a young couple with two children due to arrive the next day. As usual she hesitated . . . didn't think she could handle it. We had previously placed other members of that family and reassured her it would be an unusual experience; they were New Zealanders and she would find them most interesting. She agreed to try. The day after their arrival she called, excitedly telling me how fascinating they were. Their life style was so different from ours. They lived on an island. . . . There were hugs and kisses when they departed after ten days. The host called immediately to request other guests as soon as possible, and said that there were to be no more stipulations ever again!"

BED & BREAKFAST—LONG ISLAND

CHARLOTTE FRIEDMAN
P.O. BOX 312
OLD WESTBURY, NY 11568

PHONE: 516/334-8499
Usually live 8–4. Answering machine at other times.
OPEN: Year round.

ACCOMMODATIONS
B&Bs
Hosted private residences: 30 in summer months, 18 year round.
Almost all have air conditioning and private baths.
Some are accessible to handicapped.
Plus
Short-term (for one month) hosted possibilities.

OTHER SERVICES: Pickup at airport and train.

LOCATIONS   *Amagansett, Hampton Bays, Eastport, Bridge-hampton, Sag Harbor, Miller Place, East Quogue, West-hampton Beach, and Southampton. Also homes in New York City; Manhattan and Queens, Garden City, Baldwin, Amityville, and Glen Cove.*

SETTINGS: Range from contemporary to century-old Victorian with fireplaces in every room to 200-year-old colonial to a pre–Civil War farmhouse on several acres. Some are on or within walking distance of the beach, in historic villages, or in wooded areas.

BREAKFAST: Varies according to host. Could include cranberry bread, beach plum jam and blueberry muffins.

RESERVATIONS
Advance reservations preferred. If arrangements can be made, will accept last-minute reservations.
Minimum stay requirement: Two nights in the resort area.
Also available through travel agents.

DIRECTORY (not required for reservations): $1. Three pages of listings. *Sample:*

Southampton. Convenient location two blocks from Main Street or Job Lane shopping. One-half mile from ocean beach. One room, twin beds, private beach. Full breakfast. $65.

RATES

Singles \$35–\$45. Doubles \$45–\$85. A few in NYC go up to \$110. Weekly and monthly rates available.

Deposit requirement: One night's lodging. Full payment is due two weeks prior to arrival.

Cancellation policy: Refund of deposit, minus \$3 service charge, if cancellation is received two weeks before expected arrival date; 75 percent of payment will be refunded if cancellation is received at least five days prior to date of arrival.

HAMPTON BED AND BREAKFAST

CINDY ROBINSON

P.O. BOX 378

EAST MORICHES, NY 11940

PHONE: 516/878-8197

Live most of the time. Answering service or answering machine at other times.

OPEN: Year round.

ACCOMMODATIONS

B&Bs

Hosted private residences: 50.

OTHER SERVICES: Pickup at airport, bus, train.

LOCATIONS *Spread throughout Long Island close to bus or train stations, in rural areas, and on the water.*

SETTINGS: Some are old and quaint with antiques; some are fairly new with contemporary furnishings.

HOSTS: Teachers, retired librarians, writers, business women, carpenters, artists, domestic engineers. . . .

BREAKFAST: Varies from simple to an elaborate meal.

RESERVATIONS

Minimum stay requirement: Two nights on weekends and holidays. Two weeks' advance notice recommended for holiday reservations. If arrangements can be made, will accept last-minute reservations.

DIRECTORY (not required for reservations): $1 plus self-addressed stamped envelope. *Samples:*

> Bellport—"Shell House." 100-year-old home. 1 single room $36.11. Dbl room $48. 1 dbl rm with hi-riser $58. Share bath, no smokers. Sunfish rental, churches nearby, 1 block to Fire Island Ferry. Has dog. Country breakfast.

> Remsenburg—Modern contemporary on water, queen-sized bed with private full bath, overlooking swimming pool and water. $100 for two. Two twin rooms sharing bath—$90. 1 dbl room with private bath—$90.

RATES
Singles $30–$50. Doubles $40–$100.
Weekly and monthly rates available.
Deposit required: Charge for total stay.
Cancellation policy: One night's lodging is deducted from refund and a credit is given to be used for accommodations within one year (upon availability) if cancellation made within 12 hours of arrival date. If cancellation is made 10 days in advance, a refund minus a $10 service fee is made.

◇ ◇ ◇

BED & BREAKFAST—LEATHERSTOCKING CENTRAL N.Y.
FLORANNE/ROBERT McCRAITH
389 BROCKWAY ROAD
FRANKFORT, NY 13340

PHONE: 315/733-0040
Live 9–9 daily.
OPEN: Year round.

ACCOMMODATIONS
B&Bs
Hosted private residences: 10.   One B&B inn.
Some accessible to handicapped.

OTHER SERVICES: Car rentals. Pickup at airport, bus, and train. Theater tickets and dinner reservations.

LOCATIONS *"The Hub of New York State" includes Herkimer, Hamilton, Fulton, Montgomery, Schoharie, Otsego, Chenango, Madison, and Oneida.*

HOSTS: Business executives, engineers, farmer, antique dealer, nurse/teacher, craftspeople, caterer, lapidaries, museum curator. . . .

GUESTS COME FOR: Sightseeing, antiquing, business, outlet and specialty shopping. College-centered activities, relocation, sports, and weddings too.

BREAKFAST: All hosts serve a full breakfast with attention to special dietary needs.

RESERVATIONS
At least one week in advance preferred but will accept last-minute reservations.
Groups: Maximum of nine.
Also available through travel agents.

DIRECTORY (not required for reservations): $2. *Sample:*

Frankfort Hill. 1828 Homestead. Three miles southeast of Utica. Eight miles off I-90. This spacious, traditional home is accented by rose-covered stone fences, perennial gardens, and 200-year-old maple trees. Its 60 acres afford a spectacular view of the Mohawk Valley in all seasons, as well as an opportunity to walk or cross-country ski through wooded trails and view the wildlife on nearby ponds and streams. The cozy country kitchen, with exposed beams and a brick hearth fireplace, enhances the relaxed, informal atmosphere during a delicious breakfast. This is furnished with a combination of antique and traditional furnishings. . . . He owns a wholesale food distributing business, is a school board member, and collects antique bottles. She is a homemaker and public health nurse. . . . Frankfort Hill is convenient to all attractions in the area, including Oneida Silversmiths, Revere Copper and Brass, historical sites, forts, museums, and restaurants. Within a 45-mile radius there are six colleges. . . . One king bed with private bath $35. Twin beds with private bath $35, shared bath $30. Children 12 years and under welcome—$10 extra. Crib and baby items and babysitting available. Dog and cat in residence. No pets please.

RATES
Singles $20–$50. Doubles $30–$60.
Some weekly rates available.
Deposit required: Half of nightly rate.

Cancellation policy: Full refund if notice received at least 10 days before expected arrival date.

"Retired teachers who have traveled all over the world many times decided to try B&B through New York State. 'Unbelievable. The scenery, the food, the people—why didn't someone let us know this was here!?' We are in an area that is still undiscovered."

—The McCraiths

From parents who came for a college parents' weekend: "This was our first B&B experience and I was very pleased with everything." Under "Other comments" they wrote, "Please oil door of pink bedroom so as not to disturb others in the middle of the night when going to the bathroom." Reservation service noted the suggestion: "Done!"

BED & BREAKFAST REFERRAL OF THE GREATER SYRACUSE AREA
ELAINE N. SAMUELS
143 DIDAMA STREET
SYRACUSE, NY 13224

PHONE: 315/446-4199
  Usually 9 a.m.–11 p.m. daily.
OPEN: Year round.

ACCOMMODATIONS
B&Bs
Hosted private residences: 12.
Plus
Some unhosted private residences for overnight or weekend lodging.
Hosted short-term housing also available.

OTHER SERVICES: Pickups at transportation points for additional fee.

LOCATIONS *Currently hosts are in Syracuse and within 25 miles of the city, but other communities will be added soon.*

SETTINGS: Range from a cozy single room in a modern suburban house to an executive colonial which offers a king, a queen, and a single room with cots for children. One is a duplex on Oneida Lake.

HOSTS: Retired military officer (now a chemist), caterer, retired nurse, social worker and mail carrier husband, writer, realtor who now boards cats, radio newsman and wife, world travelers. . . . Most prefer nonsmoking guests.

GUESTS COME FOR: The crossroads of New York State with its businesses, schools (including Syracuse University), vacationers, conference attendees, house hunters, hospitals, skiing (Alpine and Nordic), golf, lakes.

BREAKFAST: Varies from simple to elaborate depending on host.

RESERVATIONS
Advance reservations preferred. If arrangements can be made, will accept last-minute reservations.
Groups: Equipped to handle up to 25, if arranged well in advance. Also available through travel agents.

RATES
Singles $25–$30. Doubles $35–$40.
Deposit required: First night's lodging fee.

BED & BREAKFAST ROCHESTER
BETH KINSMAN
BOX 444
FAIRPORT, NY 14450

PHONE: 716/223-8510, 223-8877
   Try anytime; tape machine on if not in.
OPEN: Year round. Bookings difficult Christmas week; all filled with family!

ACCOMMODATIONS
B&Bs
Hosted private homes: Five.
Most have air conditioning.
Plus
A completely furnished condominium which is available for any length of time. (It turns over every two to three months.)

OTHER SERVICES: With advance notice, dinner with the family can be arranged; $5 per person.

LOCATIONS *Most within 10 miles of downtown Rochester in beautiful quiet surroundings. One, available summers only, is on the shore of Keuka Lake.*

HOSTS: A doctor's wife who is currently writing a treatise for a museum on pre-1800 gravestone carvings, a condominium manager who collects folk art, a college professor. . . .

BREAKFAST: All full. Could include apple muffins, apple oatmeal with raisins, homemade corn bread, or croissants.

RESERVATIONS

Advance reservations preferred. If arrangements can be made, will accept last-minute reservations.

Also available through travel agents.

DIRECTORY: Please send a self-addressed stamped envelope for a descriptive list. *Sample:*

Fairport. "Woods-Edge." This home, built in 1975 and nestled in the woods where deer can often be seen, is furnished with antique country pine throughout. Hostess creates stone mosaic pictures. Husband is college professor in the field of mechanical technology. Hiking on premises. Bicycles available. Shopping and restaurants are near. Breakfast on screened porch if weather permits. Air conditioned. Located southeast of Rochester near I-90, a 20-minute drive to downtown Rochester. Two bedrooms: one with twin beds, one with double. Rates: $30–$45. Extra cots and beds available. Private bath unless both rooms are taken. Children welcome. Nonsmokers preferred. One resident cat.

RATES

Singles $30–$40. Doubles $35–$45.

The lake cottage is $55 for two.

Deposit required: One night's lodging plus 7 percent tax.

Weekly and monthly rates available.

Cancellation policy: Deposit refunded (less a $10 service fee) if cancelled at least five days before the arrival date.

It Is More than Bed and Breakfast

"Our hostesses enjoy hosting and will 'go the extra mile' to see that guests have everything they need to be comfort-

able ... will provide transportation if necessary and cook special dishes, and try to stay within specific diet guidelines if requested."

RAINBOW HOSPITALITY

GRETCHEN BRODERICK AND MARILYN SCHOENHERR
9348 HENNEPIN AVE.
NIAGARA FALLS, NY 14304

PHONE: 716/283-4794 and 754-8877
  Monday–Friday 9–7 and Saturday 9–noon.
OPEN: Year round.

ACCOMMODATIONS
B&Bs
Hosted private residences: 38.   B&B inns: 3.

OTHER SERVICES: Some hosts pick up at airport, bus, or train; baby-sitting, guided sightseeing tours.

LOCATIONS   *All in western New York: Niagra Falls, Buffalo, Amherst, Clarence, Williamsville, Orchard Park, E. Aurora, Chaffee, Colden, Derby, Lewiston, Youngstown, Wilson, Olcott, Lockport.*

HOSTS: Artist, executives, clergy, nurse, shopowner, lawyer, doctor, aerobics instructor, herbalist. . . .

GUESTS COME FOR: Niagara Falls, boating, fishing, historic villages, antiquing, conventions, international shopping, factory outlet shopping, hiking trails and winter skiing. Schools: S.U.N.Y. at Buffalo, Buffalo State University, Niagara University.

BREAKFAST: Varies according to host.

RESERVATIONS
Advance reservations preferred. If arrangements can be made, will accept last-minute reservations.
Groups: Maximum size is 25.
Also available through travel agents.

DIRECTORY (not required for reservations): $2 plus business-sized self-addressed stamped envelope. *Samples:*

Niagara Falls #NF 106 Quiet residential area overlooking Niagara River. Accommodating hostess. One double, one with twin beds, small nursery. Private bath. Baby-sitting, transportation, and full breakfast available. $25–$35.

Buffalo Area #EC103 Lovely 150-year-old gem in parklike setting. Five minutes to Buffalo Airport. Lg. twin room, porches, patio & park. $40–$45.

RATES
Singles $18–$37. Doubles $32–$50.
Some weekly and monthly rates available.
Deposit required: $10 per night per room.
Cancellation policy: Refund minus 20 percent of total charge if notice received at least three days before scheduled arrival date.

Who Else Is "At Home?"

Two single ladies from different places were placed at one B&B. Having purchased tickets at different times in different places, they arrived at the Opera to find they were seated next to each other. When they continued their conversation at "home," they discovered they had been classmates in the same school as youngsters in Canada. They talked far into the night, recalling other friends and teachers.

NORTH COUNTRY BED & BREAKFAST RESERVATION SERVICE
LYN WITTE
P.O. BOX 286
LAKE PLACID, NY 12946

PHONE: 518/523-3739
Daily, 10–10.
OPEN: Year round.

ACCOMMODATIONS
B&Bs
Hosted private residences: 28.   B&B inns: 17.
Plus
Some unhosted private residences for overnight or weekend lodging.
Unhosted housing available by the week, month, or season.

OTHER SERVICES: Car rentals, theater tickets and sport events, tours and ski packages.

LOCATIONS *Homes are in northern New York State from Lake George north to Canadian border and from Lake Champlain west to Watertown.*

HOSTS: Retired business people, teachers, foreign service, professional people, theater producer, actress, antique shop owner, former Olympic team member. . . .

GUESTS COME FOR: Recreation—cross-country and downhill skiing, skating, 1980 Olympics sites, hiking, climbing, boating, fishing, swimming, golf, tennis. History—Fort Ticonderoga, Camp Top Ridge, John Brown's Farm. Museums. Walking tours. Business reasons.

BREAKFAST: Varies according to hosts.

DIRECTORY (not required for reservations): A sample listing is sent on request. *Samples:*

Private Home PH-4 Your hosts invite you to join them in their living room or "get away" in your own private apartment. A double and single room share a spacious bath. The home is located in a new residential section, convenient to all activities and just minutes off a major hiking trail. Seasonal treats appear for breakfast. Several languages are spoken.

Country Inn CI-1 On the outskirts of town, this historic landmark offers charming accommodations in an Adirondack atmosphere. The four double rooms complete with handmade quilts are arranged so that two rooms share a bath, making it ideal for a family or two couples. There is also a Bridal Suite with its own bath and fireplace.

RESERVATIONS
Minimum stay of two nights required on weekends and holidays. Reservations two to three weeks in advance preferred. If arrangements can be made, will accept last-minute reservations.
Groups: "Our largest to date numbered 150."
Also available through travel agents.

RATES

Singles $15–$40. Doubles $30–$100. A few are higher. Some weekly and monthly rates available.

Deposit required: Varies according to placement.

Cancellation policy: Full refund less $5 service charge if canceled at least one week before arrival date.

> *"Don't know if you'll remember me or not, but ever since our delightful stay at the B&B in Keene this August, I wanted to write you to tell you how wonderful it truly was. I was really skeptical before going, because your description of it was so charming. I kept thinking to myself, how can this place be for real?! But it was and we fell in love with it. We hope to be able to return for a cross-country ski weekend this winter."*
>
> *—B. Moss, a guest*

More Sharing

> *"I booked a young couple for five days between Christmas and New Year's. They were having such a wonderful time that they called the wife's parents, who flew up from South Carolina; a brother from Texas and a sister from D.C. also arrived, making it a real New Year's Eve family reunion a la B&B in the Adirondacks."*
>
> *—Lyn Witte*

Do you have a question? When writing to a bed and breakfast reservation service, please enclose a business-sized (#10) self-addressed stamped envelope (SASE).

North Carolina

Bed and Breakfast in the Albemarle

DOROTHY WILLIFORD
P.O. BOX 248
EVERETTS, NC 27825

PHONE: 919/792-4584
   Live Monday–Friday 9–5. Answering machine at other times.
OPEN: Year round.

ACCOMMODATIONS
B&Bs
Hosted private residences: 20.   B&B inns: 3.
Most are air conditioned.

OTHER SERVICES: Private tour guides at some locations.

LOCATIONS   *In the 16 northeastern counties of North Carolina, from the Outer Banks on the Atlantic Ocean to Halifax in the west; from Murfreesboro in the north to Bath Town in the south.*

SETTINGS: Varied. On a town common, in the country, overlooking Albemarle Sound. Most are historic homes that have been restored. Some are elegant. Some are homey.

HOSTS: Farmers, historic tour guide, foreign family living here, retired military personnel, professors. . . .

GUESTS COME FOR: Four hundred years of history. The annual summer outdoor drama based on America's Lost Colony. (In 1586 Sir Walter Raleigh brought 110 people here. When he returned four years later he found that they had all disappeared.) Colonial capitals. Working plantations. Museums. Beaches on Outer Banks. Wright Brothers National Memorial. Historic houses. North Carolina Marine Resources Center. Edenton's gardens, waterfront, and 18th-century architecture. Walking tours.

BREAKFAST: All offer a Southern continental breakfast—"a little taste of the south along with sweet roll, coffee, and juice." A full breakfast is offered as an option by most hosts.

DIRECTORY (not required for reservations): $5. *Sample:*

Gates, N.C.   S$30. D$40.   NC/VA state line. Restored country farmhouse on 500 acres. Built in 1817 and listed on the National Register of Historic Places. House divided by NC/VA state line. Eat breakfast in North Carolina. Sleep in Virginia. Rooms have fireplaces, double beds and antique furnishings. On the historic Albemarle Tour Route, US Hgwy 13. Ten minutes to the Merchants Millpond State Park (canoeing, camping, fishing, hiking, and bird-watching); 20 minutes to the Chowan River. Thirty minutes to historic Edenton on the Albemarle Sound or Murfreesboro. One hour to Norfolk or Virginia Beach, VA; 1½ hours to Colonial Williamsburg. Local crafts and home-cured hams available. Share bath. Year-round availability. Rooms available—two.

RESERVATIONS
Advance preferred. If arrangements are possible, last-minute reservations are made.

RATES
Singles $20–$45. Doubles $25–$50.
A small extra charge for a full breakfast.
Deposit required: $20.
Cancellation policy: Cancellation made five business days prior to scheduled arrival date will receive full deposit refund. Less than that, deposit forfeited.

When the historic Albemarle started a four-year celebration of the 400th anniversary of the settlement of The Lost Col-

*ony, an economic development group decided to give a grant
to start a bed and breakfast program. Dorothy has taken
over the leadership and shares her enthusiasm for the area
and for B&B while finding "just the right place and people
to match travelers with."*

CHARLOTTE BED AND BREAKFAST

MRS. RUTH FOELL HILL
1700-2 DELANE AVENUE
CHARLOTTE, NC 28211

PHONE: 704/366-0979
  Usually Monday–Friday 10–5.
OPEN: Year round.

ACCOMMODATIONS
B&Bs
Hosted private residences: 10.   One B&B inn.
All have air conditioning, and a couple are accessible to handi-
capped.
Plus
One unhosted private residence for overnight or weekend lodging,
on the coast in Beaufort, North Carolina.

OTHER SERVICES: Pickup at airport.

LOCATIONS   *In North Carolina: Charlotte, Elkin, Beaufort,
Chapel Hill.
In South Carolina: Clover.
All are near public transportation.*

SETTINGS: Most of the host homes are in areas distinguished by
their settings: wooded, close to country club, near shops.

HOSTS: Health-food nutritionist, counselor, business people. . . .

GUESTS COME FOR: A vacation. Conferences. Training sessions.
Research. And some just passing through.
Attractions include Mint Museum of Art and History, Discovery
Place, The Charlotte Opera and Symphony, Davidson College,
UNCC, Queens College, Charlotte Country Day, and Charlotte
Latin.

BREAKFAST: Most serve continental.

RESERVATIONS
At least two weeks in advance preferred. If arrangements can be made, will accept last-minute reservations.
Also available through travel agents.

RATES
Singles $20–$60. Doubles $25–$85.
Weekly and monthly rates available.
Deposit required: Depends on length of stay and number in party.
Cancellation policy: Full refund if two weeks' notice given. Service fee charged if less time given.

Many Hats

Ruth is active in the Campus Ministry, the Carolina Council of World Affairs, and the Radio Reading Service for the print handicapped. She is looking forward to booking "a cross section of America and more international travelers."

Because B&Bs are all different, tell the service what you want. Think ahead of time about your needs. For a little help, turn to page 1.

North Dakota

The Old West B&B

MARLYS PRINCE
BOX 211
REGENT, ND 58650

PHONE: 701/563-4542
Live 8–8 daily. Answering machine at other times.
OPEN: Year round.

ACCOMMODATIONS
B&Bs
Hosted private residences: 15—and growing.

OTHER SERVICES: Plans are being made. Inquire about car rentals or other available arrangements.

LOCATIONS   *Throughout North Dakota. All are in rural areas. Expansion plans include listings in cities and in the Black Hills area of South Dakota.*

SETTINGS: Diverse. One is a luxurious home with indoor swimming pool. Another is a working ranch. Many are in peaceful settings. Some of the farms in the western part of the state range in size from 2,000 acres to an entire township.

HOSTS: Mostly farmers. (This will change as the service expands.)

GUESTS COME FOR: Scenery. Tranquility. "They come to experience a way of life that is quite wonderful." The Badlands, part of Theodore Roosevelt National Park. The restored town of Medora. Hunting. Fishing. Charitable gambling. Some are en route to Expo in British Columbia.

BREAKFAST: Varies. Many offer a full farm breakfast with homemade preserves and bakery. One prepares a southern breakfast complete with rabbit, biscuits, and gravy.

RESERVATIONS
Advance notice required; two weeks preferred.

DIRECTORY: $5 including updated follow-up mailings. Full description of each B&B together with activities and area attractions.

RATES

Singles $20–$50. Doubles $25–$55. Some weekly rates.

Deposit required: One night's lodging.

Cancellation policy: Full refund if notice received seven days before expected arrival date. For less notice there is a $10 service charge.

Although Marlys has lived in North Dakota all her life, it was the B&B business that gave her the opportunity to discover how different the state is from one end to the other. Her own B&B travel experiences were the inspiration for starting the service, one that continues to grow as residents become familiar with the concept.

Ohio

BUCKEYE BED & BREAKFAST

DON AND SALLY HOLLENBACK
P.O.BOX 130
POWELL, OH 43065

PHONE: 614/548-4555
Live daily 6 p.m.–7 a.m. Answering machine at other times.

ACCOMMODATIONS
B&Bs
Hosted private residences: 34.   B&B inns: 2.
Most have air conditioning and private baths and are accessible to handicapped.
Plus
One unhosted private residence for overnight or weekend lodging.
Some hosted or unhosted short-term (up to one month) housing.

OTHER SERVICES: Theater tickets.

LOCATIONS   *Throughout the state. Most are in or near urban areas.*

SETTINGS: Most, but not all, are historic homes.

258

HOSTS: Accountant, government official, orthopedic surgeon, school administrator, retired professor, civil engineer, school media chairman. . . .

GUESTS COME FOR: Conferences. Business. Getaway weekends. Antique and collectible hunting.

BREAKFAST: Most serve a full breakfast.

RESERVATIONS
Advance arrangements of at least 48 hours preferred. If arrangements can be made, will accept last-minute reservations.
Groups: Maximum size is 30.
Also available through some travel agents.

DIRECTORY: Sent on request without charge. Please send a business-sized self-addressed stamped envelope. *Samples:*

Cambridge. Once the heart of the flourishing fine glass and china district of Eastern Ohio and West Virginia. A famous brand and style of glassware bears the name that is highly prized in the annals of collecting. Now Cambridge emerges as a culturally oriented mini-city typifying the transitional nature of things both rural and industrial. Nearby Salt Fort State Park is one of Ohio's most popular vacation/recreation spots.

Charm of the South: The longest row of cookbooks you'll ever see is here in this nearly new, multilevel "smart colonial" hidden on a hillside. Your hosts' directions are a must if you expect to arrive on time. It is worth it. One could hardly imagine a more comfortable setting with a "taste of the South" in rural Ohio. You can cut the Virginia accent with the same knife you'll use to spread her homemade apple butter on your biscuit. She's a loquacious hostess with many interests in her community—from symphony to flea markets. Several room combinations, all with private baths. No pets. Full breakfast, library, and TV. $25 (s), $35 (d), extra beds, crib available.

Delaware: Small-town atmosphere 21 miles north of Columbus at intersection of US. . . . Dripping Rock Farm. One room, private bath, no pets, no children; specialty breakfast, two dogs, cat; often closed by heavy snows. After a hard day of driving, you'll find that these folks offer you a peaceful stay in a nearly new rustic home in the Olentangy River Valley.... Deck a perfect place for bird watching or to begin a hike. Good roads for cycling. Everything is friendly and relaxed here, where all family members come and go to jobs, church, tennis, or gardening. Man of the house believes breakfast to be most important meal of the day. $25. $35.

RATES
Singles $18–$28. Doubles $25–$39. A few $40–$55.
Some offer a five-nights-for-four rate.
Deposit required is 15 percent of total charge.
Cancellation policy: If notice received at least 48 hours before expected arrival date, refund minus $5 service charge made. Later than that, 75 percent is refunded.

PRIVATE LODGINGS, INC.
JANE McCARROLL
P.O. BOX 18590
CLEVELAND, OH 44118

PHONE: 216/321-3213
   Live Monday–Friday 9:30–5. Answering service at other times.
OPEN: Year round. Closed major holidays.

ACCOMMODATIONS
B&Bs
Hosted private homes: 30.
Plus
Many hosted and unhosted short-term housing possibilities in apartments, condominiums, and houses.

   LOCATIONS   *Most are within 10 miles of downtown Cleveland, on a public transportation line, and within 5 miles of a major highway.*

SETTINGS: A wide range from fairly simple to quite luxurious.

HOSTS: Realtor, relocation consultant, lawyer, public relations specialist, doctor, artist....

GUESTS COME FOR: Corporate business, conferences, schools—Case Western Reserve University, John Carroll University, Cleveland State University; for relocation, medical reasons, and cultural activities.

BREAKFAST: Varies according to host, from continental to elaborate.

RESERVATIONS
Advance reservations preferred. If arrangements can be made, will accept last-minute reservations.
Groups: Maximum size is 10.

RATES
Singles $25–$55. Doubles $30–$65.
Weekly and monthly rates available.
Deposit required: Full payment.
Cancellation policy (for B&Bs): With notice of three days or more, refund minus $10 handling fee; one to two days before arrival date, refund of 50 percent; arrival day cancellation and no-shows, no refund.

COLUMBUS BED & BREAKFAST

FRED HOLDRIDGE
769 SOUTH THIRD STREET
COLUMBUS, OH 43206

PHONE: 614/444-8888 or 443-3680
Live 8 a.m.–10 p.m. daily. Answering machine at other times.
OPEN: Year round, except for month of January.

ACCOMMODATIONS
B&Bs
Hosted private residences: 10.
Most have air conditioning.
Plus
Some short-term hosted housing available.

LOCATIONS   *All are near public transportation and both N–S and E–W interstates, and are within 10 minutes of downtown.*

SETTINGS: All are rather luxurious in historic German Village, a registered National Historic Area that features small brick houses, brick sidewalks, brick-paved streets, and wrought-iron fences. Shops and restaurants are within walking distance.

HOSTS: Artist, manufacturer, attorney, small business operators. . . .

GUESTS COME FOR: Sightseeing. A vacation. Conferences. Business. Colleges.

BREAKFAST: From continental to very full. Varies according to host.

RESERVATIONS
Advance reservations preferred. If arrangements can be made, will accept last-minute reservations.

RATES
Singles $30. Doubles $40.
Deposit required: $25.
Cancellation policy: Refund of deposit made only with a one-week notice of cancellation or if unable to fill your request.

Do you have a question? When writing to a bed and breakfast reservation service, please enclose a business-sized (#10) self-addressed stamped enevelope (SASE).

◇ ◇ ◇

Oklahoma

BED & BREAKFAST OKLAHOMA STYLE

JO ANN HAMILTON

P.O. BOX 32045

OKLAHOMA CITY, OK 73123

PHONE: 405/946-2894

Jo Ann says: "After a year of introducing the B&B concept in Oklahoma City, I am experiencing a shortage of host homes, so my reservation service is somewhat limited at the moment. Travelers should also know that we live in homes that are 'just functional'. Yes, they are comfortable and homey. This area isn't particularly known for its quaintness or attractions (the Cowboy Hall of Fame is the big one), but we do have some interesting hosts. I believe B&B should provide reasonably priced accomodations with local residents. I think it is a particularly good idea in Oklahoma City for the working woman who is traveling alone, for people who come to meetings and conferences, and for medical reasons."

RATES

Singles $20–$24. Doubles $28–$40.

Oregon

NORTHWEST BED & BREAKFAST, INC.
LAINE FRIEDMAN AND GLORIA SHAICH
7707 SW LOCUST STREET
PORTLAND, OR 97223

PHONE: 503/246-8366
Live Monday–Friday 9–6; Saturday, 9–1. Answering machine at other times.
OPEN: Year round except Christmas, New Year's Day, and Thanksgiving.

ACCOMMODATIONS
B&Bs
Hosted private residences: 275. B&B inns: 35.
Plus
Unhosted private residences for overnight or weekend lodging. Short-term (up to a few months) hosted and unhosted housing.

OTHER SERVICES: Car rentals. Pickup at airport, bus, and train. Plane reservations. Itinerary planning according to special interests. (One call or letter can set up a trip covering the represented areas with stops at one or even a dozen B&B homes or inns in the network.) Self-drive west coast tours.
Arrangements also made for self-drive cruises on waterways in France and England.

264

LOCATIONS *Throughout Oregon. Many others in the states of Washington, California, and Idaho as well as in British Columbia, Canada. A few listings are in Montana and Wyoming. B&B placements also made in selected town and country homes in England, France, and Greece.*

SETTINGS: Victorian, contemporary, Western redwood, imaginatively renovated barn, sailing ship, caboose, farms, ranches, and townhouses. They are in cities near local transportation, along the coast, in the mountains, in rural areas, and in desert territory.

HOSTS: Fifty percent have hosted for over five years.

BREAKFAST: Most hosts serve a full breakfast. Some of their specialties: clam fritters, sourdough waffles or pancakes, quiches, elaborate egg dishes, home-baked breads, muffins, sweetbreads. Home-grown fruits, vegetables, homemade jams.

RESERVATIONS
Advance reservations preferred. If arrangements can be made, will accept last-minute reservations.
Groups: Maximum size is 12 in the United States and 30 in England.
Also available through travel agents.

DIRECTORY (not required for reservations): $6.50 if purchased separately. A copy is sent to guest members. Spiral-bound, 130 pages. Updated twice annually. *Sample:*

#443—Government Camp, Oregon (Mount Hood Loop). Beautiful mountain lodge/chalet–styled home. Architecturally designed to fit into the quiet natural forest and mountain setting of the Cascades. Home, warmly furnished, fully carpeted, cedar paneled, has spacious open-beam cathedral ceilings, floor-to-ceiling windows, two separate balconies for an open, airy warm atmosphere, and three large wraparound decks for sunbathing, barbecuing, and relaxing. Spacious quarters allow maximum freedom, leisure, and privacy. Hosts, professionals in education, forestry, land-use planning, contracting, and experienced skiers, mountain climbers, backpackers. Able to provide technical advice. Traveled extensively throughout Europe and U.S. Enjoy light classical music (have full high-fi stereo system).

Knowledgeable about services in area. Easy access from main highway. Will provide transportation/reservation. Exercise equipment, private Finnish sauna, and whirlpool spa available for guests' use. Special welcome to familes with children seven or older. Dinner and lunch/reservation and fee. Hosts do not smoke; ask guests to smoke outside. Ideal place for individual and family stays as well as small group retreats and seminars. One room with king-size bed, one with queen, one with double and twin bed and sink, one with queen hide-a-bed, four private full baths. One multipurpose room with double bed and four-inch foam pads on carpeted floor. Sleeps 10 people. Guest full bath and 2/3 bath. Sleeping bags available. Rates: $30 single, $40 double. Family and group rates available.

RATES
Singles $18–$30. Doubles $25–$45. A few are higher.
Guest memberships: Single $15. Family $20.
Nonmembers pay a fee of $5 per reservation.
Payments are due in advance. Payments for last-minute reservations are made to hosts.
Weekly and monthly rates available.
Cancellation policy: Full amount less 25 percent of the first night's accommodation fee refunded if notice provided no later than 48 hours before expected arrival date. First night's fee nonrefundable if less than 48 hours.

BED & BREAKFAST OREGON
MARCELLE TEBO
5733 S.W. DICKINSON ST.
PORTLAND, OR 97219

PHONE: 503/245-0642
   Usually live 9–9. Answering machine at other times.
OPEN: Year round except Christmas week.

ACCOMMODATIONS
B&Bs
Hosted private residences: 36.   B&B inns: 7.
Most have private baths.
Plus
Some unhosted private residences for overnight or weekend lodging.
Short-term (hosted and unhosted) housing for up to two months.

OTHER SERVICES: Pickup at airport, bus, and train. Six-passenger stretch white limousine service available. Packages offered: Sightseeing, skiing, white-water rafting, horseback riding, windsurfing, and hiking.

LOCATIONS *In at least 20 communities of Oregon, including Portland, Bend, Hood River, and Corvallis. Most B&Bs are within a 10-mile radius of center city and near public transportation.*
In Washington: Long Beach, Olympia, Bingen, Friday Harbor, Port Townsend.
In California: Grass Valley, Los Angeles, San Francisco.

SETTINGS: A 60-foot (retired) sailboat, a houseboat (self-serve breakfast), country French estate, three historical landmarks, cabin in mountains, and "just nice homes."

HOSTS: Retired school teachers, antique dealers, school teachers, artist, contractors (house), draftsman. . . .

GUESTS COME FOR: Business. Conferences. Vacations. Japanese gardens, mountain sports, deep-sea fishing, lake and stream fishing, white-water raft trips, Columbia River Gorge stern wheeler tours, historical sites, wineries. . . .

BREAKFAST: About half serve continenal and half serve full.

RESERVATIONS
Some locations have a two- or three-day minimum stay requirement. Advance reservations preferred. If arrangements can be made, will accept last-minute reservations.
Groups: Maximum size is eight.
Also available through travel agents.

DIRECTORY (not required for reservations): $2. Organized geographically with information on the attractions in each area. *Samples*:

Southwest Portland. A lovely Cape Cod home in a quiet residential neighborhood. Walk to bus. Two bedrooms on the upper level with a bath. Home furnished in traditional and antiques. Your host serves breakfast in a relaxed dining area. Homemade jams and jellies for your toast. A lovely garden is perfect for coffee and relaxing. RV Parking. Nonsmoking. Double $30. Single $22. Twin $18.

Eugene. Fifteen miles to town. Forty-five miles to Florence. Your hosts, Dick and Evelyn, invite you to share their "dream home," a unique log house built from scratch on five acres of pine and fir trees. Two large bedrooms, each with private bath. The upper room can accommodate four and has its own deck. Close by there are two wineries as well as a copper company that makes beautiful kitchen ware. Forgeron Vineyards has its Bluegrass Festival the third week in July. Air conditioning. Nonsmoking. Wheelchair access. Crib available. Double $37. Single $32. Children $10.

RATES

Singles $18–$52.50. Doubles $25–$100.

Weekly and monthly rates available. Payment in full required at time of reservation.

Credit cards: VISA and MasterCard accepted but 3½ percent service fee charged.

Cancellation policy: Deposit, less $10 processing fee, is refundable with a 10-day cancellation notice.

Thank-you notes to hosts come in all shapes. This one was written on a paper towel by Caren and Ken: "Just wanted to thank you again for everything. Your kindness was appreciated. . . . The cabin was wonderful. . . . When the time comes for our second honeymoon, we will be calling you."

The northern part of Oregon has additional B&B hosts represented by Travellers' Bed & Breakfast (Seattle), page 338.

Pennsylvania

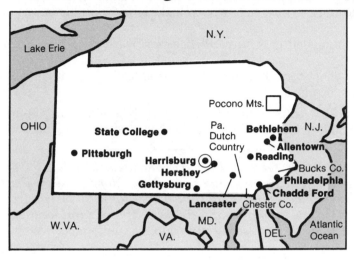

PHILADELPHIA

B&B GUESTS COME FOR: Historic Philadelphia, including Independence Hall and Liberty Bell. Universities and colleges. Museums. Mummers' Parade. Cultural performances. Sports events. Sculling on the Schuylkill along the Boat House Row. New Market and Society Hill. Conferences. Business reasons.

BED & BREAKFAST OF PHILADELPHIA
SANDRA FULLERTON AND CAROL YARROW
P.O. BOX 680
DEVON, PA 19333
PHONE: 215/688-1633
Live Monday–Friday 9–5. Answering machine or call forwarding to Sandy's home at other times.
OPEN: Open year round. Closed only Christmas, Easter, July 4, Memorial Day.

ACCOMMODATIONS
B&Bs
Hosted private residences: 100.   B&B inns: 10. Almost all have air
conditioning. Some have accommodations for children and babies.
Plus:
A few unhosted private residences for overnight or weekend lodg-
ing.
Hosted short-term housing also available, for a week, a month, two
months, or more.

OTHER SERVICES: Pickup at airport, bus, and train. Some hosts
accommodate special diets, e.g. kosher, diabetic, vegetarian.

LOCATIONS   *Greater Philadelphia area including historic
Society Hill, University City, New Hope, Valley Forge,
Brandywine Valley. City transit is reliable; suburban trains
and trolleys available and frequent. (From rural locations it
is a short drive to suburban train station that connects with
the city.)*
Delaware: Wilmington.
*New Jersey: West Berlin, Mt. Holly. And one in Moorestown
that is just five minutes from the highway and a lovely
peaceful change for those of us who are driving through and
wish a nonstandardized, personalized overnight stop. From
experience, I can say that the hostess serves a wonderful and
full breakfast.*

SETTINGS: Renovated Victorians, city brownstones, high-rises,
Main Line manor homes, horse farms, Penn Land Grant homes,
chateaus.

HOSTS: Artists, school teachers, professors, lawyers, realtors, psychologists and psychotherapists, craftspersons, retirees, gentlemen
farmers. . . . "Hosts' knowledge of their area is extraordinary.
Many are bilingual. If you book far enough in advance, hosts send
handwritten notes of welcome and directions."

BREAKFAST: All full and could include blueberry pancakes,
homemade muffins and strawberry nut bread, cold strawberry or
blueberry soup, breakfast tray in room by fireplace.

RESERVATIONS
Minimum stay requirement: Inns have two-night minimum on
weekends and for major holidays. "Our luxury homes prefer a two-
night minimum."

Two weeks in advance preferred. If arrangements can be made, will accept last-minute reservations with VISA or MasterCard deposit only.

Groups: Can handle 100 or more by using several locations if travelers have cars or if the central gathering place can be reached by public transportation.

Also available through travel agents.

DIRECTORY (not required for reservations): $5. County maps included with information on area attractions. *Sample*:

Wallingford Colonial Homestead (1685) two rms., double four-poster beds, each a pvt. bath. Full breakfast. Off-street parking. Breeze cooled. Two resident dogs and one Indian ghost. $60.

Location: Near junction of PA Rts. 320 & 252, 7 min. fm I-95 Chester exit, 17-min. drive to historic Phila. Near Swarthmore College and Widener University. Short walk to bus transport. Nat'l registered Ingleneuk Tea Room nearby.

Crowning a low hill, this sturdy stone colonial homestead seems to promise safe haven and hospitality. Built by a member of William Penn's Society of Free Traders in 1685, its two-foot-thick walls and sheltering eaves welcome the traveler to Quaker serenity. The earliest section is known as the weaving room, where hooks from the old loom harnesses are still in the ceiling beams. In 1700 the Great Hall was built, today's living room, incorporating elements of English and Swedish design. Above each fireplace at opposite ends of the room are rare built-in cupboards with extensive Philadephia paneling and original butterfly hinges. Authorities at Winterthur think these may be the earliest existent examples of this type. The floors are original random-width planking, as are the shutters on the unusual gun-port windows. Your bedroom is the loft of the weaving room; your bed an 1810 four-poster covered in an heirloom quilt. Be warned that a friendly Indian ghost drops in from time to time. Your breakfast may be served in the large fireplace-warmed dining room, originally the kitchen (1751), or on the cool terrace. Your hostess is a direct descendant of the original family. She and her husband welcome all who are interested in antiques and colonial history and will be happy to give you a personal tour of their home.

RATES

Singles $25–$60. Doubles $30–$75. Carriage houses are $85.
One-night surcharge: $5 per room.
Weekly and monthly rates available.
Deposit required: One night plus 6 percent tax, or full prepayment for graduations and special seminars.
Credit cards accepted: VISA and MasterCard.
Cancellation policy: Refund minus $20 service charge if cancellation received seven days or more in advance. Deposit forfeited if cancellation received six days or less before arrival date.

> *"After some hectic Christmas days in the city this was exactly what we needed. We will never forget the hopsitality of our hosts—we have never met something like it before. Our Swedish relatives visiting us were really overwhelmed. Thank you for your booking!"*
>
> *—A guest*

BED & BREAKFAST/CENTER CITY

MELODIE EBNER
1804 PINE STREET
PHILADELPHIA, PA 19103

PHONE: 215/735-1137
Live weekdays 9–5. Answering machine at other times.

ACCOMMODATIONS
B&Bs
Hosted private residences: 50.
Some are semihosted (do-it-yourself breakfast) arrangements. Almost all have air conditioning and private baths.
Plus
Unhosted private residences.
Some homes with efficiency apartments or private entrances ideally suited to longer-term stays.

OTHER SERVICES: Hosts pick up at airport, train, and bus. Guest membership in private clubs, host-guided tours, multilingual hosts, referrals to realtors, special events.

LOCATIONS *Most are within the boundaries of center city and include Society Hill, Rittenhouse Square, Antique Row,*

*Logan Circle, University City, and Fitler Square. A few are
in outlying areas where there are popular or otherwise well-
known institutions or attractions.*

SETTINGS: "Artists and arts collectors enjoy staying in the home of
the former director of the Pennsylvania Academy of Fine Art, the
oldest art academy in the United States. . . . Episcopal Diocesan ar-
chivists may stay in the rectory of Old Christ Episcopal Church, one
of the country's most historical churches. . . . University of Pennsylvania's Wharton School graduates are among those who have an
opportunity to stay in the Wharton House, where the founder of the
school lived for many years."

HOSTS: Retired social worker, artist, caterer, realtor, lawyer,
dancer, free-lance writers, clergy, furniture designers, interior designers, antique buffs, actors, administrators, academics, architect,
city planner, gourmet cook. . . .

BREAKFAST: Varies from help-yourself to an elaborate meal.

RESERVATIONS
Ten days to two weeks in advance preferred. If arrangements can
be made, will accept last-minute reservations.
Groups: Maximum size is 10 or 12.
Also available through travel agencies.

RATES
Singles $25–$50. Doubles $35–$68. Rates quoted for one-night
stays include a one-night surcharge of $5. Deposit required: $25 or
20 percent of total; depends on accommodation.

One Big Happy Family

*"Among our customized placements: a long-lost second cou-
sin with her relatives. Until the visit actually took place, no
one was aware of the relationship; the reservation service
admits to a bit of luck on that one."*

◇ ◇ ◇

*In addition to the Pennsylvania-based B&B reservation ser-
vices described above, some Bucks County B&B hosts are
represented by Town and Country Bed and Breakfast, page
224.*

BED AND BREAKFAST OF CHESTER COUNTY

DORIS PASSANTE
P.O. BOX 825
KENNETT SQUARE, PA 19348

PHONE: 215/444-1367
  7 a.m.–10 p.m. daily.
OPEN: Year round.

ACCOMMODATIONS
B&Bs
Hosted private residences: 30.
Plus
Some unhosted private residences for overnight or weekend lodging. Short-term (up to about three months) hosted and unhosted housing.

LOCATIONS *In Pennsylvania: Most are in the Brandywine Valley, less than an hour's drive from the historical restored area of center-city Philadelphia. Others range from suburban Philadelphia to Pennsylvania Dutch country. A few are in northern Valley Forge, Pennsylvania.*
Delaware: Several in Wilmington and north to the Pennsylvania line.
Maryland: In Warwick.

SETTINGS: From restored historic landmarks to hillside contemporaries. Some are just plain and homey; others are luxurious.

HOSTS: Horse breeders and trainers, retired engineer, dairy farmers, veterinarian, psychologist, retired bank president, physician, school nurse, insurance agent, school teachers, French caterer, artist. . . .

GUESTS COME FOR: Longwood Gardens, Winterthur, Chadds Ford (Wyeth country), Brandywine River Museum, Hagley Museum, Nemours, Rockwood, Pennsylvania Dutch Country, Valley Forge. Schools: Several including Villanova, Univeristy of Delaware, and West Chester University. Business with large Delaware companies and the high-tech area near Valley Forge.

BREAKFAST: Varies from a simple to an elaborate meal. Could include home-canned preserves and jellies; home-baked goodies; Pennsylvania Dutch specialties such as scrapple, sausages, and dried-beef gravy.

RESERVATIONS

Advance reservations preferred. If arrangements can be made, will accept last-minute reservations.

Groups: Maximum size in one house is 10. Can handle larger groups by placing them in the same neighborhood.

Also available through travel agents.

DIRECTORY (not required for reservations): $3. *Sample*:

> #25 Step back in time when you enter this restored 1750 stone gristmill, set in the heart of Brandywine country. Charmingly furnished with antiques, you will enjoy a large living room with fireplace and TV. For warmer weather, there is a screened-in porch overlooking fields with a stream for fishing or swimming. Accommodations consist of two rooms—one with double bed and the other with twin beds. There is a private bath for guests' use. Rates are $50 for double and $45 for single. Add a $5 surcharge for one night's stay. Price includes a full breakfast.

RATES

Singles $25–$60. Doubles $32–$75.

A few have a $5 surcharge for a one-night stay.

Some weekly and monthly rates available.

Deposit required is 20 percent of total stay.

Cancellation policy: If notice received at least 48 hours before expected arrival date, deposit refunded, less $10. If deposit is less than $10, no refund.

BED & BREAKFAST OF SOUTHEAST PENNSYLVANIA

JOYCE STEVENSON
BOX 278 R.D. 1
BARTO, PA 19504

PHONE: 215/845-3526
 Live much of the time; otherwise answering machine.
OPEN: Year round.

ACCOMMODATIONS

B&Bs

Hosted private residences: 28.   B&B inns: 4.

About half have private baths; many have air-conditioned rooms. Several have pools. One is accessible to handicapped.

Plus
Some unhosted private residences for overnight or weekend lodging.

LOCATIONS *Allentown, Bally, Bernville, Bethlehem, Boyertown, East Greenville, Easton, Geigertown, Kempton, Kutztown, Lancaster, Mertztown, New Tripoli, Quakertown, Robesonia, Reading, Oley Valley, Springtown, Womelsdorf, Yellow House.*

SETTINGS: In rural, suburban, and urban areas. Range from a pleasant home-away-from-home to luxurious. Many historic homes.

HOSTS: Retired realtor, retired florist, retired metallurgical engineer, artist, writer, industrial engineer, seamstress, contractor, junior high school librarian, physician, dentist, school teacher, macrobiotic cooking instructor. . . . "Not only does the home have to measure up to the usual standards of cleanliness and comfort, but I expect the hosts to be very knowledgeable about everything from restaurants (all price ranges) to horse riding, auctions, skiing, or any other whim a guest may have."

GUESTS COME FOR: Lehigh Valley—Bach Choir in May, Musikfest in August. Kutztown—Folk Festival in July. East Greenville—Goshenhoppen Festival in August. A getaway 2½ hours from New York City, 3 hours from Washington, D.C., 1½ hours from Philadelphia. Antiquing. Flea markets. "And funny little museums as well as outlet shopping. In the winter, we have cross-country skiing as well as downhill. I really believe we are undiscovered."

BREAKFAST: Varies from continental to full.

RESERVATIONS
Advance reservations generally preferred and necessary for most holiday weekends. If arrangements can be made, will accept last-minute reservations.

.DIRECTORY (not required for reservations): $1. *Sample*:

Robesonia. You will be welcomed by the bell that called children in 1875 to the Old School House. With a first-floor addition, it has been converted into a lovely home by a talented couple. Your host and hostess are bird-watchers and flower growers and they invite guests to take a quick dip in the in-ground pool. This home is equipped with ramps and can handle a wheelchair. Surrounded by cornfields teeming with wildlife. There are hiking and cross-country ski trails. An easy drive to Blue Marsh Dam for boating and fishing. They offer a double room with a private bath. Smoking allowed. No pets please. Full breakfast served in the living-dining area that has a fireplace for the use of guests. Sorry, no children. Double $48; single $36.

RATES
Singles $17–$48. Doubles $30–$59.
One-night surcharge: $5 at one home.
Some weekly and monthly rates available.
Deposit required is 25 percent. MasterCard and VISA accepted for deposit only.
Cancellation policy: Full refund less $5 service charge if given at least one week's notice before expected arrival.

Please Have Answers Ready When You Call

"Generally, I wish travelers would be explicit about interests and requirements. Sometimes they are: On learning that a prospective guest, one who was making a reservation for two people, wasn't sure which area she wished to visit, I asked, 'Have you any specific interests?' 'Yes,' she said, 'Romance.'"

BED & BREAKFAST POCONO NORTHEAST
ANN MAGAGNA
P.O. BOX 115 BEAR CREEK VILLAGE
BEAR CREEK, PA 18602

PHONE: 717/472-3145
Live daily except Tuesday, 9–noon. Most evenings, 7:30–10. Answering machine at other times.
OPEN: Year round. Closed major holidays.

ACCOMMODATIONS
B&Bs
Hosted private residences: 34.   One B&B inn.
Some are accessible to handicapped.

OTHER SERVICES: With prearrangements, possibilities include pickup at airport or bus, dinner-hour child care, guided sightseeing and hiking tours.

LOCATIONS   *The Pocono Mountains and beyond—through-out the entire northeastern section of the state. All are within a short distance of I-80, I-81, I-380, I-84, and the northeastern extension of the Pennsylvania Turnpike. Some are in real country settings—what city folks might think of as isolated.*

SETTINGS: Victorian homes in urban areas. Comfortable country homes. Historic homes. Mansions. Log cabins. Newer homes built on farmland or in converted commercial property.

HOSTS: Shopkeepers, artists, antique dealers, administrators, re-tired school teachers, building contractors, secretaries, musical di-rector, young couples with mortgages, and moms deserted by col-lege children. . . . "Some hosts appreciate the one-night bookings and some request longer visits. I can understand why guests look forward to meeting them; my job of interviewing prospective hosts is the greatest joy since peanut butter."

GUESTS COME FOR: The mountains in winter and summer. All outdoor sports, theater, antiques, many colleges and universities, business, fine arts centers, and house hunting. Some are on their way, just passing through.

BREAKFAST: Varies from simple to elaborate.

RESERVATIONS
Two weeks in advance preferred. If arrangements can be made, will accept last-minute reservations.

DIRECTORY (not required for reservations): $2. *Samples*:

Pike County, Milford. Located in the Tri-state area be-tween Pennsylvania, New Jersey, and New York, known as the gateway to the Poconos. "This small, quaint, peaceful village has many specialty shops featuring unusual gifts, baked goods, cheese, homemade jams, and more. The Queen Anne Victorian home originally built in 1863 has been completely restored. Four rooms are available for guests. Parks, flea markets, antiquing, theater, fine res-taurants, and all outdoor sports abound in this area. Your hosts invite you to step back in history and be their guest. Limited smoking. Children welcome. No pets please." Rates based on length of stay.

Monroe County, Paradise Township: Joe Jefferson Cottage.
Most Pennsylvania farmhouses were homes for ordinary,
hard-working people. This simple house acquired a famous
occupant in the 1850s when Joe Jefferson was one of the
leading American actors of the mid-19th century, most re-
nowned for his role as Rip Van Winkle. Jefferson wrote the
play, based on Washington Irving's story, while staying at
this house in 1856. Your interesting, interested hosts know
the mountain well, enjoy bird watching, are willing to hike
with you, act as tour guide on paper or in person (with
notice), render limited supervision of children, and elaborate on the history of the Poconos. Smoking is not permitted. Rates: Double, shared bath $30. Single, Shared bath
$24. In-room cot $10. Crib $10.

RATES
Singles $12–$35 Doubles $24–$50.
One-night surcharge: $5.
Weekly and monthly rates available.
Deposit required: $20 minimum.
Credit cards accepted: MasterCard and VISA for deposit only.
Cancellation policy: Refund, less $10 handling fee, if notice re-
ceived at least seven days before expected arrival date.

Attention First-Time B&B Guests!

*"Although I strive to make just the right match for all guests,
a little extra thought and attention is given to callers who are
trying B&B for the first time. . . . Some of our many converts
are businessmen who, I feel, may have been pushed by their
wives to try this 'strange way of traveling'—while thinking all
the way to the host home, 'Who in his right mind would be
doing this?' They have been won over by our gracious hosts,
who enjoy the opportunity to meet new people at home."*

REST & REPAST BED & BREAKFAST SERVICE
BRENT R. PETERS AND LINDA C. FELTMAN
P.O. BOX 126
PINE GROVE MILLS, PA 16868-0126

PHONE: 814/238-1484
Live Monday–Friday 7–11 p.m. Most any time on weekends.
Answering machine at other times.

279

OPEN: Year round except Thanksgiving, and Christmas, and month of January.

ACCOMMODATIONS
B&Bs
Hosted private residences: 30.   B&B inn: 1.
About half have private guest baths.

LOCATIONS   *All are within a 30-minute drive of Penn State University. A few are within a 15-minue drive of Juniata College in Huntington, and 10 minutes from the Greer School in Tyrone.*

SETTINGS: "Almost all are what city folks would consider rural, although some are more rural than others. The State College-Centre County area was declared after last census to be a Metropolitan area by U.S. Census Bureau, although the New York City folks who saw a bear in the middle of Rte. 26, three miles from State College, probably would refute their findings!"

HOSTS: Financial planners, educators (professors, high school and elementary school teachers), realtor, nutritionist, nurse, pharmacist, farmer, president of a high-tech company, personnel director, pilot, engineers, retaler. . . .

GUESTS COME FOR: School-related reasons. Some for vacations, conferences, business, and just passing through.

BREAKFAST: About half serve a "very nice continental breakfast"; others serve a full meal. "Our hosts share recipes with one another, via a collection made from our January potluck get-together."

RESERVATIONS
Two weeks in advance preferred, particularly for the Central Pennsylvania Festival of the Arts (second week in July) and during PSU Homecoming (second scheduled football game in October). Call several months in advance for football season.
If arrangements can be made, will accept last-minute reservations. Minimum stay of two nights required during Central Pennsylvania Festival of the Arts and Homecoming.
Groups: Maximum size 10–20.

DIRECTORY: None available, but inquiries are answered with a brochure that has a few listings. *Samples:*

B. Featured at one time in *Victorian Homes* magazine, this large host home has been restored to reflect romantic late 1800s. Located in Bellefonte's Historic District, this is one of several host homes in Bellefonte represented by Rest and Repast. All are Victorian; most are filled with period furnishings. All within walking distance of quaint downtown shopping district where the annual two-week activity-filled Victorian Christmas celebration takes place. Also within walking distance to Centre County Library and Historic Society, one of the best in the state for genealogy buffs.

D. About two miles east of State College are several contemporary homes within five minutes of each other. Each features one to three guest rooms with either twins or double bed. Each has at least one guest room with a private bath. Hosts are all professional people, most affiliated with Penn State. All prefer nonsmokers.

RATES
Singles (when available) $25–$29. Doubles $30–$40.
On football weekends: No single rates; $40–50; $5 surcharge for one-night stay.
Some weekly and family rates available.
Deposit required: $20 for each night's lodging; $40 required on football weekends.
Cancellation policy: If guest cancels at least 7 days prior to scheduled visit, the deposit minus a $10 processing fee will be refunded. On football weekends, 14 days' written notice is required for refund; $10 service charge.

> *Linda and Brent feel good about what they are doing: "We know we are filling a need. Guests write to us about having 'saved their lives' (and their budgets) and how we were an answer to an impossible housing situation here. All the time we spend on matching hosts and guests seems worthwhile when we open notes such as this one from the Soyas: 'We thoroughly enjoyed our stay at Bob & Lou's. They are special people. Their home was more than comfortable and very clean. The breakfast was delicious and prepared with Love. Thank you.' "*

BED & BREAKFAST OF LANCASTER CO.
CAROL ANN PATTON
BOX 215
ELM, PA 17521

PHONE: 717/627-1890
Live after 5:30 p.m. Monday–Friday. Answering service at other times.
OPEN: Year round.

ACCOMMODATIONS
B&Bs
Hosted private residences: 15.   B&B inns: 4.
Most have air conditioning and at least one room with a private bath.
Plus
Some unhosted private residences for overnight or weekend lodging; some with washer/dryer and pet accommodations. Hosted and unhosted short-term (up to a month) housing.

OTHER SERVICES: Car rentals.

LOCATIONS   *Most are within 15 miles of Lancaster City. (Travelers need a car for transportation out of the city.) Others are in York County and include Gettysburg, and in Dauphin County including Hershey.*

SETTINGS: Plain Mennonite farms, old stone houses with Indian doors, some luxurious residences, and quaint inns. Many are historic.

HOSTS: Business executives, farmers, nurses, attorney, realtor, caterer. . . . (Since the film *Witness*, Carol has had many requests for stays with Amish families. She would like travelers to know that the Pennsylvania Amish do not accommodate paying guests.)

GUESTS COME FOR: Pennsylvania Dutch country—food, culture, attractions. Historical sites. Museums, antiquing, flea markets. Hershey Park. Schools—Franklin and Marshall College, Linden Hall School for Girls, Hershey Medical School.

BREAKFAST: Some serve continental. Others feature ginger and spice waffles, locally grown produce, sausage, homemade breads.

RESERVATIONS
Advance reservations recommended and preferred.

282

One host has a two-night minimum stay requirement.
Groups: Maximum size is 10 or 12.
Also available through some travel agents.

DIRECTORY (not required for reservations): $2. Descriptions of private homes, farms, inns, and self-contained units. *Samples*:

> 306F Dairy farm operated by young Mennonite family.
> Guests may help if they wish. Several young children to
> play with yours. Four bedrooms, three with doubles, one
> with a queen. One bath for guests only. No smoking or
> alcoholic beverages. Just outside lovely Lititz. Full break-
> fast. Double, private bath $30, single with shared bath $20,
> children under 12 $15. Infants, no charge.

> 108H Stately old stone house filled with antiques and his-
> tory. Open-hearthed country kitchen, formal dining room
> with magnificent corner cupboard, spacious living room
> with fireplace, and veranda for summer breakfasts. Your
> host is an engineer and your hostess a former nurse. Four
> bedrooms, three with double beds, one with a canopied
> queen. Two and one-half baths for guests. Smoking outside,
> please. Warm hosts and a beautiful home. Near Ephrata.
> Full breakfast. Double with shared bath $45, single with
> shared bath $40. Children over 10 welcome. Cots $15.

RATES
Singles $20–$38. Doubles $30-$89.
Deposit required: First night's lodging fee.
Credit cards accepted (inns only): MasterCard and VISA.
Cancellation policy: Refund minus $4 service charge if notice received at least one week before expected arrival date. (One place requires a three-week notice.)

PITTSBURGH BED AND BREAKFAST
JUDY ANTICO
2190 BEN FRANKLIN DRIVE
PITTSBURGH, PA 15237

PHONE: 412/367-8080
Live hours: early morning, evenings, weekends. Answering machine at other times.
OPEN: Year round except a few weeks in summer, usually August.

ACCOMMODATIONS
B&Bs
Hosted private residences: 21.
Almost all have air conditioning and private baths. One home is
accessible to handicapped.
Plus
Some unhosted private residences available for overnight, weekend
lodging, or long-term visits.

LOCATIONS *Most are within a 10-mile radius of city
center. Almost all are near public transportation. Just a few
are outside the city limits. Suburban communities include
Shadyside, Squirrel Hill, Mt. Lebanon, and Sewickley.*

SETTINGS: A full range of "selected private homes." Three are
apartments attached to homes.

GUESTS COME FOR: Conferences. High-tech and other business
reasons. Colleges and universities including Carnegie Mellon, University of Pittsburgh, Duquesne University, Chatham College.
Cultural events. City tours.

HOSTS: Systems analysts, museum program developer, landscape
architect, business owner, secretary, actress, doctor, newspaper
editor. . . .

BREAKFAST: All serve continental.

RESERVATIONS
Only one host has a minimum stay requirement of two days. Advance reservations preferred. (Most hosts require a few days' notice.) If possible, last-minute reservations accepted.

RATES
Singles $28–$34. Doubles $30–$45.
One-night surcharge: One host charges $5.
Deposit required is 20 percent.
Cancellation policy: If notice is received at least seven days before
arrival date, deposit will be refunded, less $6 handling fee.

Rhode Island

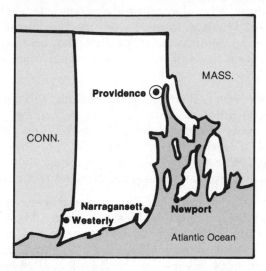

BED & BREAKFAST OF RHODE ISLAND, INC.

JOY MEISER AND KEN MENDIS
P.O. BOX 3291
NEWPORT, RI 02840

PHONE: 401/849-1298
  Monday–Friday 9–5:30.
OPEN: Year round, except national holidays.

ACCOMMODATIONS
B&Bs
Hosted private residences: 40.   B&B inns: 4.
Plus
Some short-term hosted and unhosted housing (for one or two weeks).

OTHER SERVICES: A weekend package that provides arrangements for tours at historic homes and sites, dining in an historic restaurant, and a B&B stay in an historic home.

LOCATIONS   *Throughout Rhode Island and in nearby Massachusetts communities in village, country, city, and seaside locations. Most are an easy drive or walk to the shoreline.*

SETTINGS: Historic and modern homes offering warm New England hospitality.

HOSTS: Sculptor, choral conductor and voice teacher, florist, retired Navy cook, realtor, kindergarten teacher, medical secretary, priest, marketing administrator, psychologist, antique dealer, historic preservation consultant, oceanographer, home economist, nurse. . . .

GUESTS COME FOR: Beaches, small fishing villages, and mansions along 400 miles of shoreline. Schools including Brown University, University of Rhode Island, Roger Williams College, Rhode Island School of Design, Salve Regina College, Johnson & Wales College, Naval War College. Business reasons. Relocation. House hunting. Historic sites and museums. Seafood restaurants.

BREAKFAST: Varies from simple to an elaborate meal and may include baked eggs, Belgian waffles, banana tea bread, home-style blueberry muffins, quiche Lorraine, apple pancakes, pear breakfast cake, Rhode Island johnny cakes, New England clam chowder, phoenikia with nuts, orange doughnut balls, puffed omelet, cheese souffle, glazed grapefruit.

RESERVATIONS
Minimum stay of two nights generally preferred but required during summer in resort areas.
Two weeks in advance preferred. If arrangements can be made, will accept last-minute reservations.
Groups: Maximum size is 50.
Also available through travel agents.

DIRECTORY (not required for reservations): $1. Includes information about each town represented as well as descriptions of B&Bs. *Samples*:

> #RI-106 Newport. In 1750 a well-known stone mason built this two-story house around a central chimney. He fashioned a huge walk-in fireplace that would have pleased any colonial homemaker. French doors open from the parlor to the adjoining formal dining room, where a hearty continental breakfast is served each morning. The sleeping rooms have distinctively different decor. One is furnished with Early American antiques, including Oriental-style rugs, a spindle bed, and a working fireplace. Another sunny room is furnished in French Provincial with a canopy bed and working fireplace. Rooms have wide plank flooring and

share a central sitting room with television. Located in Newport's historic Point section, this home is just a few hundred yards from the waterfront and yachting center. Both host and hostess share an interest in preserving the history of their home. Bath is shared. Rates $65 per room; $50 November 1–April 30. Breakfast: Hearty continental. Pets: Possibly with prior notice. One cat in residence. Children welcome. Smoking permitted. Two smokers in residence. Social drinking permitted.

#RI-121 North Kingstown (Wickford). The love and care which the host couple has put into this 19th-century colonial is strongly reflected in its furnishings and decor. Tasteful country charm characterizes each room, and period wall coverings and restored antiques bring visitors back to another era. Once a working farm, this home is located on 2½ acres surrounded by a picket fence, stone walls, barns, and chicken coops. Sleeping rooms are comfortably furnished with antiques. Quilted pillows, appliqued animals, and framed quilt blocks—all handmade by the hostess—help to create the country atmosphere. Guests share a centrally located bath, and an extra bath is available to guests during busy times. Both host and hostess are oceanographers and can offer suggestions about exploring marshes, tide pools, and rocky intertidal areas. Rates: May–October $40–$45 per night; off-season $5–$10 less. Breakfast: Continental; fresh baked goods, berries from garden. No pets. Children over age eight are welcome. Smoking outside only. Social drinking permitted.

RATES
Singles $30–$55. Doubles $40–$65. A few up to $75/$98 in season in heavy demand areas.
Weekly rates available.
Deposit required: $20 per room per night. A few hosts require full payment in advance.
Credit cards: VISA, MasterCard, and AMEX usually accepted for last-minute reservations only.
Cancellation policy: If cancellation is received two weeks prior to reservation date, refund is given minus $10 processing fee. No refunds within two weeks of reservation date.

What Is B&B All About?

Joy and Ken conduct workshops entitled "How to Start Your Own Bed & Breakfast Business" for people who are thinking about opening their home for B&B. Other workshops are called "Thinking of Traveling Bed & Breakfast?" for first-time B&B travelers.

BED & BREAKFAST BY THE SEA
29 GIBSON AVENUE
NARRAGANSETT, RI 02882

PHONE: 401/789-7746
OPEN: Year round.

ACCOMMODATIONS
B&Bs
Hosted private residences: Three.
Number of rooms ranges from three to five in Victorian and Cape Cod–style homes. Each of the three has one or more rooms with a private bath.

LOCATIONS *All in Narragansett in quiet residential neighborhoods.*

HOSTS: Marketing director, realtor, government staff.

BREAKFAST: Full. Features fresh baked goods, fruit, juice, coffee and creative entree.

RESERVATIONS
Minimum stay requirement of two nights on summer weekends.

RATES
Singles $30–$40. Doubles $40–$55.
Deposit required: One night's lodging.
Cancellation policy: Deposit refunded if notice received at least three days before expected arrival date and if room(s) are subsequently booked.

Narragansett's beaches are a major attraction. The history in the area—combined with the town's location, just 20 minutes' drive to Newport—inspired the Chamber of Commerce to seek housing for the many annual visitors. Each year the bed and breakfast list has grown, to the point where there is now a waiting list for the Chamber's roster. The three who have just started Bed & Breakfast By The Sea not only serve a full breakfast, but find the morning meal is a highlight of the visit. As Dave Peterson (one of the three husbands who takes an active role in hosting) puts it, "Guests respond by sharing parts of themselves; barriers quickly melt, and breakfast becomes a 'happening' which enriches their vacation—and continues to make B&B a fun experience for us."

CASTLE KEEP
DOROTHY RANHOFER, AUDREY GRIMES
44 EVERETT STREET
NEWPORT, RI 02840

PHONE: 401/846-0362
Live June 1–September 30: 8–8 daily. September 30–May 31: 3–8 p.m. Thursday–Monday.

ACCOMMODATIONS
B&Bs
Hosted private residences: 40.
Most have private baths.
Plus
Unhosted private residences by the week or month (only). Referrals (not reservations) made to B&B inns.

LOCATIONS *Newport and vicinity only. Most are within walking distance of beaches or downtown.*

SETTINGS: Victorian mini-mansions. Modern cottages by the sea. Some historic. Some luxurious. A few are "just plain homes."

HOSTS: Retired university faculty, language professor, town councilman, restaurant owner, British-born residents, garage-sale aficionado. . . .

GUESTS COME FOR: America's Cup races, yachting events, largest number of lived-in restored pre-Revolutionary houses in the country, tours of mansions, beaches, boutique shopping. Schools:

289

University of Rhode Island, Roger Williams College, St. George's School, Portsmouth Abbey.

BREAKFAST: From continental to groaning board depending on host. Some specialties include fresh fruit compote and French toast.

RESERVATIONS

Advance notice strongly suggested in season. If arrangements can be made, will accept last-minute reservations.

Note: The type of room, your dates, and desired location are top priority. This service does not usually make matches according to interests.

Groups: Maximum size is 10.

DIRECTORY: None available. Inquiries answered with a free brochure that describes a few houses. *Samples:*

> Overlooking the Ida Lewis Yacht Club, an elegant chateau. Your Swedish hostess offers breakfast in the formal dining room or on the terrace. Twin room with private bath: $60.

> The Point. An area of restored colonials and gas-lighted streets. Three homes offering the convenience of a downtown location. Doubles with shared bath: $45.

RATES

Singles $35–$40. Doubles $45–$60. A few suites in $110–$125 range.

One-night surcharge: Saturday night, $10 in season.

Weekly and monthly rates available in unhosted apartments.

Deposit required: One night or 50 percent.

Credit cards accepted: VISA and MasterCard.

Cancellation policy: Full refund if cancellations received four days before expected arrival date.

> *"Many local people utilize the service to accommodate their guests."*

Throughout Rhode Island there are also B&Bs represented by Pineapple Hospitality, page 156.

South Carolina

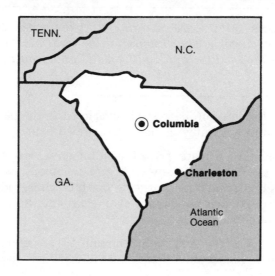

B&B GUESTS COME FOR: Gardens that feature azaleas and dog-wood in the early spring, quiet beaches in the summer, historic sites including Fort Moultrie and Fort Sumter, museums and plantations. Some come to attend conferences or for professional or school-related reasons.

CHARLESTON EAST BED & BREAKFAST

BARBARA N. AULD
1031 TALL PINE ROAD
MOUNT PLEASANT, SC 29464

PHONE: 803/884-8208
   Live Monday–Friday, 2–9. Answering machine at other times.
OPEN: Year round.

ACCOMMODATIONS
B&Bs
Hosted private residences: 17.
All have air conditioning and most have private baths.
One is accessible to handicapped.

Plus
Some unhosted private residences for overnight or weekend lodging.

LOCATIONS *Most are within a 10-minute drive of downtown historic Charleston and the local beaches in the towns of Mount Pleasant, Sullivan's Island, and the Isle of Palms.*

SETTINGS: Range from harborside overlooking the peninsula city of Charleston to a country home in a secluded fishing village.

HOSTS: Forester, private school headmistress, executive secretary, music teacher, symphony orchestra members, caterer, registered nurse, bank manager, surgeon, math teacher, radiation therapist. . . . "I visit each host about every two months, as we are all close friends and neighbors."

BREAKFAST: Varies from help-yourself to an elaborate meal. Could include: homemade breads, creek shrimp, and grits on a summer morning.

RESERVATIONS
Advance reservations preferred but not mandatory, except for March and April, when at least two weeks' notice is strongly recommended. If arrangements can be made, will accept last-minute reservations.

DIRECTORY: Descriptions of homes sent without charge (please send a business-sized self-addressed stamped envelope). *Sample*:

> #17 This recently completed modern home, with a number of skylights and bright decor, is hosted by an energetic and gracious lady who is particularly interested in meeting young couples and in having foreign visitors. Location is in a country subdivision—quiet, no traffic sounds. Accommodations: Two double rooms are available, with private bath on hall. One double room has the antique rope bed from the hostess's family in the upstate, and the second room has a queen-sized bed and wicker furnishings which are quite comfortable. There is a large patio for spring and summer breakfasts. There is a resident German shepherd, and smoking is permitted. Social drinking is allowed. $40.

RATES
Singles $20–$35. Doubles $25–$40.

One-night surcharge: $5.
Deposit required: One night's fee.
Cancellation policy: Full refund if three days' notice given.

Experience Counts

Bobbie was the administrative secretary to a physician for 25 years and is accustomed to listening for needs. Now, as service coordinator, she tries to "personalize each request, placing the guest with the appropriate host and the particular 'spirit' of that lodging."

And how is it going? "We are having the times of our lives. One of my young hostesses last week hugged me and said 'Bobbie, this has changed my life! I love it, I love it!!' We all do, and I do believe more and more travelers will use B&B homes as time progresses."

CHARLESTON SOCIETY BED & BREAKFAST
JOAN LUCAS, ELEANOR ROGERS, JANE THORNHILL
84 MURRAY BOULEVARD
CHARLESTON, SC 29401

PHONE: 803/723-4948
Live Monday–Friday, 9–5. Answering machine at other times.
OPEN: Year round.

ACCOMMODATIONS
B&Bs
Hosted private residences: 15.
All have air conditioning and private baths.
Plus
Unhosted short-term (for one or two months) housing.

LOCATIONS *All are located in Charleston's historic district and within easy walking distance of shops, restaurants, and historic points of interest.*

SETTINGS: All are historic homes.

HOSTS: Realtors, lawyer, doctors, tour guides, business women. . . .

BREAKFAST: Most serve continental.

RESERVATIONS

At least one week in advance preferred. If arrangements can be made, will accept last-minute reservations.

Also available through travel agents.

DIRECTORY: Two pages of brief descriptions are sent without charge. *Samples*:

> #10 Lovely home, built in 1853. Bedroom with double bed, private bath, overlooking formal garden. Balcony. $60 per night.

> #13 Lovely carriage house. Private entrance. Living room with fireplace. Full kitchen. Upstairs: two bedrooms, one with twins, two baths. Formal garden. $90 per couple. $150 for four people.

RATES

$65–$150 per night.

Deposit required: First night's lodging.

Cancellation policy: Full refund, less $5 for cancellations received 48 hours before expected arrival date.

HISTORIC CHARLESTON BED & BREAKFAST

CHARLOTTE D. FAIREY
43 LEGARE STREET
CHARLESTON, SC 29401

PHONE: 803/722-6606
  March 1–June 1, 9:30–6 daily.
  June–March, 1–6 p.m.
OPEN: Year round except July 4, Labor Day, Thanksgiving, and Christmas.

ACCOMMODATIONS

B&Bs

Hosted private residences: 32.

All have air conditioning, heat, and private baths.

Plus

Hosted and unhosted short-term (up to three or four months) also available.

OTHER SERVICES: Car rentals. A three-day, two-night package that includes a personalized tour of city and lunch at a restaurant. Arrangements for horse-drawn excursion rides.

LOCATIONS *All are in the historic district of Charleston, within walking distance of most major attractions and restaurants.*

SETTINGS: All are luxurious historic homes that were built between 1720 and 1890.

HOSTS: Doctors, lawyers, bankers, travel agent, retired nurse, public relations executive. . . .

BREAKFAST: Varies from simple to elaborate. Could include strawberry-filled crepes and Spanish omelets. About half the hosts are usually present for breakfast.

RESERVATIONS
Advance reservations preferred. If possible, last-minute reservations made.
Groups: Maximum size is 12.

DIRECTORY: A sampler, a beautiful color flyer of four of the homes, is sent on request without charge, as is a full list of B&Bs, their facilities, locations, and rates.

RATES
Singles $30–$100. Doubles $45–$100.
One-night surcharge: $5.
Weekly and monthly rates available.
Credit cards accepted: MasterCard, VISA, AMEX for deposit or entire fee.
Cancellation policy: Deposit less $5 service fee is refunded if cancellation notice received four days (96 hours) before expected arrival date.

"Not only was the decor impressive, but the gracious hospitality made our visit to Charleston a truly memorable occasion . . . outstanding people, who shared unstintingly their knowledge of Charleston—its history, architecture, and society. On our return, you may be assured we will ask to be accommodated with the same hosts."

—A guest from Georgia

"We sound like representatives from the Chamber of Commerce of Charleston. We are spreading the word among neighbors and friends. Not that you need more people, but you want your friends to experience Charleston—and your service—at least once in their lives."

—A guest from Virginia

Because B&Bs are all different, tell the service what you want. Think ahead of time about your needs. For a little help, turn to page 1.

South Dakota

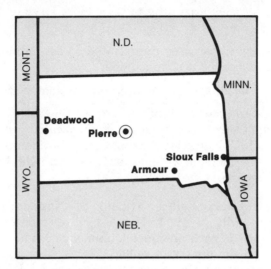

BED AND BREAKFAST OF SOUTH DAKOTA

KATHY HALES AND KAREN OLSON
P.O. BOX 80137
SIOUX FALLS, SD 57116

PHONE: 605/528-6571 and 339-0759
  Monday–Saturday, 8 a.m.–10 p.m.
OPEN: Year round except Easter, Thanksgiving, Christmas, and
  New Year's Day.

ACCOMMODATIONS
B&Bs
Hosted private residences: 15.
Almost all have air conditioning.

LOCATIONS *Spread throughout the state in rural, suburban, and urban communities.*

HOSTS: Farmers, ranchers, chemist, college dean, artist, retired
farmers, teachers, business people. . . .

GUESTS COME FOR: Mt. Rushmore, the Badlands, Lewis & Clark
Lake, Laura Ingalls Wilder Pageant, the Delbridge Museums,

Oahe Dam, ranches, Black Hills National Forest, prairie and farm-land. For business, skiing, hunting, fishing.

BREAKFAST: Varies according to host. Most serve large meals.

RESERVATIONS
Advance reservations are appreciated. Last-minute accepted. Groups up to 10 can be accommodated.

DIRECTORY: No charge for the descriptions sent. *Samples*:

SW2. Western part of state. Heart of Black Hills in old-west town of Deadwood. Spacious home located near notorious Boot Hill Cemetery. Two double. Continental breakfast. $35/first person. $5/additional person. Children welcome. Five percent state tax.

SE6. Central part of state. Armour, SD National Registry three-story built in 1904. Neoclassical elements. Beautifully furnished (with antiques) summer house and bicycle-built-for-two for guests to enjoy. Tennis, swimming pool, and golf course nearby. Near Hutterite colony. No pets, no children, and no smoking. Two double bedrooms. $30 couple, 4 percent state tax.

RATES
Singles $15–$35. Doubles $20–$40.
Deposit required: $20.
Cancellation policy: Refunds made minus $3 handling charge deducted from deposit.

Tennessee

HOST HOMES OF TENNESSEE

FREDDA ODOM
P.O. BOX 110227
NASHVILLE, TN 37222-0227

PHONE: 615/331-5244
  Answering service at all times.
OPEN: Year round.

ACCOMMODATIONS
B&Bs
Hosted private residences: 40. B&B inns: 3.
All have air conditioning. Most have private baths. Many have pools.
Plus
Unhosted lake cottages.
Hosted short-term (for as long as needed) housing.

OTHER SERVICES: Car rentals; tickets for theater, sports, and country music events; and city tours.

LOCATIONS *Spread throughout the state—in Nashville, Shelbyville, Memphis, Murfreesboro, Knoxville, Gallatin, Chattanooga, Clarkeville, Hendersonville.*

SETTINGS: Some just plain, some luxurious, some historic.

HOSTS: Surgeons, teachers, professors, administrators, decorators. . . .

GUESTS COME FOR: Opryland, the Grand Ole Opry, antique shows, Tennessee Walking Horses, Performing Arts Center, Vanderbilt, University of Tennessee, conferences, business reasons. . . .

BREAKFAST: Most serve continental.

RESERVATIONS
Advance notice preferred. If arrangements can be made, will accept last-minute reservations.
Also available through travel agents.

DIRECTORY: None available, but all inquiries are answered with a sample listing of about 20 homes. *Samples*:

> N107 Former Canadians retired. Large new home with a beautiful view. Near large shopping center, park, country music sites, and Opryland. Double room, private bath. S— $30. D—$40. Efficiency with private entrance. D—$50.

> H114 Near Opryland, Twitty City, House of Cash: National Register of Historic Homes, used as a hospital during Civil War. Colonial-style white frame and brick. All antiques. Beautiful doll collection. S—$35. D—$40. Extra $8. Nonsmokers.

RATES
Singles $26–$35. Doubles $32–$50. One is higher.
Weekly rates available.
Advance full payment (in U.S. currency) required.
Credit cards accepted: MasterCard and VISA.
Cancellation policy: 75 percent refunded on three days' notice. No refund if reservations aren't honored or if canceled within three days of expected arrival date.

RIVER RENDEZVOUS
MIMMYE GOODE
P.O. BOX 24001
MEMPHIS, TN 38124

PHONE: 901/767-5296
   No set phone hours. Answering machine when not live.

ACCOMMODATIONS
B&Bs
Hosted private residences: 12.   B&B inns: 2.
Most have private baths. All have air conditioning.
Plus
Hosted short-term housing available.

LOCATIONS   *Homes are located in cities along the Mississippi River from Memphis to New Orleans.*

SETTINGS: All are rather luxurious.

HOSTS: Retired social worker, engineer, public relations specialist, professor, teachers. . . .

GUESTS COME FOR: Conventions, historic Orpheum Theatre, music, theater, Libertyland Amusement Park, fine restaurants, Germantown Horse Show.

BREAKFAST: All are continental.

RESERVATIONS
Advance reservations preferred. If possible, last-minute reservations made.
Groups: Maximum size is 12.
Also available through travel agents.

RATES
Singles $20–$50. Doubles $25–$55.
One-night surcharge: $5.
Weekly and monthly rates are available.

BED & BREAKFAST IN MEMPHIS
HELEN V. DENTON
P.O. BOX 41621
MEMPHIS, TN 38174

PHONE: 901/726-5920
Live Monday–Friday 8–6 and Saturday 8–noon. Answering machine at other times.

ACCOMMODATIONS
B&Bs
Hosted private residences: 15.   B&B inns: 1.
All are air conditioned and have private baths.
Plus
Fourteen unhosted private residences for longer-term stays (minimum three nights).

OTHER SERVICES: Car rental arrangements. Executive secretarial services. Fees charged.

LOCATIONS   *With a few exceptions, all homes are within 15 minutes of downtown, Mud Island, universities, and the airport.*

SETTINGS: A variety in town, in suburbs, and in the country.

HOSTS: Lawyers, physicians, accountants, sales representatives, homemakers, interior designers. . . . Among them are hosts who have knowledge of at least one other language, including French, German, and Spanish.

GUESTS COME FOR: House hunting. Business reasons. Rhodes College, Memphis State University. Downtown development with luxury condos overlooking the Mississippi River. Mud Island, passive-use urban park. Victorian Village. Historic Beale Street. "Performances in the majestic Orpheum Theatre. The Peabody Hotel, where the ducks still grace the lobby at specified times. Magnolias. . . .

BREAKFAST: All continental.

RESERVATIONS
One-night surcharge: $5.
Advance reservations preferred. If arrangements can be made, will accept last-minute reservations.
Groups: Maximum size is 10.

DIRECTORY (not required for reservations): $2.50, applied to reservations when received. *Sample*:

> #N-5301 This 47-acre farm is located in northwest Shelby County and is convenient to major corporations such as duPont and Grace Chemical. Fishing (bring your own gear) and horseback riding stables nearby. This older home offers

delightful screened-in sun room where you may enjoy respite or a quiet breakfast. *Located*: Millington, approx. 8 mi. to Highway 51 North and I-240; 15 mi. to downtown, 20 mi. to Germantown. *Offering*: Two guest rooms with private bath, sitting room. [Codes indicate two rooms: one with twin beds, one with canopied double. Well-behaved supervised children allowed. TV and radio (shared). Dogs in residence. Deluxe home.]

RATES
Singles $26–$45. Doubles $32–$45. A few are higher.
One-night surcharge: $5. Weekly and monthly rates available.
Deposit required: $20 if reservations made far in advance.
Credit cards accepted: VISA and MasterCard for entire fee.
Cancellation policy: 75 percent refund for cancellations made up to three days prior to arrival date.

> *"A wonderful experience. It's a great way to visit across the states."*
>
> *—A Bed & Breakfast in Memphis guest*

NASHVILLE BED & BREAKFAST
FRAN DEGAN
P.O. BOX 150651
NASHVILLE, TN 37215

PHONE: 615/298-5674, 269-6555, 366-1115
Live Monday–Friday 8 a.m.–10 p.m. Answering service at other times.
OPEN: Year round except Christmas and New Year's.

ACCOMMODATIONS
B&Bs
Hosted private residences: 45.
All have air conditioning.
Plus
Unhosted short-term (up to six weeks) housing available.

OTHER SERVICES: Pickup at airport.

LOCATIONS *Most hosts are within 10–15 miles of Nash-*
ville, Opryland, museums, country music events, and uni-
versities. Most are close to interstate highways (Public
transportation in the area is limited.)

SETTINGS: Among the full range are some antebellum homes.
Many, including pre–Civil War homes, are on the National Register.

HOSTS: Attorney, doctors, business men and women, educators,
retirees. . . . "Nashville has lots of history and many of our hosts
are true historians."

GUEST COME FOR: Country music attractions. Universities including Vanderbilt and Belmont. Historic sites, amusement parks,
Opryland.

BREAKFAST: All serve continental.

RESERVATIONS
Advance reservations preferred. If arrangements can be made, will
accept last-minute reservations.
Also available through travel agents.

DIRECTORY (not required for reservations): $2.50. *Samples*:

Host #C-7503 [Coded to indicate two guest rooms that can
accommodate a total of four people. Well-behaved children
allowed. Private bath. Air conditioning. Hosts have a dog.
Nonsmokers only. $34 single, $50 for two guests.] . . . This
antebellum plantation home is listed on the National Register of Historic Places. From the spacious rooms to the
tester beds to the knowledgeable host, you'll think you've
stepped into a bygone era of southern grandeur. . . . Truly a
unique home and experience. In Hendersonville. Located 8
miles from downtown Nashville and Music Row; 8 miles
from the airport; 12 miles from Opryland; 2½ miles from
I-65; one room with double tester bed, two rooms each with
double tester bed. Plus your own sitting room.

Host #D-2702 [One room can accommodate three people.
Queen-sized bed; cot and crib available. Children allowed.
Private bath. Air conditioned. Nonsmokers preferred.] . . .
Your hosts on this mini-farm in Brentwood are a young

veterinarian and his family. Private guest quarters, including a patio, are in a separate wing of the house. Private entrance. Located 10 miles from the airport; 4 miles from Old Hickory Blvd., Brentwood exit; 13 miles from Opryland; 12 miles to downtown Nashville, colleges, and Music Row. No extra charge for crib. $40 for two. Cot: $10.

RATES

Singles $21–$28. Doubles $40–$50. A few are higher.

Weekly and monthly rates available.

Deposit required varies according to host.

Credit cards accepted: MasterCard, VISA, AMEX for entire fee in advance.

Cancellation policy: Full refund if notice received at least 48 hours before expected arrival date.

Do you have a question? When writing to a bed and breakfast reservation service, please enclose a business-sized self-addressed stamped envelope (SASE).

Texas

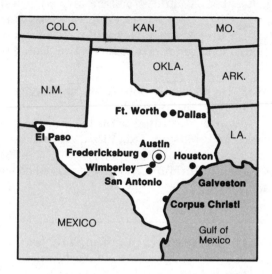

BED & BREAKFAST TEXAS STYLE
RUTH WILSON
4224 W. RED BIRD LANE
DALLAS, TX 75237

PHONE: 214/298-8586 or 298-5433
  Live Monday–Friday 8:30–5:30. Answering machine at other times.
OPEN: Year round except Christmas Day and New Year's Day.

ACCOMMODATIONS
B&Bs
Hosted private residences: 75.   B&B inns: 5.
All have air conditioning and private baths. Many have pools and hot tubs.
Plus
Some unhosted private residences for overnight or weekend lodging.
Hosted short-term (two weeks to six months) housing.

OTHER SERVICES: Pickup at airport, bus, and train. Theater tickets and restaurant reservations possible.
Note: It is almost essential to have a rental car. Although many homes are very near public transportation, it is not too frequent on weekends, when many tourists need it.

306

LOCATIONS *Most are in the Dallas/Ft. Worth area, but there are many others all over the state from Sherman to Galveston, including Austin, Houston, Sam Rayburn Lake, San Antonio, and Waco.*

SETTINGS: Some lakeside getaways, some ranches, new condos/townhomes, "just plain" clean and comfortable, historic, and some very luxurious estates.

HOSTS: Artists, writers, lawyers, teachers, business owners. . . .

GUESTS COME FOR: Conferences. Business reasons. School-related activity at the many colleges and universities in the state. House hunting. Vacations and touring: State Fair of Texas, Dallas Cowboys, Billy Bob's of Texas, Fort Worth Stockyards, Six Flags, Texas Rangers, Hill Country and Lakes District of Texas, Bay (Galveston) of Texas.

BREAKFAST: Varies from help-yourself to an elaborate meal that could include German wurst, and scrambled eggs, Taquitas (Mexican omelets in tortillas), fruit cup, homemade breads, sourdough pancakes, strawberries, and locally grown (five months of the year) cantaloupe.

RESERVATIONS
Two weeks to a month in advance preferred. If arrangements can be made, will accept last-minute reservations.
Minimum stay: Some hosts require two nights.
Also available through travel agents.

DIRECTORY (not required for reservations): $2. *Samples*:

Dallas. "Iris Canopy." Home with an historical marker has this lovely double bedroom featuring iris coverlet, canopy, and prints on the wall. Many antiques in large two-story red brick, prairie-style architecture. Private bath, no shower. Hosts have traveled B&B and hosted folks from many countries. Convenient to bus line, Convention Center, and arts district. No smokers, please. Single $50, double $60.

Houston-Galveston. "Bayside." Halfway between Houston and Galveston on the bay is this fine home right on the water. Area is reminiscent of San Francisco, with many sailboats in view from the living-dining room. Glass windows across entire side of home make pelican watching a favorite hobby of the hosts. Pool in front yard may be used by guests if hostess is not giving a swimming lesson. Twin beds in room just off breezeway and a private bath. NASA is 15 minutes away, about 45 minutes to Houston and 30 minutes to Galveston. Wonderful couple who have a collie dog and a St. Bernard. She is a gourmet cook and will prepare omelets or quiche for breakfast. Single $45, double $50.

RATES
Singles $25–$50. Doubles $30–$70.
One-night surcharge: $5.
Some weekly and monthly rates available.
Deposit required: $20.
Cancellation policy: Deposit refunded minus a $7 service charge if cancellation received three working days before arrival date.

BED & BREAKFAST SOCIETY OF AUSTIN
KATHY SMOLIK
1702 GRAYWOOD COVE
AUSTIN, TX 78704

PHONE: 512/441-2857
  Live 8–8 daily. Answering service at other times.
OPEN: Year round.

ACCOMMODATIONS
B&Bs
Hosted private residences: 10.
All have air conditioning and private baths.
Plus
Unhosted private residences for overnight or short-term (up to two or three months) housing.

OTHER SERVICES: Theater tickets.

LOCATIONS   *Most are in the inner city, but some are suburban. Austin is rather compact. Within a half hour you can reach neighborhoods and areas with homes that provide parking, are close to large hotels used for seminars, and are near amenities such as lakes, recreational facilities, and parks.*

SETTINGS: Varied. One has a clean room in a comfortable house. Another is in a cottage behind a main house. Still another is a ranch house in the Hill Country.

HOSTS: Interior decorators, physicians, realtors, retired teachers. . . .

GUESTS COME FOR: Business and pleasure. "The university area, Hill Country, lakes, Capitol, symphony, ballet. . . ."

BREAKFAST: Varies according to host.

RESERVATIONS
At least one week in advance preferred.

RATES
Singles $25–$50. Doubles $35–$50. $10 for each additional person. Some weekly and monthly rates available.
Deposit required: Full payment in advance.
Cancellation policy: Refund minus $10 handling charge if notice received at least three days before expected arrival date.

> *Kathy has a roster of frustrated innkeepers—including herself. In addition, she has done considerable B&B traveling. Now her dream is to open the first B&B inn in this unique city. If that interests you as a traveler, you might inquire if she has found the right older home in the right place and made it all happen.*

SAND DOLLAR HOSPITALITY
PAT HIRSBRUNNER
3605 MENDENHALL
CORPUS CHRISTI, TX 78415

PHONE: 512/853-1222
   Monday–Saturday 9–5.
OPEN: Year round except Christmas.

ACCOMMODATIONS
B&Bs
Hosted private residences: 16.
All have air conditioning and private baths.
Plus
Some unhosted private residences for overnight or weekend lodging.

Unhosted short-term (up to one month) housing available includes a new condominium on the gulf.

OTHER SERVICES: Will arrange B&B reservations for other locations in area and state.

LOCATIONS *All within a 10-mile radius of center city and within a 20-minute drive of beaches.*

SETTINGS: The range includes "budget" ("just plain"), moderate (most are in this category), and deluxe with hot tub and pool among the amenities.

HOSTS: Dietitian, teachers, many retirees. . . .

GUESTS COME FOR: Vacations and business. Attractions include Aransas Wild Life Refuge—home of whooping crane—and King Ranch—world's largest ranch. Tours. Beaches. Fishing.

BREAKFAST: Full.

RESERVATIONS
If arrangements can be made, will accept last-minute reservations.

DIRECTORY: Single-page directory sent without charge in answer to all inquiries. *Sample*:

"Dolphin"—Lovely home in newer neighborhood has one room with queen-sized bed and one with a double. Both rooms share a full bath and are nicely furnished. Attractive covered patio will lure you outdoors with your morning coffee or afternoon refreshment. Pampered pets accepted. Kitchen, laundry, TV. Bus service nearby; close to shopping. No smoking or children please. Single $35. Double $40.

RATES
Singles $20–$35. Doubles $25–$40.
Weekly rates at 20 percent discount.
Deposit required: $5 per night single or $7.50 per night double.
Cancellation policy: With 48-hour notice, all but $5 is refunded.

BED AND BREAKFAST OF FREDERICKSBURG

KATHY KOPP
307 WEST MAIN STREET
FREDERICKSBURG, TX 78624

PHONE: 512/997-4712
Live 7 a.m.–11 p.m. daily. Answering machine at other times.
OPEN: Year round.

ACCOMMODATIONS
B&Bs
Hosted private residences: 15.   B&B inns: 3.
All have air conditioning and private baths.
Plus
Unhosted private residences available for overnight or weekend lodging.
Short-term (up to five or six months) housing available.

OTHER SERVICES: Car rentals. Airport and bus pickup. Train pickup in San Antonio (70 miles away). Theater tickets. Arrangements for family reunions, special seminars, meetings, and small conventions.

LOCATIONS   *All in the Fredericksburg area. "Some are located on acreage in outlying areas. However, Fredericksburg itself is a quiet, country town when compared to larger cities. Your accommodation may be only blocks from Main Street, yet have the atmosphere of a country setting."*

SETTINGS: Include unique and historic, from budget to deluxe, plain to luxurious.

HOSTS: Retirees, beauticians, school teachers, ranchers, ministers, oilmen, and world travelers. Ethnic families, housewife, active nurses, business women, minister, dentist, lawyer, waitress, banker's wife. . . .

GUESTS COME FOR: Texas-German culture and architecture. "Hauptstrasse" (Main Street) with its shops, bakeries, "biergartens," and restaurants. Museums, state parks, historic buildings, and churches.

BREAKFAST: Half serve continental and half serve full breakfasts. Offerings could include German brötchen; coffee cakes;

311

cooked cheese (Handkaese); homemade jellies, jams, and wines; and sausages of all types, "wonderful delights they have developed or inherited from many eons back."

RESERVATIONS
Last-minute reservations accepted. Also available through travel agents.

DIRECTORY: Several pages of descriptions sent without charge. *Samples:*

#2. This popular hostess has many return guests. Her beautifully remodeled early-1900s home was moved from a downtown location and is tastefully decorated and comfortable. It is convenient to Main Street shopping and is in a quiet tree-filled neighborhood. Two bedrooms are available with double beds and shared bath between the two rooms. Central H & A. The gracious hostess is a native of Fredericksburg, and guests may find themselves in a lively gathering on her spacious and beautiful patio/garden. Single $38.50. Double $49. Restriction: No smoking. Breakfast: Continental, plus.

#7. This very special guest house is a rock barn, over 100 years old. The restoration is beautiful and unique, with much country flavor. Available is a downstairs sitting area, kitchen, bath with sunken Mexican tile tub, and an upstairs loft-type bedroom. Both the gracious hosts are professional people who have created a charming setting for their home and guest house. This getaway is only 1.5 miles from town and has become one of our most popular B&Bs. Heating is by wood cookstove and central heat, air conditioning. Single $49. Double $54.50. Extra persons $16.50. Restrictions: No toddlers. No smoking preferred. Breakfast: Fix-your-own, full. Beds: Loft twins, can be pushed together to make king; sitting room has twin-size trundle.

RATES
Singles $27.50–$49. Doubles $38.50–$71. A few higher.
Deposit required is 50 percent of total cost of lodging.
Credit cards: VISA, MasterCard, AMEX accepted for entire fee.
Cancellation policy: Full refund, minus $10 handling and service charge, if made at least three days before scheduled arrival date.

BED AND BREAKFAST SOCIETY OF HOUSTON
MARGUERITE SWANSON
921 HEIGHTS BOULEVARD
HOUSTON, TX 77008

PHONE: 713/868-4654
  Monday–Friday 9–5; other times by chance.
OPEN: Year round.

ACCOMMODATIONS
B&Bs
Hosted private residences: 25 (and growing).
All have air conditioning and private baths. Some have pools, hot tubs.
Plus
Some unhosted private residences for overnight or weekend lodging.
Hosted short-term (six weeks to two months) housing available.

OTHER SERVICES: Pickup at airport shuttle points.

LOCATIONS *Throughout Houston metropolitan area, plus Brenham, Bryan, Alvin.*

SETTINGS: Wide range from average to luxurious.

HOSTS: Social worker, antique dealer, career counselor, real estate broker, and retired. . . .

GUESTS COME FOR: Oil-related business. Relocations. NASA. Many schools including University of Houston, Rice University, Baylor College of Medicine. Galveston. Gulf Coast beaches. Medical consultations. Conferences. A vacation.

BREAKFAST: From simple to elaborate possibilities. Regional specialties could include huevos rancheros, jalapeno cornbread, muffins, omelets, quiche.

RESERVATIONS
Advance reservations of at least two weeks preferred.

DIRECTORY: Representative listings sent without charge on request. *Samples:*

  Montrose. Lilac and burgundy accents are a refreshing surprise inside this traditional older recently redecorated home. Furnished throughout with family antiques and modern art. Home is convenient to the University of St. Thomas, museums, parks, and cafes. The guest suite is upstairs, two twin beds, private bath, bathtub. $25–$35.

Montrose. One of the few really old homes in Houston, this three-story house has a small second-floor apartment which is used for bed and breakfast. Old crochet and unusual old furniture make this place like a trip to the past. Convenient to everything downtown and to the famous Galleria area. A bonus is the charming hostess whose hobby is cooking. $30–40.

RATES
Singles $25–$50. Doubles $35–$60.
One-night surcharge: $5.
Some weekly rates available.
Full payment in advance required.
Cancellation policy: Full refund less $5 service charge if cancellation received three days before expected arrival date.

> *"The place where we are staying in Houston is one of the best B&Bs we have stayed in here or abroad."*
> —*A guest from Minnesota*

BED & BREAKFAST HOSTS OF SAN ANTONIO
HOME LODGING SERVICE

LAVERN CAMPBELL
166 ROCKHILL
SAN ANTONIO, TX 78209

PHONE: 512/824-8036
  Monday–Friday, 9–5. Answering machine at other times.
OPEN: Year round.

ACCOMMODATIONS
B&Bs
Hosted private residences: 25.   One B&B inn in San Marcus. One in San Antonio.
All have air conditioning and most have private baths. Some are accessible to handicapped.

OTHER SERVICES: Pickup at airport and train.

LOCATIONS *Most are within a 10-mile radius of center city. Almost all are near public transportation.*

BREAKFAST: Varies from simple to elaborate according to host.

RESERVATIONS
Advance reservations preferred. If arrangements can be made, will accept last-minute reservations.

DIRECTORY: Two pages of descriptions sent without charge. *Samples:*

> #C. A gregarious young couple eager to serve a full breakfast that includes bacon, eggs "as you like them," hash browns, and Danish pastries. They will also escort their guest to "off the beaten path" places that most visitors miss. Their guest bedroom has a queen-size bed and private bath. There's a hot tub on the terrace. Single $48. Double $53.50. Nonsmokers.

> #N. In the historic King William area, within walking distance of downtown San Antonio attractions, this charming couple have restored their beautiful Victorian home. They have an upstairs bedroom with two beds, a refrigerator, balcony, and bath. With advance notice, this hostess will prepare an authentic Mexican dinner for her guests. Single $46. Double $59. Smokers accepted.

RATES
Singles $27–$53. Doubles $42.50–$80.
Weekly and monthly rates available.
Full advance payment required.
Credit cards accepted: MasterCard and VISA.
Cancellation policy: $5 service charge for cancellation received at least three days before scheduled stay. No refunds for later cancellations.

BED AND BREAKFAST OF WIMBERLEY TEXAS

LARRY LATTOMUS
P.O. BOX 589
WIMBERLEY, TX 78676

PHONE: 512/847-9666
Usually live Monday–Friday 9–5. Answering machine at other times.
OPEN: Year round.

ACCOMMODATIONS
B&Bs
Hosted private residences: Four.
Plus
A couple of unhosted units available for short-term lodging.

LOCATIONS *Wimberley, 35 miles from Austin, 60 miles from San Antonio.*

SETTINGS: Range from a guest house that was featured in a recent *Austin Homes and Gardens* magazine, to a small ranch near town with a pool, well-maintained grounds, and horses, to (hosted) rooms located over an office that are just intended to be clean and neat places to stay.

HOSTS: Naval Academy retiree, stockbroker, realtor. . . .

GUESTS COME FOR: A small town with winding rivers, rolling hills, shops, and tourist attractions.

BREAKFAST: All serve continental.

RESERVATIONS
Advance preferred.

RATES
Singles $25–$40. Doubles $50–$75.
Deposit required: First night's lodging or 25 percent of total.
Cancellation policy: Return of 50 percent of deposit with notice of three days before expected arrival date.

Utah

THE BED 'N BREAKFAST ASSOCIATION OF UTAH

BARBARA BAKER AND NADINE SMITH
P.O. BOX 16465
SALT LAKE CITY, UT 84116

PHONE: 801/532-7076
   Live Tuesday through Friday "most any time." Answering mach-
   ine at other times.
OPEN: Year round. (Some hosts are seasonal.)

ACCOMMODATIONS
B&Bs
Hosted private residences: 19. B&B inns: 14.
Almost all have air conditioning and private baths.
Plus
Some short-term (two to six weeks) housing.

OTHER SERVICES: Pickup at airport, bus, or train for a small fee.

   LOCATIONS   *Spread throughout the state in rural, suburban, and urban areas.*

HOSTS: A retired newspaper editor, the mayor of a small town,
business people, museum guide. . . .

GUESTS COME FOR: "The best skiing in the world!" Mormon Genealogical Library, Mormon Temple and Mormon Tabernacle Choir, national parks and recreation areas, annual Shakespearean Festival in Cedar City.

BREAKFAST: Most serve a full meal. "Good home-cooked meals often including home-grown produce. Gardens are big out here."

RESERVATIONS
Minimum stay of two days required for city locations.
Advance reservations preferred. If arrangements can be made, will accept last-minute reservations.
Groups: Can book groups of up to 20 in Salt Lake City only.

DIRECTORY: None available, but inquiries are answered with some sample listings. *Samples:*

> Fairview—Accommodations for eight in a converted old church. Crow's nest lookout at top. Children over 12 welcome.

> Cedar City—Accommodations for eight. Children over 12 only. Picnic area. Site of Shakespearean Festival in summer.

RATES
Singles $20–$30. Doubles $30–$45. A few are higher.
One-night surcharge: $5 in Salt Lake City.
Weekly and monthly rates available.
Deposit required: Cost of first night, or two nights for five days. Increases by one night's cost every five additional days.
Cancellation policy: No refund if cancellation received less than seven days from expected arrival date.

Some additional B&Bs in Utah are available through Mi Casa–Su Casa, page 27.
A few in Salt Lake City and Park City are represented by Bed & Breakfast—Rocky Mountains, page 76.

Vermont

B&B GUESTS COME FOR: Scenic beauty. Fall foliage. Hiking, fishing, cycling, canoeing, downhill and cross-country skiing. Maple sugaring. Granite quarries. Shelburne Museum. Concerts. Plays. Restaurants. Craft fairs. Antiquing. Lake Champlain.

AMERICAN BED & BREAKFAST IN NEW ENGLAND

P.O. BOX 983
ST. ALBANS, VT 05478

Although this service provides information about its listings by mail only, the directory (see below) includes telephone numbers of individual hosts.

ACCOMMODATIONS
B&Bs
Hosted private residences: 44.

LOCATIONS *Most private home B&Bs are throughout the state of Vermont.*
In Maine: One in Waldoboro.

In Massachusetts: Berlin, Groton, Littleton, Northampton, Sturbridge.
In New Hampshire: Lisbon.
In New York: Cortland and Dannemora.

SETTINGS: All are in quiet settings with rural surroundings. Some are on dairy farms. Some are high in the mountains. Some are in villages.

HOSTS: Farmers, meteorologist, high school principal, lawyer, physician. . . .

GUESTS COME FOR: A vacation. House hunting. Nearby schools and colleges.

BREAKFAST: Most offer a full breakfast that "varies from good New England cooking to high cuisine."

RESERVATIONS
Made directly with hosts by guests.
Advance reservations preferred and strongly recommended for foliage season. When possible, last-minute reservations accepted.

DIRECTORY: $3 plus a business-sized self-addressed stamped envelope. The list includes name of B&B, description of location, number of rooms, and direct telephone number.

RATES
Singles $20–$24. Doubles $25–$40.

Bob Precoda, a former Peace Corpsman, was one of the first to recognize that the time was right in New England for B&B as a people-to-people program. He established his initial list by knocking on doors and meeting potential hosts in rural Vermont. His initial style—of publishing a list that travelers use for their own direct bookings—has remained.

GREEN MOUNTAIN B&B
MARGERY SENECAL
STAGE ROAD
BENSON, VT 05731

PHONE: 802/537-2081
Live 11–1 daily. Answering machine at other times.
OPEN: Year round.

ACCOMMODATIONS
B&Bs
Hosted private residences: Five and growing.

LOCATIONS *Shoreham, Belmont, Middletown Springs, Brandon, Benson—for now. Eventually listings will be state-wide.*

HOSTS: Realtor, writer, teachers. . . .

BREAKFAST: Varies according to host.

RESERVATIONS
Advance reservations required; two weeks' notice preferred but will make reservations up to 48 hours before arrival time.

DIRECTORY: One is planned. Until the service grows, descriptions of the limited listings are sent without charge.

RATES
Singles $25–$30. Doubles $35–$45.
Some weekly or monthly rates available.
Deposit required is 20 percent of room rate plus state tax.

With the encouragement of a relative who has a reservation service in a neighboring state, Margery has initiated this home business that she can do while she is restoring a 1790 farmhouse. She offers a personalized service, matching hosts and guests according to needs.

VERMONT BED AND BREAKFAST

SUE AND DAVE EATON
BOX 139 BROWNS' TRACE
JERICHO, VT 05465

PHONE: 802/899-2354 or (Vermont only): 1-800-442-1404
   Calls taken live or on answering machine 7 a.m.-10 p.m.
OPEN: Year round except Christmas and Thanksgiving.

ACCOMMODATIONS
B&Bs
Hosted private residences: 28.   B&B inn: 1.
Guests book their own reservations directly.

LOCATIONS *Spread throughout the state in rural and urban areas and include: Brandon, Burlington, Calais, Essex Junction, Hinesburg, Huntington, Jeffersonville, Jericho, Middlebury, Newbury, Norwich, Putney, Reading, Richford, Richmond, South Strafford, Vergennes, Dorset, East Dorset, St. Johnsbury, Waterbury, Springfield. More to come.*

SETTINGS: New, old, and historic homes. A cozy log home with mountain views, some homes-away-from-home, some luxurious.

HOSTS: Social worker, IBM employees, business people, international entrepreneur, hotel manager, insurance manager, concert pianist, dance instructor, teacher, retired nurse, realtor, lawyer. . . .

BREAKFAST: Varies from help-yourself to an elaborate meal and could include eggs Benedict, egg/sausage/cheese souffle, French toast served with berries and maple syrup, omelets, egg/cheese frittata, homemade muffins and breads, or "Dutch baby," an oven pancake served with dark sweet cherries or blueberries and Vermont maple syrup.

RESERVATIONS
Made directly by guest with host. Sue will make some reservations in the fall under certain circumstances.
Advance reservations appreciated. Fall reservations should be made very early. When possible, last-minute reservations accepted. Groups: B&B in Vergennes can handle 12.

DIRECTORY: $3. Includes addresses and phone numbers and directions with descriptions. *Samples:*

Calais. The Fitch House at Kent's Corner. A charming home, circa 1860, on 200 acres in an historic district. Ten miles northeast of Montpelier with mountain views enhancing a peaceful and friendly atmosphere. Accommodations include three double rooms and one single wth two shared baths. $30 couple, $22 single. Tax included. [Directory includes name, address, telephone number, directions—and a sketch of the B&B.]

A Century Past. A charming historic house with a beautiful view, dates back to 1790. Located on Vt. Route 5 in the village of Newbury. Canoe on the unspoiled Connecticut River in summer and enjoy cross-country or downhill skiing in winter. Hunting and fishing also close by. Accommodations include three rooms; two with a double bed, one with twin beds. Shared bath. Cozy sitting room with fireplace. $29 double occupancy. $20 single.

RATES
Singles $20–$45. Doubles $29–$60.
One-night surcharge: Some hosts add $3 per room.
Some weekly and monthly rates available.
Deposit required: Amount varies with each host home.
Cancellation/refund policy varies with each host home.
All fees are paid directly to the host.

Throughout Vermont there are B&Bs represented by Pineapple Hospitality, page 156.
Along the southern border there are also B&Bs represented by Berkshire Bed and Breakfast, page 191, and Covered Bridge Bed & Breakfast, page 85.

Virginia

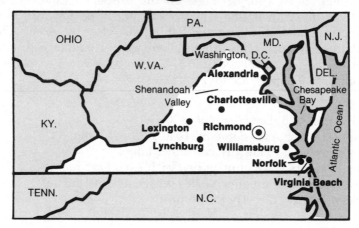

PRINCELY BED & BREAKFAST, LTD.

E. J. MANSMANN
819 PRINCE STREET
ALEXANDRIA, VA 22314

PHONE: 703/683-2159
  Live Monday–Friday, 10–6. Answering machine at other times.
OPEN: Year round.

ACCOMMODATIONS
B&Bs
Hosted private residences: 31.
All have air conditioning and private baths.
Plus
Some unhosted residences for overnight or weekend lodging. One hosted and two unhosted homes for short-term (two to three months) housing.

LOCATIONS *All are in Alexandria. Many are in historic Old Town.*

SETTINGS: *Sixty percent are historic homes built between 1750 and 1830.*

HOSTS: TV cameraman, caterer, political science professor, sculptor, lawyer. Many are world travelers.

GUESTS COME FOR: The nation's capital. Mount Vernon. Conferences. Seven Universities. Business reasons.

BREAKFAST: All serve "continental plus."

RESERVATIONS
One to two weeks in advance required.
Minimum stay of two nights required.
Phone arrangements preferred.
Groups: Maximum size is 30.

RATES
Singles $50–$60. Doubles $65–$75. A few higher.
One-night surcharge: $10.
Monthly rates available.
Deposit required: One night's lodging.
Cancellation policy: Full refund less a $10 service fee with a minimum of one week's notice.

BLUE RIDGE BED AND BREAKFAST
RITA Z. DUNCAN
ROCKS & RILLS, RTE. 2, BOX 259
BERRYVILLE, VA 22611

PHONE: 703/955-1246
   Live Monday–Friday, usually 10–9. Answering machine at other times.
OPEN: Year round.

ACCOMMODATIONS
B&Bs
Hosted private residences: 33.   B&B inns: 3.
Almost all have air conditioning and private baths.
Plus
One unhosted private residence for overnight or weekend lodging.
Short-term housing also available.

OTHER SERVICES: Pickup at airport, bus, and train stations. Theater tickets, passes to horse racing and historical sites.

LOCATIONS *Waterford, Lincoln, Millwood, Woodstock, Taylorstown, Winchester, Hamilton, Paris, Middletown, Purcerville, Berryville, Boyce, Linden, Hinton.*
In West Virginia: Summit Point.
In Maryland: Leedsville.
In Pennsylvania: Greencastle.

SETTINGS: On farms, in villages, on the mountains. Some are historic homes.

HOSTS: Retired school administrators, lawyers, writers, widows, young couples, engineers, artists, real estate broker; retired doctor, shop owners, full-time innkeepers, school teacher. Some hosts are bilingual or proficient in American Sign Language.

GUESTS COME FOR: Historic sites, antique shops, scenery, apple country, gardens, festivals, cuisine.

BREAKFAST: Varies from simple to an elaborate meal. Could include country cooking, quiche, omelets, fresh country eggs, homemade muffins, or pancakes.

RESERVATIONS
One to two weeks in advance preferred. If possible, will accept last-minute reservations.
Groups: Maximum size is 50.
Also available through travel agents.

DIRECTORY: No charge for two pages of descriptions. *Sample:*

Bluemont. Not far from the Appalachian Trail, this expanded log cabin home is located on the Blue Ridge less than two hours' drive from Washington, D.C. Originally built by Daniel Morgan of Revolutionary War fame. Guests can hike or canoe on the nearby Shenandoah River.

RATES
Singles $25–$75. Doubles $20–$85.
Some weekly and monthly rates available.
Deposit required is 20 percent.
Cancellation policy: Entire amount refunded if cancellation received two days before expected arrival date.

SHENANDOAH VALLEY BED & BREAKFAST RESERVATIONS

NANCY AND JOHN STEWART
P.O. BOX 305
BROADWAY, VA 22815

PHONE: 703/896-9702 or 896-2579
Live 4–11 p.m. weekdays, occasional weekends. Answering service at other times.
OPEN: Year round. Closed December 20–January 1.

ACCOMMODATIONS
B&Bs
Hosted private residences: 15.
Plus
Hosted short-term housing also available.

OTHER SERVICES OFFERED: Arrangements made for local events.

LOCATIONS *All are within a 10-mile radius of a center city or town, but near I-81, along a 50-mile distance. Communities include Middletown, Maurertown, Woodstock, Front Royal, Tenth Legion, Rawley Springs, Harrisonburg, Churchville, Staunton—all in Virginia.*

SETTINGS: Range includes historic, garden tour, and contemporary homes. All are in the Valley, between the Alleghenies and the Blue Ridge Mountains, an area rich in history and scenery.

HOSTS: Interior designer, antique dealer, architect, bookkeeper, educator, retirees, sheep farmer, nurse, Mennonite homemaker, real estate agent.

GUESTS COME FOR: Touring. Sightseeing. Scenery. Schools: James Madison University, Bridgewater College, Eastern Mennonite College, Massanutten Military Academy, Shenandoah Conservatory, Mary Baldwin.

BREAKFAST: Most serve a hearty continental.

RESERVATIONS
Minimum stay of two nights preferred.
Advance notice of at least a week preferred. If possible, last-minute reservations made—with credit card prepayment.

DIRECTORY (Not required for bookings): $1. Detailed descriptions.
Sample:

Churchville, near Staunton: Entlee Farm, a spacious, restored country home, provides a Currier and Ives setting on
Whiskey Creek. Located on the old coach road to Staunton
from Jenner's Gap, the house served in earlier times as an
inn for weary travelers. Its original log portion, built prior
to 1800, was expanded before the Civil War. The Churchville Cavalry served with the Valley Army and camped on
the hill behind the house, trading places periodically with
the Union Cavalry. Today horses and pasture surround the
house. In the 1930s the latest addition was added along
with the carriage house. Decorated with antiques from the
Victorian era . . . a player piano. . . . Den furnished in luxurious leather. . . . Hostess formerly worked in public relations and in government service; active in theater, gardening, entertaining, and music. . . . Host, a retired army colonel, teaches at a military school nearby; owns, breeds, and
trains harness horses also. . . . One guest room with double
brass bed. . . . Other with twin beds. . . . Guest bath shared
by the two rooms. . . . Crib, highchair, toys, fenced-in
yard. . . . Room to park RVs. Pets permitted. $35 single;
$40 double. $5 crib.

RATES
Singles $24–$40. Doubles $40–$75.
Some monthly rates available.
Credit cards accepted: MasterCard and VISA for deposit only or for
a guaranteed reservation.
Cancellation policy: With an advance three-day cancellation no-
tice, the deposit will be returned, less a $10 service fee per room.

Traditions

*John Stewart, a former Viennese and a retired James Madi-
son University professor, has become an expert on Shenandoah Valley folklore and can advise on almost any local
history topic in English, German, or French.*

*His wife, Nancy, remembers her childhood days in New
Market, Virginia, when she sold her mother's homemade
cottage cheese on Saturdays to Main Street residents. One
customer's home had a sign, "Eat and sleep with Mrs.
Driver." Respect for the doctor's wife caused town residents
to assume the best: Mrs. Driver took B&B guests! Nancy
feels that she and John—through their reservation service—
have revived a local tradition that was alive from the 1880s
to the 1940s.*

ROCKBRIDGE RESERVATIONS

ELIZABETH B. ANDERSON
SLEEPY HOLLOW, P.O. BOX 76
BROWNSBURG, VA 24415

PHONE: 703/348-5698
Live Monday–Friday 10–4. Answering machine at other times.
OPEN: Year round.

ACCOMMODATIONS
B&Bs
Hosted private residences: 12. B&B inns: 2.
Most have private baths.
A few are accessible to handicapped.
Plus
A few unhosted private rooms for overnight or up to about a week.

OTHER SERVICES: Theater tickets.

LOCATIONS *Most are in Lexington, Virginia, and in the surrounding Rockbridge county. A few are on the edges of adjacent counties. Some are within walking distance of downtown and some are rural sites, all within a half-hour drive to town.*

SETTINGS: "Some are more luxurious than others. One of the in-town inns is clean and attractive, but not elegant. Some houses are both elegant and historic, while others are well-loved farm homes."

HOSTS: "Several are retired. Some are young professors at the local colleges; they have traveled abroad and enjoyed B&B elsewhere."

GUESTS COME FOR: Sightseeing. Conferences. Business. Washington and Lee University, Virginia Military Institute, Southern Seminary Junior College—all with related museums. Blue Ridge Parkway. "Lexington is a small southern town in a very rural, mountainous area, with a special ambience of warmth and welcome. An undiscovered area for travelers."

BREAKFAST: All serve continental.

RESERVATIONS
Minimum stay of two days required.

Advance notice preferred. If arrangements can be made, will accept last-minute reservations.

Groups: Maximum size is 12. Advance notice required.

Also available through travel agents.

RATES

Singles $45. Doubles $45.

Deposit required is 25 percent of total charge, plus state and local taxes upon confirmation.

Cancellation policy: Entire deposit refunded if cancellation received at least two weeks in advance.

> *Think Ahead!*
>
> *"I wish travelers/callers would call with a better idea of what they want as to accommodations. I have to be sure to ask all the right questions to get the answers that make it easy for me to know my clients. That's hard work!"*

GUESTHOUSES, INC.

SALLY REGER

P.O. BOX 5737

CHARLOTTESVILLE, VA 22903

PHONE: 804/979-8327

Live Monday–Friday 12–5. Answering service at other times.

OPEN: Year round.

ACCOMMODATIONS

B&Bs

Hosted private residences: 100. B&B inns: 5.

Almost all have air conditioning and private baths.

Plus

Some unhosted private residences for overnight or weekend lodging. Short-term, hosted and unhosted housing available by the month. Some are converted mother-in-law apartments; others are cottages on the property.

LOCATIONS *Some are in the city of Charlottesville; several are very close to the University of Virginia. Many are in the surrounding rural areas, including Luray, with some splendid views of the Blue Ridge Mountains.*

SETTINGS: Range includes antebellum homes, modest local residences, and luxurious estates.

HOSTS: Realtors, businessmen, artist, physician, antique dealer, attorney, retired professor. . . .

GUESTS COME FOR: University of Virginia. Conferences. Business. Relocation. Garden Week tour. Monticello. Ash Lawn (home of James Monroe). Wineries. Nearby Shenandoah Valley and Blue Ridge Mountains.

BREAKFAST: Varies from help-yourself to an elaborate meal.

RESERVATIONS
Advance reservations preferred. If arrangements can be made, will accept last-minute reservations.

DIRECTORY (not required for reservations): $3. A 32-page booklet printed on glossy paper with a photo of each home and full information including individual rates. *Samples:*

> Maho-Nayama—Attention to detail is evidenced in the landscaping and furnishings of this beautiful Japanese-style home. Hand-split cedar shakes are laid in such a way as to give the impression of a thatched roof. The large master bedroom has a king-sized bed with custom furnishings. The master bath has a sunken tub. Occasionally, arrangements can be made for private rental of the home when three additional bedrooms make it most desirable for a family. A private tennis court is available. The house is located in a rural wooded area 67 miles northeast of town. It was on the 1974 Virginia Garden Tour and was featured in the May 1982 issue of *Commonwealth* Magazine.

> Chathill is a delightful country house, in a rural setting only a few minutes' drive from the Farmington Country Club, Boar's Head Inn, and the University of Virginia. During the summer months, visitors can enjoy the swimming pool and the informal gardens that surround it. Accommodations consist of a paneled sofa-bed/sitting room with a fireplace and a queen-sized bed and adjoining bath. The quarters offer the same restrained elegance and comfort shown throughout this charming dwelling, which is so reminiscent of an English country house built in the style of a Palladian villa.

RATES
$44–$72. A few higher for cottages and suites.
One-night surcharge: $4. Weekly and monthly rates available.
Deposit required is 25 percent of total charge.
Cancellation policy: For most reservations, full refund minus $15
service fee if thirty days' notice given. No refund for less than 72
hours' notice.

SOJOURNERS BED AND BREAKFAST
ANN AND CLYDE MCALISTER
3609 TANGELWOOD LANE
LYNCHBURG, VA 24503

PHONE: 804/384-1655
Live Monday–Saturday mornings until 10, evenings after 6 p.m.,
and on Sundays. Answering machine at other times.
OPEN: Year round.

ACCOMMODATIONS
B&Bs
Hosted private residences: 10.
Almost all have air conditioning and private baths.

LOCATIONS   *Most are within 10-mile radius of Lynchburg.
A few are rural. Local bus transportation is excellent.*

SETTINGS: Range includes several in historic area, a log cabin,
and a country estate.

HOSTS: Professional genealogists, retired military personnel, language professor, photographer, retired college administrator, furniture craftsman, caterer. . . .

GUESTS COME FOR: Appomattox State Park, site of Civil War
Confederate surrender; Booker T. Washington Plantation; Poplar
Forest, vacation home of Thomas Jefferson; historical and genea-
logical research; visits to residents of Westminster-Canterbury re-
tirement home. Schools—Lynchburg College, Randolph-Macon
Woman's College, Sweet Briar College, Virginia Episcopal School,
Liberty University. Blue Ridge Parkway, less than an hour's drive
away.

BREAKFAST: Varies from simple to elaborate. Homemade breads a specialty.

RESERVATIONS
Advance reservations preferred. If possible, last-minute accepted.

RATES
Singles $32–$40. Doubles $36–$50.
Discount for reservations that run more than three consecutive nights.
Deposit required: One night's lodging fee.
Cancellation policy: No refund if canceled less than seven days before expected arrival date. Deposit refunded, minus $5 service fee, if canceled more than a week in advance. Full refund if unable to book.

BED AND BREAKFAST OF TIDEWATER VIRGINIA

SUSAN HUBBARD AND ASHBY WILLCOX
P.O. BOX 3343
NORFOLK, VA 23514

PHONE: 804/627-1983
Monday–Friday 8 a.m.–10 p.m.
OPEN: Year round.

ACCOMMODATIONS
B&Bs
Hosted private residences: 33.   B&B inns: 2.
Almost all have air conditioning and private baths.
Some short-term (hosted and unhosted) housing available.
One first-floor apartment is accessible by ramp.

LOCATIONS   *Throughout Tidewater (coastal) Virginia in Norfolk, Portsmouth, Chesapeake, Virginia Beach, Hampton, Newport News, the Eastern Shore, and the Northern Neck of Virginia.*

SETTINGS: A wide assortment. Some historic.

HOSTS: Psychologist, several artists, decorators, housewives, veterinarian, teacher. . . .

GUESTS COME FOR: The Atlantic Ocean and the Chesapeake Bay, the world's largest naval base, Waterside, Norfolk's Festival Marketplace. Fishing, swimming, surfing, boating, harbor cruises. The Virginia Opera, the Chrysler Museum, Virginia Stage Company (Wells Theatre), the MacArthur Memorial, colonial and historical homes. Williamsburg, an hour's drive from here. And since 1983 Ashby and Susan have helped with housing for couples in the in-vitro fertilization clinic at Eastern Virginia Medical School.

BREAKFAST: Varies from help-yourself to an elaborate meal. One host fixes oyster fritters for breakfast; another has sausage and fried apples, or a casserole of ham, mushrooms, eggs, and cheese.

RESERVATIONS
Advance reservations preferred. If arrangements can be made, will accept last-minute reservations.

DIRECTORY: A free sampler is sent on request.

RATES
Singles $25–$40. Doubles $30–$75.
Deposit required is 20 percent of total charge.
Cancellation policy: Refund minus $10 service charge for cancellations received more than three days before arrival. No refund of deposit if cancellation is later.

BENSONHOUSE OF RICHMOND
LYN M. BENSON
P.O. BOX 15131
RICHMOND, VA 23227

PHONE: 804/648-7560
   Live 1–5, Monday–Friday. Answering service at other times.
OPEN: Year round.

ACCOMMODATIONS
B&Bs
Hosted private residences: 40.
Most have private baths.
Some have elevators and stairglides.
All summer guests are placed in air-conditioned homes.
Plus
Unhosted short-term (from three weeks to many months) housing

in private fully furnished cottages, apartments, and condominiums in quiet residential areas.

LOCATIONS *All are within a 15-mile radius of Richmond. Most are within historic districts, are located on bus lines and just 10 minutes from sites and attractions.*

SETTINGS: "Many, but not all, are rather luxurious."

HOSTS: Travel business owners, retirees, many attorneys, teachers, architects, dentists, small-business owners . . . .

GUESTS COME FOR: Relocation. Business. Weddings. Schools: University of Richmond, Medical College of Virginia, Virginia Commonwealth University. Museums. Historic sites. A base for touring: The mountains, beaches, and Washington, D.C., are two hours away. Williamsburg is an hour's drive.

BREAKFAST: Half-serve continental. Half-serve a full meal.

RESERVATIONS
One to three weeks in advance preferred. "No calls after 7 p.m. for 'same night' please." Also available through travel agents.

DIRECTORY: A sample listing of about 15 homes is sent on request. Please enclose a self-addressed stamped envelope.

RATES
Singles $28–$72. Doubles $36–$85. Very elegant or estate homes are higher.
Deposit required: 25 percent.
Credit cards accepted: American Express, MasterCard, VISA. Cancellation policy: If notice received at least five days before expected arrival date, refund minus $15 service charge made.

Thank you for steering us to our hosts. You chose wisely. From the glass of wine upon arrival, to the art gallery opening with our hosts, to the welcoming four-poster bed, to breakfast the next morning, we could not have been better cared for.

—Guest from Downington, Pennsylvania

THE TRAVEL TREE
JOANN PROPER, SHEILA ZUBKOFF
P.O. BOX 838
WILLIAMSBURG, VA 23187

PHONE: 804/253-1571
   Live Monday–Friday, 5–9 p.m.
OPEN: Year round.

ACCOMMODATIONS
B&Bs
Hosted private residences: About 12.
All have air conditioning. Most have private baths.

LOCATIONS   *In residential communities surrounding the historic area of Williamsburg.*

SETTINGS: Some cozy and comfortable and some luxurious.

HOSTS: Retired military, engineer, physician, chemist. . . .

GUESTS COME FOR: Colonial Williamsburg, Busch Gardens, The Old Country, Yorktown, Jamestown, conferences, College of William and Mary, house hunting, and business reasons.

BREAKFAST: All serve continental.

RESERVATIONS
Advance notice of three days required. More notice, up to a month, suggested for spring through fall, Thanksgiving, and Christmas.

DIRECTORY: Written inquiries are answered with a brochure that includes suggestions such as "Enjoy the comforts of home away from home in a spacious room complete with dining alcove and private entrance," or "Delight in the view from the bay window of a guest cottage with pullman kitchen."

RATES
Singles $28–$60. Doubles $35–$75.
Deposit required: $20.
Cancellation/refund policy: Full refund, minus $10 service charge, if cancellation received seven days before expected arrival date.

Washington

B&B ASSOCIATES

CLAIRE HASLEBACHER
ROUTE 2, BOX 126
CHENEY, WA 99004

PHONE: 509/299-3973
   Live 9–5 daily. Answering machine at other times.
OPEN: Year round.

ACCOMMODATIONS
B&Bs
Hosted private residences: Five.

LOCATIONS *All in central eastern part of Washington, in Spokane, Cheney, and Medical Lake.*

SETTINGS: In Spokane, a Victorian home built by a former mayor. In Cheney (11 miles east of Spokane), within walking distance of the university. Some are in the country.

GUESTS COME FOR: Eastern Washington University. Fairchild Air Force Base. Business.

BREAKFAST: Varies from continental to full according to host.

RESERVATIONS
Advance preferred.

RATES
Singles $20. Doubles $25–$45.
Deposit required: One night's lodging for advance bookings.

While Claire lived in Alexandria, Virginia, for four years, she was a B&B hostess. When she returned home to Cheney, she missed meeting travelers, so decided to start her own service, one that is quite new as this book goes to press.

TRAVELLERS' BED & BREAKFAST (SEATTLE)
JEAN KNIGHT
P.O. BOX 492
MERCER ISLAND, WA 98040

PHONE: 206/232-2345
Live Monday–Friday 8–8. Answering machine at other times.
OPEN: Year round.

ACCOMMODATIONS
B&Bs
Hosted private residences: 102.　B&B inns: 25.
Many have private baths.
Plus
Hosted and unhosted short-term (one month to one year) housing.

OTHER SERVICES:　Itineraries planned for Washington state plus Vancouver and Victoria, B.C. City tours of Seattle/Vancouver or Victoria arranged. Also sightseeing tours to Mt. St. Helens, Mt. Rainier, and San Juan Islands. Car rentals. Pickup at airport.
Bed & Breakfast in London (England) program: Rates $18–$31 for one person, $31–$50 for two.

LOCATIONS　*Throughout the state of Washington. Others are in northern Oregon and British Columbia. Downtown B&Bs are in Seattle, Washington; Portland, Oregon; and in Vancouver and Victoria, British Columbia.*

SETTINGS:　Range from luxurious to plain family homes. A houseboat and yachts are included.

HOSTS: Doctors, lawyer, teacher, artists, musician, nurse, retired servicemen, teachers, retired nurses, bank managers, realtors. . . .

GUESTS COME FOR: Spectacular northwest scenery, mountains, and lakes of Washington and British Columbia. Cruise the San Juan Islands. Skiing. Mt. St. Helens. Visit to Victoria, British Columbia. Fishing (salmon/trout). Hydroplane races. Mountain climbing (Mt. Rainier).

BREAKFAST: Menus vary. Tropical fruit salads. Eggs Benedict with asparagus. Dutch pancakes. Unusual egg casseroles.

RESERVATIONS
Advance reservations preferred but not necessary.
Groups: Maximum size is 25.
Also available through travel agents.

DIRECTORY (not required for reservations): $5. A small book with some maps and photographs. Describes over 80 listings. *Sample:*

> Mercer Island. Antiqua. The Pink Room: A very romantic room furnished in carefully chosen antiques. A French Provincial four-poster double bed has 75 yards of fabric in its custom-designed canopy; subtle colors used are dusky pinks and browns. The wallpaper matches. The walls have romantic painting, prints, and old English engravings. A large crystal chandelier hangs over an antique tea table. In the corner stands an antique pump organ. A door opens onto a patio and garden full of flowers in spring and summer . . . the Brown Rooms . . . The Blue Room. . . . This home is most interesting, with an intriguing art collection and extensive antique clock collection. The dining room is elegant. A continental breakfast is gracefully served while enjoying the view and listening to relaxing music. . . . A night to remember! Guests have use of a small sitting room with TV; also use of a refrigerator. Stairs. No smoking, please. The Pink Room: $45 double. The Brown Room: $45 double. The Blue Room: $40 single.

RATES
Singles $25–$60. Doubles $35–$70.
Some weekly and monthly rates available.
Deposit required.
Credit cards accepted: MasterCard and VISA.
Cancellation policy: $15 fee charged for notice of 72 hours or more. Less notice than that, one night's lodging is charged.

People Make a Difference

"We had a little time left upon arriving in Seattle before our trip home so we drove over to Mercer Island. We drove completely around the Island and could not believe how many lovely homes there are and also how many homes were for sale. We did not have time to check with a realtor but wondered what price range the homes sell for there. We are looking for a place to retire and have almost made up our minds after seeing your beautiful country.

"Thank you for your very efficient handling of our accommodations. I especially like the personal service I received. I don't think I will ever want to stay in a hotel or motel again. I love the bed and breakfast people. Maybe I will be calling you again, or better yet, maybe I will be your neighbor!"

—A guest from Burbank, California

PACIFIC BED & BREAKFAST AGENCY
IRMGARD CASTLEBERRY
701 N.W. 60TH
SEATTLE, WA 98107

PHONE: 206/784-0539
Live Monday–Friday 9–4. Answering machine at other times. TELEX 329473 ATTPBB 580.
OPEN: Year round.

ACCOMMODATIONS
B&Bs
Hosted private residences: 65.　B&B inns: 38.
Plus
Some unhosted private residences for overnight or weekend lodging. A few listings accessible to handicapped.

OTHER SERVICES:　Pickup at airport and bus for a fee.

LOCATIONS　*Most city locations are near bus lines and within a 10-mile radius of downtown Seattle. Many guesthouses and small inns listed are located throughout the state of Washington and in British Columbia.*

SETTINGS: Contemporary guesthouses, Victorians, private suites and apartments, country inns, cottages, vacation rentals.

HOSTS: German language professor (and gourmet cook), retired librarian, chef, real estate salesman, textile artist, high school principal, accounting professor, computer specialist, art professor, attorney. . . .

GUESTS COME FOR: Mountains, ocean, the Sound, lakes, alpine meadows, desert, the Columbia River. Skiing, hiking, birdwatching, fishing, lakes, boating. Historic districts, museums, art galleries, universities, opera, cultural offerings, shopping. . . .

BREAKFAST: Most are full. Could include: apple turnovers, caviar omelet, quiche, Norwegian specialties, fancy egg dishes, German waffles, blueberry pancakes, coddled eggs, salmon souffle. "Most of my hosts are fabulous cooks."

RESERVATIONS
At least one week in advance preferred. If arrangements can be made, will accept last-minute reservations.
Groups: Up to 20 or 30 can be booked.
Also available through travel agents.

DIRECTORY (not required for reservations): $3. Although inquiries are answered with some sample listings and information about the area's attractions, detailed descriptions of all homes are in the directory. *Samples:*

> #1 Grand old sycamore trees surround this stately spacious turn-of-the-century home, which is located in a peaceful close-in neighborhood, one block from a bus line. One of Seattle's finest city parks is its backyard. You are minutes away from our fine art museum and the conservatory and tennis courts. The guest rooms on the first floor are comfortable and feature private baths. Enjoy the elegant living room, furnished with heirloom antiques, and play the baby grand piano. Your breakfast will be served in the grand dining room on fine china and will probably include delicacies prepared by the hostess. Both host and hostess are gracious, outgoing, and love entertaining.

> #2 A true Victorian, built in 1890 across from a fine city park, offers you charm and elegance. Admire the stained-glass windows, the original woodwork, the fine period furniture, all painstakingly restored by the hostess. The loca-

tion of this home is superb, both for the tourist and business traveler. Guests enjoy the piano in the parlor but most of all, the legendary breakfasts offered here. A [writer from a] national magazine was an incognito guest here and later wrote his experience. "The skylight view from the shower will make your spirits soar."

RATES

Singles $25–$49. Doubles $30–$85.

One-night surcharge: $5.

Weekly and monthly rates available.

Deposit required: $20.

Credit cards accepted: MasterCard and VISA for entire fee.

Cancellation policy: Deposit refunded, less $10 service fee, if cancellations received by five days before arrival date.

Note: Some inns require prepayment of first night and will refund only with 72 hours' notice or if room can be rerented.

"Your brochure isn't just words but true facts, especially the friendly and inviting hosts. The company was delightful. You not only shared your rooms and breakfast but your lovely city of Seattle. I appreciate your tips on everything from riding the buses to sightseeing. Pacific B&B doesn't just talk about service, but provides it."

—A guest from Nebraska

Some perfect matches: The nurse looking for a job who was placed with an RN who could give tips. . . . The "looking for a house in the neighborhood" type who was placed with a real estate hostess. . . . The opera singer who needed a quiet place to practice for three weeks and ended up in a private apartment with a deaf hostess.

In many parts of Washington there are additional B&B hosts represented by Northwest Bed & Breakfast, page 264. Some have also been selected by Bed & Breakfast Oregon, page 266, and by Bed & Breakfast International, page 35.

West Virginia

Some West Virginia B&Bs are available through Blue Ridge Bed and Breakfast, page 325, and through services with nationwide listings, page 6.

Wisconsin

BED & BREAKFAST GUEST-HOMES
EILEEN WOOD
RT. 2
ALGOMA, WI 54201

PHONE: 414/743-9742
7 a.m.–9 p.m. "If no answer we are only out for a short time."
OPEN: Year round.

ACCOMMODATIONS
B&Bs
Hosted private residences: 23.
Plus
Some cottages, small homes, apartments available by the week.

LOCATIONS *Although many homes are along the 80-mile length of Door County, a peninsula that is considered the Cape Cod of the Midwest, Eileen has begun to expand to areas throughout the state of Wisconsin, including Milwaukee and Madison areas.*

SETTINGS: Small-town, urban, rural, and waterfront.

HOSTS: Teachers, building contractor, writer, retired business executive, lawyer, investment consultant, milk truck (dairy farm pickup) driver, charter fishing captain, engineer. . . .

GUESTS COME FOR: A vacation. The Door County area is known for its scenery, swimming, fishing, five state parks, dairy farming, and shipbuilding, and as a major cherry- and apple-producing territory.

BREAKFAST: Most full and may include quiche, highbush cranberry jelly, kringle, cheese/sausage strata, eggs Benedict.

RESERVATIONS
Two to three weeks in advance preferred. If arrangements can be made, will accept last-minute reservations. July, August, and October are busiest months.

DIRECTORY (not required for reservations): $5, refundable with two-night stays. Includes all B&Bs listed with Eileen as well as almost every inn in the state. *Sample:*

> Maplewood. Six miles south of Sturgeon Bay. Two guest rooms, each with double bed. Room for child on hideaway in separate room. Shared bath. Full breakfast. Home is adjacent to Annaphee State Trail (hiking, biking, snowmobiling, skiing). There are four state parks within 20 miles. Easy drive to Lake Michigan, Green Bay swimming, boating, fishing waters. Hosts with grown family enjoy sharing their colonial home. Double $35. Nonsmokers please.

RATES
Singles $20–$40. Doubles $30–$45.
Some cottages, small homes, apartments from $280/week or $50/day for four.
Some family rates available.
Weekly and monthly rates available.
Deposit required is 25 percent of total charge.
Cancellation policy: Full refund less $7 with a minimum of 72 hours' notice.

> *"Hosts made us feel warm, wanted, and well cared for. We would have loved to stay longer. They were great fans of their area and shared their enthusiasm with us."*
> *—Guests from Michigan*

BED & BREAKFAST OF MILWAUKEE
CAROLYN HATZIS
3017 N. DOWNER AVENUE
MILWAUKEE, WI 53211

PHONE: 414/342-5030
 Live 8 a.m.–10 p.m. daily.
OPEN: Year round.

ACCOMMODATIONS
B&Bs
Hosted private residences: 10.
All have private baths and one has chair lift on stairs.
Plus
Some short-term (one to two months) housing available.

LOCATIONS *Most are within three or four miles of center city and within walking distance of Lake Michigan. All are on bus routes.*

SETTINGS: Historic homes. English Tudor homes. One is private apartment in restored downtown area.

HOSTS: Social workers, lawyer, professor, business persons, artist. . . .

GUESTS COME FOR: A vacation. Symphony, music, ballet. Sports, boating, swimming. Ethnic diversity. Business reasons. University of Wisconsin–Milwaukee.

BREAKFAST: All continental. Special diets and requests honored.

RESERVATIONS
Advance reservations preferred. If arrangements can be made, will accept last-minute reservations.

RATES
Guest membership fee is $35.
Singles $30–$40. Doubles $30–$75.
Weekly and monthly rates available.
Deposit required: $10 for each day.
Cancellation policy: Refund of deposit with one week's notice.

Wyoming

*B&B hosts along Route 80 are represented by Bed & Breakfast—
Rocky Mountains, pages 76–77.*
*Some Wyoming B&Bs are also available through Northwest Bed &
Breakfast, page 264.*

B&Bs in Canada

◇ ◇ ◇

Eastern Canada

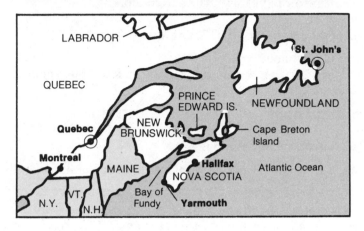

NOVA SCOTIA
NEW BRUNSWICK
NEWFOUNDLAND AND LABRADOR
PRINCE EDWARD ISLAND
QUEBEC

NOVA SCOTIA

Nova Scotia Tourist Bureau
129 COMMERCIAL STREET
PORTLAND, ME 04101

PHONE: 1-800-341-6096 (In Maine: 1-800-492-0643)

The bureau distributes printed material from three groups that
have screened B&Bs:

CAPE BRETON BED & BREAKFAST

RAY PETERS
C/O CAPE BRETON DEVELOPMENT CORPORATION
P.O. BOX 1750
SYDNEY, NOVA SCOTIA B1P 6T7, CANADA

PHONE: 902/564-3600
OPEN: May–October for most available B&Bs, but some operate year round.

ACCOMMODATIONS
B&Bs
Hosted private residences: 63.

OTHER SERVICES: Some B&Bs offer the option of lunch or dinner.

LOCATIONS   *In all areas—urban and rural—of Cape Breton, but not necessarily in every community. Four in the south, 9 on the western shores, 30 in the (historic) east, 13 in Central Lakes region, 7 in northern Highlands.*

BREAKFAST: Full. Some even serve trout.

RESERVATIONS
Booked directly with host by guest.

DIRECTORY: Free brochure includes name, address, location, number of guest rooms, and phone of each B&B. Organized according to areas listed under "Locations" above.

RATES
Singles $20. Doubles $24.

In 1974 this program started with five B&Bs in the northern section where there were no accommodations for visitors. The Cape Breton Development Corporation still encourages the development of B&Bs along the lines of its rules, regulations, and standards. (The Corporation offers financial assistance on a loan and grant basis to hosts.) Each year about half a dozen more are added to the brochure. The Corporation is also the source for the signs with logo in front of each home, and provides individual soaps and matches with the Cape Breton B&B logo. Travelers who fill out comment slips often mention the clean, comfortable accommodations and add personal notes:

"... *Very educational ... a way to help people to get to know each other. ...*" *From Alberta.*

"*After spending what seemed to me an exorbitant amount of money at a motel the night before, this B&B was like coming home. Mrs. Allia was so helpful that it made planning the rest of the trip so much easier. ...*" *From Ontario.*

FARM & COUNTRY VACATION ASSOCIATION
C/O JANE REID STEVENS
NEWPORT STATION, HANTS COUNTY
NOVA SCOTIA, BON 2BO, CANADA

PHONE: 902/798-5864
OPEN: Most B&Bs are open June–October, but others are open year round.

ACCOMMODATIONS
B&Bs
Hosted private residences: 41.
Many offer other meals. Several include evening snacks with rates.

LOCATIONS   *All over Cape Breton.*

BREAKFAST: Most offer a full breakfast.

RESERVATIONS
Booked directly with host by guest.

DIRECTORY: *Nova Scotia Farm & Country Vacations & B&B Homes* is a free pamphlet with keyed map and introductory section about each area; it includes names, addresses, phone numbers, and directions for each listing. *Sample:*

#24 Gateway Farm. Gateway to the Maritimes. Our farm is situated 5 miles from Yarmouth town, about five minutes' drive to ferries, 8 miles to airport, and 60 miles to Digby, where you can take the C.N. marine ferry to New Brunswick. We have a very large dairy farm, about 150 head of cattle of all ages; baby calves born daily. We invite you to experience how a real farmer spends his day by visiting with us. Also the river with good fishing, 1 mile from ocean. Lots of room for walking, hiking, or a picnic. Our home is over 100 years old, with three guest rooms and one-half bath on the second floor, full bath on first floor. Crib and folding cot available on request and children welcome. Open May 1 to November 1. Rates: Bed & Breakfast $15 per adult, $8 per child under 12 yrs., $25 per couple. Meals on request. Reservations please.

RATES
Singles $15–$25. Doubles $20–$30.
A few have weekly rates.

HALIFAX-METRO BED AND BREAKFAST
LORNE PERRY
P.O. BOX 1613, STATION M
HALIFAX, NOVA SCOTIA B3J 2Y3, CANADA

PHONE: 902/434-7283
  Available with answering machine 24 hours a day.
OPEN: Year round.

ACCOMMODATIONS
B&Bs
Hosted private residences: 25.
"There are few private baths, but facilities are ample.
Most of our homes have two or more baths and no more than two guest rooms."

LOCATIONS *Halifax and Dartmouth.*

SETTINGS: From quite good to "out of this world."

HOSTS: Museum guide, social worker, businessman, graphic artist, musicians, housewife, teachers. . . .

GUESTS COME FOR: Boat tours, sailing, beaches, scenery, history, medical and business reasons.

BREAKFAST: Most serve a full meal.

RESERVATIONS
If arrangements can be made, will accept last-minute reservations.

RATES
Singles $25. Doubles $35.
Deposit required: At least first night's lodging.
Cancellation policy: Deposit refunded, less $15 processing fee, if notice received 48 hours before reservation date.

> *"Our hosts and hostesses really care. They are proud of their province and sincerely like people. You will find them helpful and informative. . . . It's not a business transaction. It's more like a friendly relationship."*

SOUTH SHORE BED & BREAKFAST ASSOCIATION

MARGARET CAMPBELL
P.O. BOX 82
BRIDGEWATER, NOVA SCOTIA B4V 2W6, CANADA

PHONE: 902/543-5391
OPEN: Year round. (Some B&Bs are seasonal.)

ACCOMMODATIONS
B&Bs
Hosted private residences: 26.

LOCATIONS *All on the south shore between Yarmouth and Halifax, Nova Scotia.*

SETTINGS: All in picturesque areas. Most are on rivers, the ocean, or lakes. Most are restored historic homes.

GUESTS COME FOR: A vacation. The scenery. Sightseeing. The culture and heritage of the region. Sportfishing. Photography.

BREAKFAST: All serve a full meal.

RESERVATIONS
Booked directly with host by guest.
Last-minute reservations are accepted, when possible.

DIRECTORY: The free brochure with keyed map includes descriptions, addresses, and telephone numbers. *Sample:*

> A recently restored home built in 1841 is located on the lighthouse route, two miles from the Barrington Tourist Bureau, one mile to Sand Hill's Provincial Beach and Pic-

nic Park. Enjoy the sun, sand, and sea. Picnic lunches and additional meals on request. Tent sites available. Open all year. $25 single, $32 double. Off season: $15, $25.

RATES
Singles $20–$25. Doubles $30–$35.

◇ ◇ ◇

NEW BRUNSWICK

NEW BRUNSWICK DEPARTMENT OF TOURISM
P.O. BOX 12345
FREDERICTON, NEW BRUNSWICK E3B 5C3, CANADA

PHONE: Toll-free in all of North America: 1-800-561-0123
FROM NEW BRUNSWICK: 1-800-442-4442

ACCOMMODATIONS
B&Bs
Hosted private residences: About 30.   B&B inns: 3.
Many offer the option of a full farm vacation.
Because of traveler demand, the Department is encouraging more residents to participate as hosts in their homes. Inquire about current arrangements.

LOCATIONS   *In 13 communities throughout New Brunswick.*

SETTINGS: On farms, in small towns, and in or near cities.

BREAKFAST: Usually features homemade food that could include freshly made muffins or bread and jam. Recipes often shared.

RESERVATIONS
Booked directly with host by guest.

DIRECTORY: Names, addresses, telephone numbers, and rates are included in the annual Accommodations Book (which includes farms, hotels, motels, country inns, and B&Bs) that is sent without charge. Individual B&B inn brochures sent on request. All accommodations suggested by this office have been inspected by the tourism department.

RATES
Singles $20. Doubles $24.
One thatched-roof five-room B&B across the street from a major hotel in St. Andrews: $45 single, $55 double.

◇ ◇ ◇

NEWFOUNDLAND AND LABRADOR

GOVERNMENT OF NEWFOUNDLAND AND LABRADOR
DEPARTMENT OF DEVELOPMENT AND TOURISM
P.O. BOX 2016
ST. JOHN'S, NEWFOUNDLAND A1C 5R8, CANADA

PHONE: 1-800-563-NFLD (Continental U.S. and most of Canada)
112-800-56-NFLD (From British Columbia)
709/737-2830 (Newfoundland and Labrador)
TELEX: 0164949
OPEN: Year round. "The West Coast has some brilliant maples in September." Some B&Bs are open summer only.

ACCOMMODATIONS
B&Bs
Hosted private residences: 30. This number is likely to increase because the government is encouraging more local families to welcome paying guests in their homes, "particularly in the interesting little coastal communities off the beaten track, in an environment which reflects the traditional character and lifestyle of the Province."

LOCATIONS   *In all areas—in the villages, in town, in rural parts, and by the water.*

GUESTS COME FOR: Festivals. Scenery. The people. "You know, we are classified as the friendliest people in North America. There are large stretches of wide open spaces. Even if you should get the four seasons in one day up here, the environment is so free, you don't mind it."

BREAKFAST: Varies according to host.

RESERVATIONS
Booked directly with hosts by guests.
Last-minute calls accepted. Wherever you enter Newfoundland, there is a tourist office from which you can make reservations, but it is a good idea to have advance arrangements.

DIRECTORY: B&Bs were called Hospitality Homes until four years ago. They are all listed with names, addresses, phone numbers, and rates in the *Newfoundland and Labrador Travel Guide* that is issued annually without charge in April. (The guide is comprehensive and includes all available accommodations, tours, sites, and events.)

RATES
$22–$35.

> *Hosts say: "Something happens to our guests. They join right in and for a short time become part of our family."*

◇ ◇ ◇

PRINCE EDWARD ISLAND

VISITOR SERVICES OF PRINCE EDWARD ISLAND
P.O. BOX 940
CHARLOTTETOWN, P.E.I. C1A 7M5, CANADA

PHONE: 902/892-2457.
  Toll free, mid-May–mid-September, from Nova Scotia and New Brunswick only: 1-800-565-7421.
OPEN: Generally May–October. Most B&Bs open in June. A few are open year round. Perhaps by the time you read this, winter tourist packages that include cross-country skiing may be offered; inquire about the current arrangements.

ACCOMMODATIONS
B&Bs
Hosted private residences: 68.
Most have two guest rooms. Some have just one; others have up to four.

OTHER SERVICES: With advance arrangements, some serve dinner to guests. Some deep-sea fishing or clam-digging arrangements.

LOCATIONS   *All over Prince Edward Island.*

SETTINGS: Some in old farmhouses, by the water, in town; from bungalows to "standard Cape Cod homes."

HOSTS: Many retired farmers, some professionals, teachers, government employees, hotel staffers. . . .

GUESTS COME FOR: A vacation. A honeymoon. For business.

BREAKFAST: Usually option of continental or full meal offered.

RESERVATIONS

Advance (at least a month) reservations strongly recommended for July through first two weeks of September.

Book your own directly; or toll-free calling from the maritimes allows you to call in your last-minute request to Visitor Services; you are asked to return the call in a few days to see what they have been able to book for you.

DIRECTORY: Although the accommodations guide published and distributed by Visitor Services includes everything available—tourist homes, places with and without breakfast, hotels, motels, cottages, farm vacations—if you request a free copy of the booklet called *The Bed and Breakfast and Country Inns Association of Prince Edward Island* you will be aware of the B&Bs that have organized as an association and set standards to help the traveler who is looking for a "real B&B" without a public dining room. This new group works closely with the Visitor Services office. Their directory includes, in addition to the name, address, phone number, and rates of each location, a descriptive paragraph written by the hosts about their own B&B. *Sample:*

> Alberton: Welcome to a holiday of rural family living. Our farm home is on the Dock Road, between Elmsdale and Alberton on Rte. 150, off Rte. 2. We milk a herd of 50 dairy cows, and our daughter will be pleased to show you the calves, bantam hens, and ducks. She will also give children rides on our pony. There is safe swimming in the Mill River or at sandy ocean beaches, and a golf course, all about three km from us. We have three guest rooms, one with one double bed, and two with two double beds. Bath and shower shared by guests. Open June 1 to October 31. Rates: $15 per person, $5 add'l adult, $3/child 12 years and under. Breakfast $3/adult, full breakfast, $1.50 light breakfast.

RATES
Singles $16–$18. Doubles $16–$35.
Breakfast, as an option, is usually extra; rate depends on place and choice of light or full meal.
Some weekly rates are offered.
Deposit preferred for peak season.

> *Until three years ago, Prince Edward Island B&Bs were generally called tourist homes. Whatever the name, residents are quite used to the system and they observe that "guests find it delightful—and are requesting it more and more."*

◊ ◊ ◊

QUEBEC

GÎTE QUÉBEC
THÉRÈSE TELLIER
3729, AVE. LECORBUSIER
STE-FOY, QUEBEC G1W 4R8, CANADA

PHONE: 418/651-1860
  Always live daily, 7 a.m.–midnight.
OPEN: Year round.

ACCOMMODATIONS
B&Bs
Hosted private residences: 40. Some are seasonal.
Many have pools.
Many accommodate families and can provide cribs.

OTHER SERVICES: Many tips on hidden discoveries, including special restaurants. Advance reservations made for you.

> LOCATIONS *Most are within a 10-mile radius of the center of Quebec, "the oldest town in North America." Almost all are near public transportation. One is a renovated historical home near Île d'Orléans in the St. Lawrence, about 15 miles from Old City. "Everyone who comes to Quebec thinks they want to be in Old Quebec next to the Chateau Frontenac. That area is no longer residential and has government offices, hotels, restaurants, cafes, yes, but no homes! Quebec is a big city, but many of my B&Bs are beautiful places that*

*are about 10 minutes by car, some are 15 minutes' walking,
to Old City."*

SETTINGS: City homes, apartments, historic homes, all in lovely
residential areas of greater Quebec.

HOSTS: Lawyer, nurses, artist, many teachers, retirees.... All
speak English and French. Many speak a third language, perhaps
Italian or Spanish (Thérèse Tellier personally visits each host at
least twice and sometimes up to four times a year.)

BREAKFAST: All serve a full meal.

RESERVATIONS
Minimum stay of two nights required.
Advance reservations preferred. If arrangements can be made, will
accept last-minute reservations.
Groups: Maximum size is 20.
Also available through travel agents.

RATES
Singles $30. Doubles $50.
Deposit required: $15 (money order or certified check only please)
together with a self-addressed stamped envelope.
Cancellation policy: If notice is received at least two weeks before
expected arrival date, full deposit is returned.

Individual Attention

*"We try to locate our customers in the area of their prefer-
ence. We try to match people of the same age, taste, profession. We also provide them before their arrival with road
map, city map, documentation with points of interest. We
inquire about their arrival time to make sure that they are
expected and well received. We call during their stay to inquire if they are satisfied with their accommodation. Many
of our guests have heard about our organization through
friends and relatives whom we have placed."*

MONTREAL B&B GUESTS COME FOR: Vacations. Conferences.
Business. The city with Mount Royal in the center. The city made
an island by the St. Lawrence River. The harbor area. Botanical
Gardens. The Olympic Stadium. Sports Centers. Place des Arts
(cultural center). The subway and underground city of shopping.
McGill University. Visits to the Laurentian Mountains or Eastern
Townships, 60 miles away.

MONTREALERS AT HOME—YOUR DOWNTOWN BED AND BREAKFAST

BOB FINKELSTEIN
3458 LAVAL AVE. (AT SHERBROOKE STREET)
MONTREAL, QUEBEC H2X 3C8, CANADA

PHONE: 514/289-9749
  Live June, July, August, and September, daily 8:30 a.m.–9 p.m.
  All other months: 8:30–6 daily.
OPEN: Year round.

ACCOMMODATIONS
B&Bs
Hosted private residences: 57.
Plus
Some unhosted private residences for overnight or weekend lodging.
Short-term housing, hosted and unhosted, available for up to three
months.

OTHER SERVICES: Some hosts pick up at airport, bus, and train.
Some offer guided tours, baby-sitting, guest entrance to health or
golf clubs. . . .

  LOCATIONS   *All are in downtown and the center of Montreal.*

HOSTS: Teacher, engineer, fashion model, urban planner, free-
lancer, editor, translator, playwright, homemaker, blue-ribbon
chef, nurse, salespeople. . . . "Our hosts have a yearly reunion and
we exchange our impressions of the B&Bs we ourselves have
stayed in."

BREAKFAST: All full. Most hosts offer a complimentary morning
paper with breakfast.

RESERVATIONS
Advance reservations appreciated. If arrangements can be made,
will accept last-minute reservations.
Groups: Maximum size: 40.
Also available through travel agents.

DIRECTORY: None available, but a one-page sample list is sent
without charge. *Samples:*

Near Westmount Park: Richard, an art gallery administrator, and Francine spoil their guests with Quebecois hospitality. As a city councilor, Richard was instrumental in the preservation of the Latin Quarter. Your hosts would love to suggest one of Montreal's sensational restaurants, and have personal knowledge of the antique district. They offer a double with private bath and a single in a warm and inviting home.

Quebec City Landmark: Yesterday's charm with today's conveniences. This listed landmark home, built in 1671, faces the beautiful St. Lawrence River. Your hostess, a blue-ribbon chef, offers guests a memorable breakfast featuring "Quiche Floriane." For an unforgettable stay, you are invited to experience the warmth and hospitality of a typical Quebecois home. Two enchanting doubles.

RATES
Singles $25–$30. Doubles $35–$45. A few higher.
One-night surcharge: $5.
Weekly and monthly rates available.
Deposit: $15 per night requested.
Cancellation policy: $15 service charge made on all cancellations.

"Always Leave a Number Where You Can Be Reached"
One evening a guest was notified that he had won the lottery for more than a million dollars. The guest and host family celebrated until dawn. (Since then, the guest has been back.)

MONTREAL BED & BREAKFAST
MARIAN KAHN
5020 ST. KEVIN, SUITE 8
MONTREAL, QUEBEC H3W 1P4, CANADA

PHONE: 514/738-9410 or 738-3859.
    Live 8:30 a.m.–7 p.m. daily. Answering machine at other times.
OPEN: Year round.

ACCOMMODATIONS
B&Bs
Hosted private residences: At least 40.

Plus
Short-term unhosted unhousing.

OTHER SERVICES: Car rentals, discounts on sightseeing and walking tours in the city.

LOCATIONS *All are near excellent public transportation. Most are within 20 minutes' traveling time (with public transportation; less by car) of downtown Montreal. Others are country B&Bs near skiing and year-round recreation spots.*

SETTINGS: Range from modest walk-up apartments to eleven-room Tudor-style luxury homes.

HOSTS: Librarian, travel agent, real estate agent, fashion designer, hospital employees, boutique owners, musician, teachers. . . .

BREAKFAST: Full breakfast offered at all homes.

RESERVATIONS
Advance reservations preferred. If possible, last-minute reservations made.
Groups: Maximum size is 40.
Also available through travel agents.

DIRECTORY: None available, but free brochure about service includes a few descriptions. *Samples:*

Off St. Louis Square: This unusual renovated row house with interior spiral staircase belongs to a writer and former model. One street from St. Denis Street, Montreal's Latin Quarter. One double, with private bathroom.

Snowdon: Lillian's large home with three rooms for guests (two doubles, one single) is filled with fine objects and a wonderful collection of Canadian art. Formerly a travel agent, she now lets the world come to her.

RATES
Singles $25–$50. Doubles $35–$70.
One-night surcharge: $5.
Weekly and monthly rates available.
Deposit required: $25 per room for stay of three nights or less, $50 per room if more than three nights.

Cancellation policy: If cancellation received by seven days before expected arrival date, full refund made.

Hosts Really Do Enjoy Their Role

Montreal Bed & Breakfast started in 1980. Eighty percent of the hosts who started with Marian Kahn are still welcoming visitors to the city.

Allow extra time for round trip mail to and from Canada.

Ontario

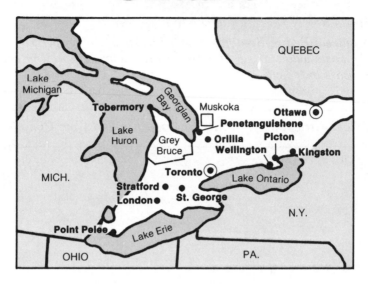

TORONTO

B&B GUESTS COME FOR: A multicultural city that is particularly clean and has an extraordinary public transit system. Four
thousand restaurants. A vacation. Conferences and business. Festivals. Theater. University of Toronto.

ALL SEASONS BED AND BREAKFAST
SHIRLEY DOOBAY
383 MISSISSAUGA VALLEY BOULEVARD
MISSISSAUGA, ONTARIO L5A 1Y9, CANADA

PHONE: 416/276-4572
  Anytime. ("People really are reasonable.")
OPEN: Year round.

ACCOMMODATIONS
B&Bs
Hosted private residences: 20.
Many are air conditioned and have private baths.

LOCATIONS *Most are in the city of Toronto and near public transportation. Others are in Mississauga and neighboring areas. A few are rural. Mississauga is a half-hour drive from the core area of Toronto. 1½ hours' drive from Niagara Falls.*

SETTINGS: Most are in residential neighborhoods. Some are Victorian homes in the central area of town. Most are single-family homes. A few are apartments and a couple are penthouses.

HOSTS: Realtors, business people, seamstress, travel consultant, social worker . . . people who host primarily because they enjoy the cultural exchange.

BREAKFAST: Varies according to host. "Most serve a delicious hot cooked meal."

RESERVATIONS
Advance reservations preferred. If arrangements can be made, will accept last-minute reservations.

RATES
Singles $30–$35. Doubles $40–$45.
Deposit required.
Cancellation policy: If received less than seven days before expected arrival date, deposit is forfeited.

Shirley Doobay has been involved in an international student exchange for many years; she has been a host for several students too. A couple of years ago, she decided to expand those experiences and to establish this network of local hosts.

THE DOWNTOWN TORONTO ASSOCIATION OF BED AND BREAKFAST GUEST HOUSES
SUSAN OPPENHEIM
P.O. BOX 190, STATION B
TORONTO, ONTARIO M5T 2SWI, CANADA

PHONE: 416/598-4562 or 416/977-6841
Live daily at least 9:30–10:30 a.m. Answering machine at other times.
OPEN: Year round.

ACCOMMODATIONS
B&Bs
Hosted private residences: Eight.
Also one yacht with two double and one king-sized cabin.
Baths are for guests only. (Never more than three to a bath.)
Parking (for average-sized cars) provided.
All have more than one room, "guest house atmosphere."
Smoking permitted outside in the gardens.
Sorry, no pets allowed.

OTHER SERVICES: "The house is yours." Special diets catered to.
Help-yourself tea at night.

LOCATIONS *All within half an hour of the center of the city
by public transportation. All are on 24-hour transportation
lines.*

SETTINGS: Downtown restored Victorian homes in ethnic neighborhoods within walking distance of other ethnic neighborhoods.
One is a coach house. And then there's the yacht.

HOSTS: Musicians, professors, yachtsman, art instructor, yoga instructor, massage therapist. . . .

GUESTS COME FOR: Business. Festivals. Theater. Multicultural
city. Restaurants. University of Toronto.

BREAKFAST: All gourmet. "Breakfasts reflect our creativity."
Plentiful. Often served on platters. Some menus feature chicken
and fresh corn quiche, frittatas or souffles, potato pancakes, bagels
and homemade muffins, freshly ground coffee. Homemade jams
and scones.

RESERVATIONS
Minimum stay requirement of two nights; three on long weekends.
Advance reservations preferred. If arrangements can be made, will
accept last-minute reservations.

DIRECTORY: None available, but the free brochure includes a few
descriptions. *Sample:*

> A six-bedroom semidetached Victorian brick home in
> downtown Toronto. There are three double rooms with two
> three-piece washrooms strictly for guests. The hostess is a
> torch singer/lyricist with four pianos (two of which are in

the 600-square-foot living room) and extensive record collection ranging from Chopin to Richie Havens to Ella Fitzgerald. The B&B operation is into its fifth year with international guests who offer marvelous stimulation for resident children, Aura, 12, and Eden, 8. The kitchen has been used as a set in television and films. Cooking is a special item here and the house is a three-minute walk from Kensington Market (an open-air collection of every nationality in Toronto). The menu ranges from mango oatmeal, glazed maple syrup pears to fresh salmon and dill havarti omelets and spicy freshly smoked tuna quiches. Rolls and croissants are supplied by natural foods bakery. Fresh muffins made on premises. Fruits such as melons, kiwi, papayas featured in season. Breakfasts can also be arranged for nonguests. Please inquire as to seating availability and pricing ($5–$8 C).

RATES
Singles $35. Doubles $40–$48.
Some weekly rates available in off season.
Deposit required: Half of full fee in form of personal check.
Cancellation policy: Deposit refundable only if room can be rebooked.

Small in a Big City
Susan has seen many times more the number of homes than those that she represents. She selects people who give the feeling of "staying with Aunt Martha." They are all hosts who have restored their homes, appreciate the opportunity to share a cosmopolitan, clean, safe city, and contribute in some way to spreading the word about what "this B&B team" offers.

METROPOLITAN BED & BREAKFAST OF TORONTO
ELINOR BOLTON
309 ST. GEORGE STREET
TORONTO, ONTARIO M5R 2R2, CANADA

PHONE: 416/964-2566 or 928-2833
Usually live 9 a.m.–10 p.m. daily. Answering service at other times.
OPEN: Year round.

ACCOMMODATIONS
B&Bs
Hosted private residences: 50.

LOCATIONS   *All in Toronto, convenient to the public transit system.*

SETTING: All are comfortable homes-away-from-home. A few are historic. Some are luxurious.

HOSTS: Music conductor, artists, executives, chefs, airline stewardess, real estate agents, accountants, lawyers, film technician, teachers, architect, nurses, retirees, appraisor. . . .

BREAKFAST: Varies from simple to elaborate according to host. "Some of our breakfasts are famous."

RESERVATIONS
Booked directly with host by guest or through Metropolitan Bed & Breakfast office.
Advance reservations preferred and strongly recommended for holidays and July and August. Last-minute reservations accepted when possible.
Also available through some travel agents.

DIRECTORY: (necessary if you want to book directly with the host): $2. An informative booklet that includes a map of the city. Telephone number, but not address, is part of each listing. *Sample:*

Pine Villa. Area: Danforth/Greenwood. Accommodations: Two doubles at $40 (double beds)/one double at $45 (twin beds); one single at $25 (single bed). The hostess of this sparkling new townhouse has two years at the College of Cooking and super breakfasts are her specialty. Chicken crepes are only one of the fine dishes she serves. The home is air conditioned with plenty of parking. It is very prettily decorated. It's only two minutes to a free pool in a park nearby. Dinners and car service can be arranged. Close to the subway and streetcars, it is very easy to get downtown from this home. It's a 10-minute drive to the Science Center, and the Beaches area is just a 10-minute drive in the other direction. The Eaton Centre is also easy to reach. French is spoken fluently. Close to: All downtown attractions.

RATES
Singles: $27–$48. Doubles: $34–$60. Many have children's rates.
Weekly rates at some in the off season only.
Deposit required: One night's lodging fee.
Cancellation policy: Varies, but generally a full refund is made if
notice received two weeks before expected arrival date. Inquire
when you book.

TORONTO BED AND BREAKFAST
RANDY LEE
P.O. BOX 74, STN. M
TORONTO, ONTARIO M6S 4T2, CANADA

PHONE: 416/233-3887
   Live evenings and weekends. Answering machine at other times.
OPEN: Year round.

ACCOMMODATIONS
B&Bs
Hosted private residences: 30.
Some offer short-term hosted housing for three to four months.

OTHER SERVICES: Some hosts offer additional meals, baby-
sitting, laundry facilities.

LOCATIONS   *All are in metropolitan Toronto area only.*

SETTINGS: They represent a wide range of facilities.

HOSTS: Musician, teacher, sales manager, insurance broker, personnel trainer, artist, caterer, realtor, accountant, airplane mechanic, hair stylist, chef, union negotiator, nurse. . . .

BREAKFAST: Varies from help-yourself to an elaborate meal. All
hosts offer a full breakfast.

RESERVATIONS
Booked directly with host by guest.
Ten days in advance preferred. Last-minute reservations accepted.
Groups: Maximum size is 20.
Travel agents should contact Randy Lee.

DIRECTORY: $3 includes postage. A pamphlet that includes description of facilities, location, transportation, restrictions, season, and rates for each entry. *Sample:*

> Anna's Place. Open year round. Available: One room with queen-size bed, adjacent private bathroom. $35 for two. One room with single bed, shared bath, $25 night. "We live in a new townhouse on a quiet street between Dupont and Davenport. Very close to downtown. You are easily accessible to both subway lines. We come from Europe, were brought up in the arts, and speak English, German, Swedish, and Hungarian. . . . Two small girls knock on your door in the morning to tell you "Breakfast time". You shall be served a large breakfast from the menu you circled the night before, and during breakfast we can discuss your schedule for the day. . . . You will have a key to come and go when you please. You will be treated as a member of the family, which includes the use of the piano (we have no TV), laundry facilities, the occasional ride, and a nightcap. No pets please."

RATES
Singles $25–$35. Doubles $35–$55. A few offer seventh night free. Deposit required is 50 percent of total.

◇ ◇ ◇

NIAGARA REGION BED & BREAKFAST SERVICE
GITE D'ACCUEILL DE LA RÉGION DU NIAGARA
MONIQUE FERLAND WETHERUP
2631 DORCHESTER AVENUE
NIAGARA FALLS, ONTARIO L2 2Y9, CANADA

The address for Monique Ferland Wetherup's nearby service:

NIAGARA-ON-THE-LAKE BED & BREAKFAST
P.O. BOX 1515
NIAGARA-ON-THE-LAKE, ONTARIO L0S IJ0, CANADA

PHONE: 416/358-8988
Live Monday–Friday, 9–9. Answering machine at other times.
OPEN: Year round.

ACCOMMODATIONS
B&Bs (all hosted private residences)
In Niagara region: 40.
In Niagara-on-the-Lake region: 20.

French-speaking hosted private residences: 15.
Almost all have air conditioning.

> *Gîte d'Accueil de la Région du Niagara: Une agence de réservations servant les villes de Niagara Falls, Welland, et St. Catharines. Les francophones ou amis des francophones sont invités à partager nos foyers francophones et à apprécier notre culture franco-ontarienne.*
>
> *This service is open to Francophones (French-speaking people) or anyone who would like to experience a different culture.*

OTHER SERVICES: Home-cooked dinners available if requests made in advance. Car rentals, pickup at bus or train. Tour guide provided. Attraction and dinner reservations made. Reservation and purchase of theater tickets. Some provide baby-sitting service.

LOCATIONS *Welland, Niagara Falls, St. Catherines, Fort Erie, Vineland, and Niagara-on-the-Lake.*

SETTINGS: Range from simple to luxurious. On fruit farms, beachfront, and country properties, and some homes in town.

HOSTS: Artists, business men and women, retirees, consultants, housewives, teachers. . . .

GUESTS COME FOR: Niagara Falls. Shaw Festival. Victorian and historical town of Niagara-on-the-Lake. Handcrafts. Wineries. Welland Canal Locks. Bus tours. French-speaking communities. Folkloric evenings.

BREAKFAST: All serve a full meal. Specialties could include Canadian bacon, crepes, quiches, muffins. Guests in French-speaking homes might experience a champagne breakfast, a barbecue breakfast, or perhaps a candlelight breakfast with crystal dishes and silverware.

RESERVATIONS
Advance reservations preferred. If arrangements can be made, will accept last-minute reservations.

Groups: Maximum size is 45. (Bus tours accommodated.)
Also available through travel agents.

RATES
Singles $35–$60. Doubles $40–$65. Seventh night is free.
Weekly and monthly rates available.
Deposit required: $25.
Credit cards accepted: MasterCard, VISA, and AMEX.
Cancellation policy: If cancellation received at least two weeks before expected arrival date, full refund minus $10 service charge.

> *"B&B travelers are mainly people, who, regardless of price, are opting for the personal touch. Our hosts have restaurant recommendations, entertainment advice, and out-of-the-way sightseeing information."*

CENTRE D'ACTIVITÉS FRANÇAISES
CLAUDETTE PAQUIN
C.P. 1270, 63, RUE MAIN
PENETANGUISHENE, ONTARIO L0K 1P0, CANADA

PHONE: 705/549-3116
 Monday–Friday 9–5.
OPEN: Year round.

ACCOMMODATIONS
B&Bs
Hosted private residences: 12.

LOCATIONS *All within a 20-mile radius of Penetanguishene.*

SETTINGS: In towns, on beaches, on farms. Some homes are older. Some are modern.

HOSTS: Long-time residents, doll maker, many farmers. . . .

GUESTS COME FOR: Georgian Bay. Boating, sailing, swimming. Historic sites. Martyr Shrine. Festivals. Cross-country skiing.

BREAKFAST: All serve a full meal.

RESERVATIONS
Advance preferred. If arrangements can be made, will accept last-minute reservations.

DIRECTORY: None is published. If you stop into the center, they have photos of each home and a description. *Sample:*

> Pension Lancia. This chalet on Georgian Bay's waterfront is an ideal location for the amateur photographer. The cathedral ceilings and plants create a welcoming and pleasing atmosphere. The hosts and their children will be glad to greet you. English, Dutch, and German are spoken.

RATES
$25 for one person. $5 for each additional person in same room.

> *This hosting program evolved through a government grant to develop tourism in the area. Center staff members initially screened hosts. Now the Center keeps the program going and does the bookings.*

KINGSTON AREA BED & BREAKFAST
RUTH MACLACHLAN
410 WESTVIEW ROAD
KINGSTON, ONTARIO K7M 2C3, CANADA

PHONE: 613/542-0214
   Daily 9 a.m.–10:30 p.m.
OPEN: Year round.

ACCOMMODATIONS
B&Bs
Hosted private residences: 30.
Plus
Some hosted short-term (up to three months) housing.

OTHER SERVICES: Pickup at airport, bus, or train can be arranged.

> LOCATIONS   *All are in Ontario. Most are within a 10-mile radius of the center of Kingston. Those in the city are near public transportation. A few are in the countryside near Kingston. A few farther away are in Bath, Westport, Winchester, Morrisburg, Rockport, Gananoque, Seeley's Bay, Newboro.*

SETTINGS: Most are recently built homes in urban settings. A few restored Victorians. A few rural.

HOSTS: Retired university professor, professional musicians, school teachers, owners of antiques and craft shop, insurance broker, shop keeper, graphic artist, retired nurse, children's bookstore owner, retired city planner. . . .

GUESTS COME FOR: "We started appealing to tourists and then found that business and professional men and women—professors, engineers, nurses—began to use our service. The social workers in the local hospitals began to request information to accommodate relatives visiting the sick. Graduating students from our local university and colleges would phone seeking accommodation for parents and relatives. A bride and groom may make arrangements for out-of-town wedding guests. Families often have reunions in Kingston and inquire about the possibilities of using B&B. . . . People often take short course/seminars and want accommodation near the university/college/hospital. Some are apartment hunting or in the process of undertaking real estate transactions. Others come investigating employment possibilities. The tourists find much to do."

Lake Ontario offers opportunities for sailing, windsurfing, swimming, boat cruises, power boats. St. Lawrence River: sailing, swimming, boat cruises among the Thousand Islands, power boats, canoeing, windsurfing. Restored old buildings downtown. Restored (early 1800s) Old Fort Henry. Museums. Historic sites. Galleries. Shopping. Restaurants. Bicycles for rent. Walking tours. Rideau (hiking) Trail starts at Kingston.

BREAKFAST: All full. Most hosts serve good plain food with special attention to table settings. "We serve hot things hot, cold things cold. Breakfast is a time to get to know your guests. Often hosts join guests for coffee and conversation."

RESERVATIONS
Advance reservations preferred. If arrangements can be made, will accept last-minute reservations.
Groups: Maximum size is 20.
Also available through some travel agents.

DIRECTORY (not required for reservations): $1 for pamphlet that includes B&B descriptions. *Sample:*

West End of Kingston: Open year round. Rates: Single $25, double $36, twin $39. "We live in a Cape Cod–style house with a spacious addition and two four-piece bathrooms, situated on a large lot in a delightful subdivision. All guest rooms have cross ventilation. Our large dining room overlooks a beautiful garden. Bus routes and several restaurants close by. We are Kingston enthusiasts, know the area, and are only 10 minutes from downtown." Hosts' interests: Canadiana, log building, canoeing, camping, the outdoors, music, Scottish country dancing.

RATES
Singles $25. Doubles $36–$39. A few (those with private bath) higher.
Weekly and monthly rates available.
Deposit required: First night's charge.
Cancellation policy: A refund of room deposit will be made if notice received at least one week before expected arrival date.

What Is B&B All About?

"We personalize hospitality. Some guests want to be in a home where German, French, or Dutch is spoken. Some request an en suite bathroom, or a certain size of bed, or air conditioning, or to be downtown—or all of these things! Others indicate their wishes for a farmhouse, or a Victorian home, or a room with a view. In all cases, we try to oblige. However, we think that because of the social nature of B&B, the hosts are as important, if not more important, than the physical structure and surroundings of the house."

COUNTRY HOST
MRS. GRACE CRONIN
R.R. #1
PALGRAVE, ONTARIO L0N 1P0, CANADA

PHONE: 519/941-7633
   Daily 9 a.m. to midnight.
OPEN: Year round.

ACCOMMODATIONS
B&Bs
Hosted private residences: 30.   B&B inns: 2.

OTHER SERVICES: Most northern hosts offer transportation to and from the famous Bruce Trail for hikers. With advance notice they also prepare dinners and pack picnics and lunches. "My hosts will transport a guest's car from home to home so that it is there—when they come off the Bruce Trail after a day's hike—complete with night attire, change of clothes for dinner, perhaps a bottle of wine, all of the things they would ordinarily have had to carry while hiking. Hosts even take guests to and from the trail."

LOCATIONS *The northern network of Country Host homes extends almost 300 miles, from just outside Toronto, following the Niagara Escarpment north and west through some of Ontario's most picturesque areas, to Tobermory at the tip of the Bruce Peninsula.*
The southern network of Country Host homes is located at the Point Pelee area, Canada's most southerly point, on Lake Erie near Leamington, where the most spectacular bird migration in North America takes place spring and fall. Homes are also located on Lake Nipissing at North Bay and a few within 50 miles of west Toronto.

SETTINGS: Some are fully restored Victorian mansions; others are modern. Some are century-old farmhouses with acreage. Some are working farms. All are on good roads.

HOSTS: Several artists, a retired doctor, farmers, mining executive, librarian, teachers, travel agent, realtor. . . .

GUESTS COME FOR: Peace. "We get a lot of guests who have stressful jobs trying to relax through a change in environment. They usually hike in summer and ski in winter."

BREAKFAST: All full, wholesome meals. Most homes offer fruit and vegetables from their gardens in season. A few Austrian and German hosts serve recipes from their native countries.

RESERVATIONS
Advance reservations preferred at all locales. Point Pelee reservations for the month of May only are often made six months in advance. If arrangements can be made, will accept last-minute reservations.
Groups: Equipped to handle up to 20 at lodges.

DIRECTORY: None available, but Grace Cronin suggests this sample:

Lamont—One of Scotland's most ancient clans and the name of an attractive guest home nestled on the craggy

Niagara Escarpment at Kimberley, in the heart of the lovely Beaver Valley. The owners, Mary and Graham, are of Scottish descent, and the warmest of welcomes awaits guests to their home with its in-ground pool. Hikers on the world-famous Bruce Trail, birders, hang-gliders, camera buffs, and nature lovers are especially attracted to this area in summer; cross-country and downhill skiers are close to some of the finest in the province; fishing is an all-year sport in the Beaver River and nearby Georgian Bay. Additional meals are provided if requested in advance.

RATES
Singles $28–$30. Doubles $35–$40.
Weekly and monthly rates available.
Deposit usually required; varies according to season and location.
Cancellation policy: Refund minus $10 processing fee made if cancellation received 14 days before expected arrival date.
Exception: Point Pelee area, where 30 days' notice is required for cancellation refund.

How One Service Started

"The idea of organizing a B&B network in our lovely part of the country had appealed to me since my husband and I had enjoyed them in the British Isles a few years previously; so Country Host was born, starting in the nearby picturesque Hockley Valley. It grew north gradually at the request of hikers, naturalists, and birders who like comforts, rather than 'roughing it' while pursuing their hobbies or favorite recreation. Then a southern network of homes was established to accommodate bird-watchers primarily. Our greatest satisfaction has come from guests' completely unsolicited calls—after using our homes—to report reactions, to share their thrills of discovery, perhaps sighting a new bird or rare plant, or their enthusiasm for completing a part of, or even the entire 430-mile-long Bruce Trail."

BED AND BREAKFAST PRINCE EDWARD COUNTY

MRS. ANN WALMSLEY

BOX 1500

PICTON, ONTARIO K0K 2T0, CANADA

PHONE: 613/476-6798
  Live 9–9 daily.
OPEN: Year round.

ACCOMMODATIONS
B&Bs
Hosted private residences: 20.

LOCATIONS *Spread throughout Prince Edward County, halfway between Montreal and Toronto, in Picton, Bloomfield, Wellington, Rednersville, Black River, Lake on the Mountain, and Sandbanks area.*

SETTINGS: On the water, near the beach, farm and country locations.

HOSTS: Social worker, artist, realtor, lawyer, school teacher, librarian, nurse, farmers, engineer.

GUESTS COME FOR: "This is a pastoral and rural area on Lake Ontario which attracts city people who wish a change of pace."

BREAKFAST: All full. "Emphasis is on good country cooking."

RESERVATIONS
Advance reservations preferred.
Groups: Maximum size is 40.

DIRECTORY: None available, but inquiries are answered with a brochure that includes area attractions and a page of some home descriptions. *Samples:*

Big Island: This old stone home of architectural merit (1846) is on the Bay of Quinte and is located 300 yards from a fully equipped marina with docking facilities. There is also a conservation area nearby. The location of this home lends itself to sailors, bicyclists, bird-watchers, and nature lovers. In the winter the blazing kitchen fireplace beckons cross-country skiers. Breakfast is often served in the charming dining room with a view of the water. The hosts are warm and welcoming and are enthusiastic to share their interest in travel, horticulture, genealogy, and crafts. Double room $35. Huge room (with special accommodation for families) $38.

Modern Guest House: Privacy on the Lake on the Mountain. Twin bedroom, pull-out bed in the living room. Completely equipped kitchen for light meals. Bathroom (bathtub in main house a step away). Deck facing water. Hostess is an excellent cook who invites guests to her home for breakfast. $270 per week for two, includes breakfast. French spoken. Great for a city escape, honeymoons, or a quiet holiday.

RATES
Singles $25–$40. Doubles $35–$45. A few higher.
Deposit required: First night's lodging fee.
Weekly and monthly rates available.
Cancellation policy: No refund with less than one week's notice.

"When a guest phones, I believe they sense an honesty and a real effort to match them with suitable hosts. In order to be enthusiastic, I must be convinced that my hosts will be able to carry out my expectations. I feel they do, and therefore it adds up to a well-run and happy network."

—Ann Walmsley

PRINCE EDWARD COUNTY BED & BREAKFAST INDEPENDENTS
CARL STEEVES
P.O. BOX 502
WELLINGTON, ONTARIO K0K 3L0, CANADA

PHONE: 613/399-2569
OPEN: Year round.

ACCOMMODATIONS
B&Bs
Hosted private residences: Six.

LOCATIONS *In a range of about 15 miles. All are in the country. The nearest city, Belville, is 22 miles away.*

SETTINGS: Some are Victorian homes or restored farmhouses.

HOSTS: Most are retired. Antique refinisher/dealer, potter, marine museum curator. . . .

GUESTS COME FOR: "Vacationland of lakes and bays." Beautiful sand dunes and large flat beaches in Sandbanks Provincial Park. Good fishing. Scenic drives. Antiquing. Windsurfing. Cross-country skiing. A getaway.

BREAKFAST: All serve a full cooked meal.

RESERVATIONS
Booked directly with host by guest.
If arrangements can be made, hosts will accept last-minute reservations.

DIRECTORY: Pamphlet with descriptions, names, addresses, and phone numbers sent without charge. *Sample:*

> Sandling House. A gracious country home, 130 years old, in the village of Cherry Valley, five miles south of Picton and five miles from the famous Sandbanks and beaches. Antique store on premises. A large garden. Three spacious bedrooms, one with twin beds. Rates: $35 double, $25 single. Includes full breakfast. Adults, nonsmokers, air conditioned.

RATES
Singles $25. Doubles $30–$35.
Cancellation policy: Individualized. Some suggest, "Let us know as early as you can."

> *This group of independents banded together to disseminate information about what they offer. Among the retirees are a couple who moved from the city and started (tried) B&B with one room so they wouldn't really feel that much "away." After meeting people from all over the world in their first season, they opened other rooms—up to a total of three— to B&B guests.*

AMBASSADOR BED & BREAKFAST GUEST HOMES
GRACE & MORRIS BRUNK
266 ONTARIO STREET
STRATFORD, ONTARIO N5A 3H5, CANADA

PHONE: 519/271-5385
 Live 9–9 daily.
OPEN: Year round except the last two weeks of October.

ACCOMMODATIONS
B&Bs
Hosted private residences: 10.
Hosted short-term (by the week or month) housing.

OTHER SERVICES: Some homes offer kitchen facilities.

LOCATIONS *Most are centrally located within walking distance of theater and downtown restaurants and shopping. (One is in Mennonite territory, 20 minutes from Stratford.) Most are close to bus and train depots. Taxi service is good and fairly reasonable.*

SETTINGS: Range from a century-old Victorian, filled with period furnishings and a bit of Stratford history, to very modern homes. One with a log cabin addition is by a creek just five minutes from the city.

HOSTS: School teachers, retired and active; former hotel employees; retired farmers.

GUESTS COME FOR: The Stratford Shakespearean Festival Theatre, Rothman Art Gallery, antique shops, tours through Mennonite territory, Kitchener's Farmers Market. Business reasons.

BREAKFAST: Varies according to host, from help-yourself to an elaborate meal.

RESERVATIONS
Advance notice always preferred; at least two weeks during summer. If arrangements can be made, will accept last-minute reservations.
Groups: Maximum group size: 50. Some homes can handle 20, but most have room for 6–10 people.
Also available through travel agents.

DIRECTORY: None available, but inquiries are answered with some flyers on individual B&B guest homes that travelers can book through this service.

RATES
Singles $25–$45. Doubles $28–$50. A few are higher.
Ten percent discount for three-night stays.
Weekly rates in off season: $45 and up.
Deposit required: $25 (Canadian) or $20 (American).
Cancellation policy: All but $5 handling refunded if notified within 48 hours of expected arrival date.

What's in a Name?

"The name "Ambassador" implies that we are here to promote good relationships, peace, and goodwill among people of all nationalities, and walks of life. (We acknowledge the 200 independent residents who list their homes with the Shakespearean Theater.) We feature personalized service. Good relationships and good conversation happen here.

"We have had some folks who have been coming back for over five years. It is interesting to catch up on the latest news. We have made some very personal friends. A guest from last year is immigrating to Canada from Italy to spend the last part of his life here with us. He is a man of 78 years, born in Stratford, England."

STRATFORD AND AREA VISITORS' AND CONVENTION BUREAU
38 ALBERT STREET
STRATFORD, ONTARIO N5A 3K3, CANADA

PHONE: 519/271-5140
  Monday–Friday 9–5.
OPEN: Year round.

ACCOMMODATIONS
B&Bs
Hosted private residences: 33.   B&B inns: 2.
Hosted short-term housing available in off season only.

LOCATIONS *Stratford, St. Marys, Shakespeare, New Hamburg, Embro, St. Pauls, Staffa, Mitchell.*

SETTINGS: Many are Victorian with period furnishings.

HOSTS: Farmers, genealogist, builder, teachers, antique dealer. . . .

GUESTS COME FOR: Shakespeare Festival, May–October. Theater-related lectures, music concerts, Mennonite farm countryside, beaches, barn theaters, and parks where canoes, paddle boats, and bicycles are available for rent.

BREAKFAST: Most are continental and could include scones, muffins, apple strudel, and homemade jams. Some offer cooked breakfast for an extra charge.

RESERVATIONS
Booked directly with host by guest.
Advance reservations preferred. When possible, last-minute reservations are accepted.
Groups: Maximum size is 40, who can be booked into seven houses located within a few blocks of each other.

DIRECTORY: Mailed without charge in answer to inquiries. Published annually, in February. (Requests for theater programs are also filled.) Map included has a reminder that no overnight parking is allowed on city streets between 4 and 6 p.m. Description of each B&B includes host name, address, and phone number. *Samples:*

> Devon Place. Our home is a short walk through Queen's park to the Festival Theatre and a five-minute drive to downtown. Our accommodation is clean and comfortable with a friendly atmosphere, and the rooms are tastefully decorated. Double $28. Twin $30.

> Glenaby Farms. "Down on the farm" hospitality welcomes you to our 15-room home built by our family in 1861. Nestled on the edge of woods on a quiet country road. Homemade dinners featuring cabbage rolls, schnitzel, cinnamon buns, and apple strudel. Even the quilts on each bed are homemade. Smoking room. Single $25. Twin $40. Double $30–$50. $5 each extra person.

RATES
Singles $20–$40. Doubles $25–$50. (One at $95.)
Deposit required: At least $10 per room.
Cancellation policy: Refund given if notice received far enough in
advance, otherwise if room can be rented by host home.

Friendly Advice
*"We recommend that you pay on arrival. You and your host
will find it easier to do business while you are still strangers."*

MUSKOKA BED AND BREAKFAST ASSOCIATION
MARG MILNE
BOX 1431
GRAVENHURST, ONTARIO P0C 1G0, CANADA

PHONE: 705/687-4395
OPEN: Most hosts welcome guests from May through October, but if
you make advance arrangements, winter and spring visits are
possible too. High season includes July, August, and the "Caval-
cade of Color," the first two weeks of October.

ACCOMMODATIONS
B&Bs
Hosted private residences: Nine.

LOCATIONS   *In small towns in the southern part of the regional municipality called Muskoka, 100 miles north of Toronto. Populations average between 5,000 and 8,000 people.*

SETTINGS: Some rural, some in towns, some lakeside.

HOSTS: Retired school teachers, other retirees, a community
worker. . . .

GUESTS COME FOR: Cruises on a 100-year-old restored steam-
boat, R.M.S. *Segwun.* Professional summer theater. National
Parks historic house. Visits with relatives and friends in the area.
Water activities at lakefront properties.

BREAKFAST: All serve a full meal.

RESERVATIONS
Booked directly with host by guest.

Advance arrangements for high season strongly recommended. (For some places, reservations are made three months ahead of time.)

DIRECTORY: Sent free on request. Listings include name, address, directions, facilities, and phone. *Sample:*

> Housey's Rapids—Old log home with large fireplace and modern facilities on private 60-acre lot by Kahshe Lake. Enjoy outdoor recreation: Swim at our sandy beach; rent a boat for fishing (no motors); walk our woodland trails. Or relax in our quiet, homey surroundings. English and French spoken. Season: May to October; winter by reservation.

RATES:
$20–$45.

> *Most Muskoka B&Bs had been operating for a couple of years when they recently decided to form an association and distribute their brochure. (As a group, they have voluntarily asked the municipal health unit to inspect members' homes annually.) Enthusiasm runs high—among hosts and guests.*

GREY BRUCE BED & BREAKFAST ASSOCIATION
R.R. 5
OWEN SOUND, ONTARIO N4K 5N7, CANADA

PHONE: 519/371-2071. Toll free in Ontario, 1-800-265-3127.

ACCOMMODATIONS
B&Bs
Hosted private residences: 23.

> LOCATIONS   *On farms, in town, in rural areas. In 15 communities on a peninsula where the largest town has a population of 20,000.*

HOSTS: Most are retired or semiretired long-time residents who are happy to provide a quiet place for others on the peninsula.

GUESTS COME FOR: Swimming in Lake Huron, seven miles of sandy beach. Fishing. Hunting. "The natural paradise" with its flora and fauna; orchids in the southern area.

RESERVATIONS
Booked directly with host by guest.
If you arrive in town without reservations, the tourist office (telephone listed above) will call the host for you. When possible, last-minute reservations accepted.

DIRECTORY: Pamphlet, available free on request, includes name, address, and telephone number of each B&B.

RATES
Singles $25. Doubles $30.

SOUTHWESTERN ONTARIO COUNTRYSIDE VACATION ASSOCIATION

MRS. E. A. HENDERSON
HONEY BROOK FARM
R.R. 1
MILLBANK, ONTARIO NOK 1LO, CANADA

PHONE: 519/595-4604
Live most of the time. Answering machine at other times.
OPEN: Year round. (Some hosts close to guests in winter.)

ACCOMMODATIONS
B&Bs
Hosted private residences: 15.

OTHER SERVICES: All homes offer B&B, but in addition, some offer up to three meals a day for full-time vacationers. Some offer tours of the area and pickup at transportation points.

LOCATIONS *All in the countryside, covering about 100 miles from Fergus and Elora southwest to Chatham, including Kitchener and Waterloo area and the outskirts of London.*

SETTINGS: None are in a large center. The largest community has a population of 10,000 people.

HOSTS: Dairymen, farmers, antique lecturer, government employees, caterer, retirees. . . .

GUESTS COME FOR: Stratford Shakespearean Festival. Recreational facilities of Grand River and Thames River Conservation areas. Lakes. Swimming. Maple sugar time. Museums. Festivals—including Oktoberfest, music, clogging, foods. Mennonite culture. The annual Mennonite Relief Sale that includes a famous quilt auction.

BREAKFAST: All hosts serve a full meal.

RESERVATIONS
Booked directly with host by guest.
If you call Mrs. Henderson, she will suggest hosts who would be an appropriate match for you (but the Association does not have any system for knowing who has openings).
Advance reservations strongly recommended for summer season. Hosts will accept last-minute reservations, when possible.

DIRECTORY: A brochure with descriptions, names, addresses, and phone numbers sent without charge upon request. (Canadians: Please enclose a self-addressed stamped envelope.) *Sample:*

> Welcome to Kelly's Corner, 120 acres with our own beach on Lake Huron. There are large verandas for your comfort and a modernized farm home. Excellent meals with fresh fruits and vegetables and home baking. Five miles from Goderich or Bayfield . . . loads of sightseeing. Children welcome; pets if they stay outside. B&B rates: $25 single, $40 double.

RATES
Singles $20–$30. Doubles $25–$40.

> *"Most of us have been in business for a long time. Four years ago we formed the association, with a membership that set standards of cleanliness, comfort, and hospitality. Other members are still being added. . . . I don't know how anyone could operate without liking people. Many of our guests come from recommendations, and from all over the world. We all have much repeat business."*
>
> *—Mrs. E. A. Henderson*

OTTAWA DOWNTOWN BED & BREAKFAST

ALBERT HOUSE
478 ALBERT STREET
OTTAWA, ONTARIO K1R 5B5, CANADA

PHONE: 613/236-4479
Live 6 a.m.–11 p.m. daily.
OPEN: Year round.

ACCOMMODATIONS
B&Bs
Hosted private residences: Six.

LOCATIONS *All are centrally located in downtown core on main bus lines, within walking distance of all tourist attractions.*

SETTINGS: With the exception of the Albert House, which has 15 guest rooms, they have 3–5 guest rooms. Edwardian house and "old-fashioned family homes" included.

HOSTS: Professor, civil servant, ex-stewardesses, teachers. . . .

BREAKFAST: Varies from a tray continental to a full meal.

RESERVATIONS
Book your own directly.

DIRECTORY: A short list with name, address, telephone number, number of rooms, style of house, and type of breakfast served at each B&B. Sent on request.

RATES
Singles $30–$39. Doubles $29–$43.

A host reports: "Often you pick up the best tips in the world sitting around a B&B breakfast table!"

OTTAWA AREA BED & BREAKFAST

SUZAN BISSET
P.O. BOX 4848, STN E
OTTAWA, ONTARIO K1S 5J1, CANADA

PHONE: 613/563-0161
Live 8–8 daily. Answering service at other times.
OPEN: Year round.

ACCOMMODATIONS
B&Bs
Hosted private residences: 50.   B&B inn: 1.
Almost all have air conditioning and private baths.
Plus
Some short-term (one month) hosted housing available.

OTHER SERVICES: Pickup at airport, bus, and train. Some hosts offer picnic baskets, baby-sitting, city tours, and vegetarian homes.

LOCATIONS   *Most are in Ottawa area. Three are rural.*

SETTINGS: Most are rather luxurious. Variety includes Georgian, Tudor, colonial, historic, and one experimental farm.

HOSTS: University professor, lawyers, military, government executives, high-tech employees, pilot, social worker, teachers, nurses, some retirees, and artists. . . . "Whenever possible, we try to match guests who are professionals with hosts in a similar profession."

GUESTS COME FOR: Capital of Canada, world's longest skating rink, tulip festival, National Arts Centre, Winterlude (Winter Carnival). Free activities include museums, the House of Parliament, art galleries, historical sites, skating on the Rideau Canal, biking on miles of parkways and trails. Some guests come for business reasons, for house hunting, or for schools: Carleton University, Ottawa University, Algonquin College.

BREAKFAST: All serve a full meal.

RESERVATIONS
Advance reservations preferred. If arrangements can be made, will accept last-minute reservations.
Groups: Maximum size is 15.

DIRECTORY: None available, but inquiries are answered with descriptions of a few homes. (Please send a self-addressed stamped envelope or international reply coupon, whichever is applicable.)
Sample:

> D-1: One double room. Twin beds. Queensway & Richmond Road. Executive-style two-story air-conditioned home. Ideally suited to family bookings or the young at heart. In-ground pool; VCR and Intellivision in beautifully

finished game room. No smoking in sleeping accommodations only. Single $25. Double $35. Family rates on request.

RATES
Singles $25. Doubles $35.
Some family rates available.
Deposit required: One day's charge.
Credit cards accepted: MasterCard.
Cancellation policy: Full refund if notice received five days before expected arrival date.

LONDON AND AREA BED AND BREAKFAST ASSOCIATION
MRS. SERENA A. WARREN, COORDINATOR
720 HEADLEY DRIVE
LONDON, ONTARIO N6H 3V6, CANADA

PHONE: 519/471-6228
OPEN: Year round.

ACCOMMODATIONS
B&Bs
Hosted private residences: 12.

LOCATIONS   *Most are in London near public transportation. A few are a half hour's drive out of town.*

SETTINGS: Modern, Tudor, Victorian in the city. Farmhouses in country settings.

GUESTS COME FOR: Business and pleasure.

BREAKFAST: All serve a full meal.

RESERVATIONS
Booked directly with hosts by guests.
Two weeks in advance preferred. If arrangements can be made, will accept last-minute reservations.

DIRECTORY: A brochure is sent without charge. (Please enclose a business-sized self-addressed stamped envelope or an international reply coupon.) Name of host, address, phone, and directions included with each listing. *Samples:*

#10 Warren: Air-conditioned home in prestigious residential area of West London. Sun room for relaxation. Near Springbank Park, 10 minutes from Theatre London. Bus service at the door. Three bedrooms and full bath. Regular breakfast. Single $20. Double $25. Twin $30.

#6 Humberstone: Charming turn-of-the-century house with turret and fireplace. Offering two double and one twin bedroom. No smoking in bedrooms, lounge provided. Direct from Highway #401. Near downtown. Adults preferred. No pets please. Full breakfast, if requested. Single $25. Double $30. Twin $32.

RATES
Singles $20–$25. Doubles $25–$35. A few are higher.
Weekly rates available.
Deposit required: One night's lodging.
Cancellation policy: Deposit refunded if notice received at least seven days before expected arrival date.

"We started the Association in May 1982. To date it is an enriching, rewarding experience."

ORILLIA AREA BED & BREAKFAST
EUNICE STREETER AND ELEANOR LAITY
76 MISSISSAGA ST. W.
ORILLIA, ONTARIO L3V 3A8, CANADA

PHONE: 705/326-7743 and 487-3135
Monday–Friday 9–1, 2–5. 795-315 after 5:30 and on weekends. Answering machine at other times.
OPEN: Year round.

ACCOMMODATIONS
B&Bs
Hosted private residences: Nine (fewer in winter).
Plus
Hosted short-term (up to three weeks) housing.

LOCATIONS *Homes are all within a 10-mile area. Most are in the country where there is no public transportation. Many are on lakes. There is regular bus service between Toronto, located 80 miles to the south, and Orillia.*

SETTINGS: Range from plain rustic to comfortable modern, near golfing, theater, swimming, boating, riding, and skiing.

HOSTS: Chiropractor, teacher, chaplain, clerk. . . . Many foreign languages spoken: German, French, Estonian, and Polish.

GUESTS COME FOR: Golf, fishing, lakes, swimming, boating, horseback riding, skiing. Theater. Stephen Leacock Home. L.B.K. Ranch and Wildlife Preserve. Wye Marsh Preserve. Big Chute Marine Railway, Martyr's Shrine. Muskoka countryside in the Canadian Shield.

BREAKFAST: Varies from simple to elaborate, according to host.

RESERVATIONS
Can be made through the service or directly with the hosts.
If arrangements can be made, will accept last-minute reservations.

DIRECTORY: $1 to cover mailing costs. A list of names, addresses, restrictions, and rates.

RATES
Singles $25–$30. Doubles $30–$45. A few are higher.
Some weekly or monthly rates may be available.

Allow extra time for round trip mail to and from Canada.

Western Canada

MANITOBA
ALBERTA
BRITISH COLUMBIA

MANITOBA

B&B OF MANITOBA
MARLENE AND LEN LEOWEN
7 SANDALE DRIVE
WINNIPEG, MANITOBA R2N 1A1, CANADA

PHONE: 204/256-6151
Live Monday–Friday, 24 hours a day, by answering service that answers, "Accountable Management."

ACCOMMODATIONS
B&Bs
Hosted private residences: 20.

LOCATIONS *Most homes are just a short drive to major shopping centers. Some are within 10 minutes of downtown; others are close to city parks and entertainment centers.*

SETTINGS: Vary from plain to luxurious.

HOSTS: Many retired or semiretired, a couple of doctors, some school teachers. . . . "All friendly."

GUESTS COME FOR: Vacations, conferences, and business. "Winnipeg is a good stopping point for wildlife hunters and fishermen." Professional sports. Paddlewheel river boats. Rainbow Stage (outdoor theater).

BREAKFAST: Varies. Could be continental or could include bacon and eggs.

RESERVATIONS
Booked directly with hosts by guests. "If you prefer, you may call or write the office for assistance."
Two weeks' advance notice preferred. If arrangements can be made, will accept last-minute reservations.

DIRECTORY: A brochure sent without charge on request includes list of areas where B&Bs are located, hosts' names, addresses, locations, phone numbers, numbers of rooms with bed size, e.g., "two doubles, one single."

RATES
Singles $20–$25. Doubles $25–$32. A few are higher.
Weekly and monthly rates available.
Reservation and cancellation policy: Varies according to individual host.

◇ ◇ ◇

ALBERTA

BED & BREAKFAST BUREAU–CANADIAN CARE INC.
DON SINCLAIR
BOX 7094, STATION 'E'
CALGARY, ALBERTA T3C 3L8, CANADA
AND
BOX 369
BANFF, ALBERTA T0L 0C0, CANADA

PHONE: 403/242-5555 (Calgary)
        403/762-5070 (Banff)
   Live 8–8 daily.
OPEN: Year round except for Statutory holidays.

ACCOMMODATIONS
B&Bs
Hosted private residences: Over 100.
More than half have private baths.
Some are accessible to handicapped.
Plus
Some hosted short-term housing available for up to one month.

OTHER SERVICES: Theater tickets. Arrangements for local tours
and attractions such as skiing, heli-skiing, trail rides, rafting. Car
rentals. Pickup at airport, bus, and train.

LOCATIONS   *Throughout western Canada, with hosts in all
major centers in the provinces of Alberta, British Columbia,
Manitoba, Saskatchewan. Others are in the Yukon and
Northwest Territories.*
*In Alaska through cooperative arrangements with other
B&B reservation services.*

SETTINGS: Apartments, condos, suburban homes, farm and ranch
homes. "The emphasis is on cleanliness and warmth of welcome."

HOSTS: "We cover the whole gamut with respect to occupations
and professions, and every age group." Included are lawyers, engineers, doctors, teachers, senior citizens, salespersons, business
people, realtors. . . .

GUESTS COME FOR: Skiing in the Canadian Rockies October–
May. Scenery. Centennial celebrations. Expo 86 in Vancouver,
British Columbia; 1988 Winter Olympics in Calgary.

BREAKFAST: All hosts serve a full meal.

RESERVATIONS
Two weeks in advance preferred. If arrangements can be made,
will accept last-minute reservations. Most reservations are made
through the mail. (Reminder: Round-trip mail can take weeks.)
Groups: Equipped to handle up to 50. Can handle larger groups in
all major centers with adequate notice.
Also available through travel agents.

RATES
Singles $20–$30. Doubles $30–$40.
Some family rates available.
One-night surcharge: $5.

Weekly rates available, with 10 percent discount over one week. Deposit required: $20 minimum, or 25 percent on stays over four days.

CALGARY BED & BREAKFAST–AAA BED WEST LTD.

JAN SCOTT CAMERON
BOX 7094, station 'E'
CALGARY, ALBERTA T3C 3L8, CANADA

PHONE: 403/242-5555
  Daily 8–8.
OPEN: Year round except on Statutory holidays.

ACCOMMODATIONS
B&Bs
Hosted private residences: Over 60.
Almost all have private baths.
Some accessible to handicapped.
Plus
Hosted short-term (up to one month) housing.

OTHER SERVICES: Car rentals. Pickup at airport, bus, and train. Theater tickets. Arrangements for local tours, trail rides, skiing, heli-skiing, ranch stays, tours to Banff, Lake Louise Jasper, Columbia Ice Fields.

LOCATIONS   *All major centers and the surrounding areas throughout the Province of Alberta, including Calgary, Edmonton, Banff, Jasper, Waterton, Lethbridge, Medicine Hat, Peace River, Red Deer. In addition, B&B hosts live on working cattle ranches and grain farms, most of which are adjacent to Banff, Jasper, and Waterton National Parks, in the Alberta foothills of the Rocky Mountains.*

SETTINGS: Range from well-located and prestigious suburban homes and acreages to central apartments and condominiums.

HOSTS: Represent a wide range of occupations, professions, and age groups. Fifty percent have hosted for over three years.

GUESTS COME FOR: The scenic farmlands in the eastern portion, rolling foothills on to the Rocky Mountains in the west. Calgary

Stampede and Edmonton Klondike Days held every July. The 1988 Winter Olympics in Calgary.

BREAKFAST: All full. "Good down-home cooking generally."

RESERVATIONS
Two weeks in advance preferred. If arrangements can be made, will accept last-minute reservations.
Groups: Maximum size is 50.
Also available through travel agents.

RATES
Singles $20–$30. Doubles $30–$40. A few are higher.
Weekly rates available, with 10 percent discount over one week.
Deposit required is 25 percent ($20 minimum) on stays over four days.
Cancellation policy: Reservation fee, less $5 service charge, refunded if cancellation received at least one week before scheduled arrival date. One-half of reservation fee refunded if cancellation received less than one week but more than 48 hours before arrival date.

ALBERTA BED AND BREAKFAST
JUNE M. BROWN
4327 86TH STREET
EDMONTON, ALBERTA T6K 1A9, CANADA

PHONE: 403/462-8885
   Live 7 a.m.–10 p.m. daily. Sometimes it is an answering service.
OPEN: Year round.

ACCOMMODATIONS
B&Bs
Hosted private residences: 50.

OTHER SERVICES: Circle tour arranged through Canadian Rocky Mountains with B&Bs available in seven of eight locations; the exception is Lake Louise.

LOCATIONS   *In Alberta—Calgary, Bragg Creek, Canmore, Banff, Jasper, Hinton, Edmonton, Cochrane, and Westerose. In British Columbia—Kamloops, halfway point between*

Banff and Vancouver. Kamloops is a four-hour drive from Vancouver, site of Expo 86.

SETTINGS: Some are attractive homes-away-from-home and some are large, beautifully furnished homes.

HOSTS: Artist, realtor, musician, caterer, senior-citizen day center director, teacher, travel agent, secretary, registered nurse. . . .

GUESTS COME FOR: Bow River in Calgary, Alberta "with the best trout fishing in North America." The Canadian Rocky Mountains in Banff and Jasper. The Calgary Stampede held for 10 days in July. Klondike Days held for 10 days in Edmonton in July, immediately following the Calgary Stampede.

BREAKFAST: Continental "plus" at most homes.

RESERVATIONS
Advance reservations preferred. Because regular mail tends to be very slow, air mail is suggested. For fast service, telephone reservations accepted. Will accept last-minute reservations, but not during Stampede days in Calgary.
Groups: Small (up to six) can be accommodated.

DIRECTORY (not required for reservations): $3. *Samples:*

Calgary: South East Area. Host is British and owns a beautiful home with lovely furnishings, and offers one bedroom with double bed, one bed-sitting room with a queen-size hide-a-bed, and one guest bath. Another bath downstairs. She is within walking distance of Fish Creek Park, the Bow River, a swimming lake, a designated fishing area, nature walks, bicycle paths, and a small museum. Host does not mind smokers. There are no children in this home. There is one small dog. To downtown Calgary, and the Calgary Tower, it is 20 minutes by car. $25 single. $35 double.

Edmonton: South. Lovely home in nice area with good accessibility to University of Alberta, Jubilee Auditorium, and route to Calgary or Jasper. Hosts are near the Confederation Swimming Pool and tennis courts. No pets, no children in this home, and they prefer nonsmokers. This host offers additional meals, and would like you to know she serves a full breakfast. Accommodation is one bedroom/double bed, second bedroom/single bed, and one guest bath. $25 single, $35 double.

RATES
Singles $20–$25. Doubles $30–$35.
$10 nonrefundable booking fee for Banff.
$10 nonrefundable booking fee for Jasper.
Some family rates available.
Weekly and monthly rates available.
Deposit required: $15 per two persons for each location, excluding
Banff and Jasper.
Cancellation policy: For each location booked, excluding Banff and
Jasper, a refund of $10 is made if cancellation is received three
days prior to confirmed reservation date.

> *"Hostess was very gracious and accommodating, and her
> apartment is quite beautiful. The location could not have
> been better. We were able to walk everywhere we wanted to
> go—Muttart Conservatory, Centennial Library, Schoctor
> Theatre, Northwoods Inn, Convention Centre. We were very
> impressed with your beautiful city, and everyone was very
> helpful and warm."*
>
> —*A guest from Ontario*

WELCOME WEST VACATION LTD.

MARILYN KAISER
1320 KERWOOD CRESCENT, S.W.
CALGARY, ALBERTA T2V 2N6, CANADA

PHONE: 403/258-3373
  Live at all times.
OPEN: Year round.

ACCOMMODATIONS
B&Bs
Hosted private residences: 25.

OTHER SERVICES: Some hosts offer transportation to and from
the airport, and to points of interest. Laundry facilities. Baby-
sitting. Additional meals at reasonable rates.

LOCATIONS *Calgary, Edmonton, Canmore, Banff. Most
are within 10 or 15 miles of center of Calgary.*

SETTINGS: In addition to city locations, some are in farm and ranch homes on acreage. One is a summer cabin in the mountains near a lake, a 10-minute drive from Banff.

HOSTS: Teachers, retirees, all professionals in their approach to B&B. . . .

GUESTS COME FOR: A vacation. Cross-country skiing. A stopover on the way to Banff and/or Jasper.

BREAKFAST: All serve a full meal.

RESERVATIONS
Advance preferred. If arrangements can be made, will accept last-minute reservations.

RATES
Singles $20–$25. Doubles $30–$35. Family rates available.
Ten percent discount for stays over five days in one location.
Deposit required: $25 for advance reservations.
Cancellation policy: A refund of $15 is made if cancellation is received seven days prior to reservation.

How Do Hosts Speak of Paying Guests?

One host said, "We have enjoyed all the company we have had."

◇ ◇ ◇

BRITISH COLUMBIA

VICTORIA GUESTS COME FOR: A vacation in the Garden City with its attractions that include Butchart Gardens, Provincial Museum, Parliament Buildings, Craigdarroch Castle, Scenic Marine Drive, tea at the Empress Hotel. Some come for medical reasons. Many come for business reasons.

ALL SEASON BED & BREAKFAST AGENCY
MAUREEN VESEY
BOX 5511 STATION B
VICTORIA, BRITISH COLUMBIA V8R 6S4, CANADA

PHONE: 604/595-2337 (604/595-BEDS)
Live most of the time. Answering machine at other times.
OPEN: Year round.

ACCOMMODATIONS
B&Bs
Hosted private residences: 25.

OTHER SERVICES: Some hosts pick up at ferry or airport. Some hosts are bilingual (French, Spanish, Dutch, German). All Season's guest packet includes a bookmark that asks, "Why be a tourist when you can be a houseguest?"

LOCATIONS *All are in Victoria area within a 10-mile radius of center city. All are on public transit lines.*

SETTINGS: "We specialize in waterfront and garden single-family homes."

HOSTS: Teachers, chef, nurse, retired dietitian. . . .

BREAKFAST: All serve a full meal.

RESERVATIONS
Advance reservations preferred. If arrangements can be made, will accept last-minute reservations.

DIRECTORY (not required for reservations): $1 to cover postage. In addition to descriptions of all of Maureen's listings (each named by its owner), the publication includes ads for selected private B&B homes up-island and one inn in Victoria. *Sample:*

> Rose Home. On waterfront. Ten minutes to city. Your host and hostess would like to share their waterfront home, with a fantastic view of Olympic Mountains. Suite with private entrance. Living room with fireplace. Private bath. Hosts' hobbies and interests: Gardening, boating, fishing, golf, music, and home-related activities. Twin $45. Additional adult $7.50 (Chesterfield bed in living room.) No pets. (Three cats and a small dog live here.) No children. Nonsmokers preferred. Ten percent discount for seniors. Steps and sloping driveway.

RATES
Singles $25–$30. Doubles $35–$40. A few on the waterfront are higher.
Some hosts offer seventh night free.
Deposit required: One night's lodging fee.
Cancellation policy: If notice is received 72 hours before expected arrival date, refund minus $5 handling charge is made.

A B&B Major

Maureen studied hotel administration and majored in bed and breakfast. She wrote papers on "Alternative Tourism" and "Opening a B&B House." Since opening her reservation service in 1983, she has established the policy of having each guest receive what she calls official adoption papers, a certificate signed by the host, adopting the guest by name and promising to provide comfortable, clean accommodations; to supply visitor information; and to make the B&B stay as enjoyable as possible.

V.I.P. BED & BREAKFAST CO.
JOANNE RIDLEY
1786 TEAKWOOD ROAD
VICTORIA, BRITISH COLUMBIA V8N 1E2, CANADA

PHONE: 604/477–5604
  Almost anytime.
OPEN: Year round.

ACCOMMODATIONS
B&Bs
Hosted private residences: 20.
Most homes have two B&B rooms.
Some hosts welcome pets and children.

OTHER SERVICES: Meet buses. Arrange sightseeing tours. Babysitting. Escorted tours of garage sales, "the final resting places of all treasures of the world." Special arrangements for Conversational English sessions for foreign visitors—two-hour sessions that could involve reading a newspaper or highlighting attractions in the city.

LOCATIONS *Close to Victoria's center, near the University of Victoria, shopping malls, golf courses, Butchart Gardens, and the airport and ferry terminals.*

SETTINGS: Traditional older homes, contemporary homes, country places, and some near the waterfront.

HOSTS: One composer and one organist each have grand pianos in their homes and play for guests. Others include retired or semiretired professionals, professors, teachers, military personnel, musicians. . . .

BREAKFAST: "Big enough to eliminate lunch."

RESERVATIONS
Advance reservations preferred. If arrangements can be made, will accept last-minute reservations.

RATES
Singles $30. Doubles $45.
Family and weekly rates negotiable.

In addition to enjoying her (five-year-old) role as head of a service that has a motto of "Something more than bed and breakfast," Joanne hosts in her own home. Her enthusiasm for matching guests with "just the right host"—knowing the stair situation, whether a car is needed, where fishing boats are available—allows her imagination to come up with unique and exciting ideas. Recently she offered two nights at a B&B together with an escorted tour of garage sales as an item to be sold at a fund-raising television auction. Result: Big success! The same can be said for her Conversational English packages.

TRAVELLER'S BED & BREAKFAST
ELSIE LAIRD
1840 MIDGARD AVENUE
VICTORIA, BRITISH COLUMBIA Z8P 2Y9, CANADA

PHONE: 604/477-3069
Almost anytime. Answering machine sometimes.
OPEN: Year round.

ACCOMMODATIONS
B&Bs
Hosted private residences: 10. One home can take groups up to 12 or 14.

OTHER SERVICES: Pickup at ferry or bus. Attention to special dietary needs. Boat rentals at one B&B. Baby-sitting. Tours. Salmon-fishing charters.

LOCATIONS *Most are in residential areas throughout the city of Victoria.*

SETTINGS: Varied. On large acreage in the country, with a sea view, downtown, near the University of Victoria, and in the gorge area.

HOSTS: Housewives with spouses who are retirees, teachers, realtors, professionals. . . .

BREAKFAST: "Very good and full." Could be juice, fruit salad, bacon and eggs, sliced tomatoes, potato patties, scones, bread with homemade jam. Maybe pancakes, quiche, or souffle. "When guests stay several days, we try to vary the menu."

RESERVATIONS
Advance reservations preferred. Will accept last-minute reservations.
Groups: Can accommodate up to 10.

RATES
Singles $25–$30. Doubles $36–$45. Seventh night free.
Some family rates available.
Deposit required (when time allows): First night's lodging.

> *"Some first-time guests are surprised to find that Victoria is not a little village. It is a major tourist-oriented town. We find that our guests are well educated and well traveled; they choose B&B as a complementary alternative style of travel that allows them to meet local residents. They return—and return again, and send friends—and friends of friends and relatives. They send stacks of thank-you notes—after having paid!"*

VANCOUVER B&B GUESTS COME FOR: The scenery. A cultural mecca. Expo.

COTTAGE BED AND BREAKFAST REGISTRY
BELLE CURD
3534 WEST KING EDWARD AVENUE
VANCOUVER, BRITISH COLUMBIA V6S 1M5, CANADA

PHONE: 604/738-7561
Live all the time. (Please do not call late at night.)
OPEN: Year round.

ACCOMMODATIONS
B&Bs
Hosted private residences: 30.
Plus
Some short-term housing arrangements.

OTHER SERVICES: Car rentals; pickup at airport, bus, and train; boat charters and tours.

LOCATIONS *In British Columbia: Vancouver, North Vancouver, Kelowna, Vernon, Campbell River, Victoria, Parksville, Naniamo, Richmond, Summerland, New Westminster, White Rock, and Whistler.*
In Alberta: Calgary.

HOSTS: Housewives, retired couples, self-employed professionals. "Many are new adventurers."

BREAKFAST: All serve a full meal. Some include homemade marmalades and jams, hot muffins, pancakes with pure maple syrup, or quiches.

RESERVATIONS
Advance reservations suggested. (Reminder: Mail is very slow.) If possible, last-minute requests accommodated.
Groups: Maximum size is nine.
Also available through travel agents.

RATES
Singles $20–$40. Doubles $30–$45. Two-bedroom suites are higher. Family rates available.

Weekly and monthly rates also available.
Deposit required: One night's lodging fee.

> *Belle says: "Because my husband and I were B&B hosts before we owned Cottage Bed & Breakfast Registry, we are very careful about our placing guests where they can expect the unique experience of B&B. Maybe our greatest success story is about the Englishman who came for a week and stayed for five months!"*

TOWN & COUNTRY BED & BREAKFAST IN BRITISH COLUMBIA, CANADA

PAULINE SCOTEN AND HELEN BURICH
P.O. BOX 46554, STN. "G"
VANCOUVER, BRITISH COLUMBIA V6R 4G6, CANADA

PHONE: 604/731-5942
  Monday–Friday, 8–6.
OPEN: Year round.

ACCOMMODATIONS
B&Bs
Hosted private residences: 200.
A few are self-contained small lodges, or offer full farm vacations.
Some have facilities for handicapped, RV space, camping space.

LOCATIONS   *Homes are in most areas of British Columbia. Pauline Scoten and Helen Burich have personally inspected the homes except where distance has made that impractical.*

SETTINGS: Modest to luxurious, urban to rural.

HOSTS: Retired teacher, retired public health nurse, design architect, flight attendant, landscape gardener, musician, caterer, social worker, farmers, rancher. . . .

BREAKFAST: Varies from help-yourself to an elaborate meal. Most serve a full breakfast that could include eggs Benedict, shrimp quiche, and various omelets.

RESERVATIONS
Booked directly with host by guest.
Advance arrangements recommended.

Last-minute reservations accepted by many.
Some B&Bs have a minimum stay requirement.

DIRECTORY: $7.95 includes postage to the United States. Full description of each B&B includes address and telephone number of each host.

RATES
Singles $25–$30. Doubles $30–$55. A few higher.
Some weekly and monthly rates available.
Deposit required.
Cancellation policy varies with each host.

WESTERN COMFORT BED & BREAKFAST REGISTRY
BARBARA SMITH
180 EAST CARISBROOKE ROAD
NORTH VANCOUVER, BRITISH COLUMBIA V7N 1M9, CANADA

PHONE: 604/985-2674
   Live dawn till dusk daily. Answering service at other times.
OPEN: Year round.

ACCOMMODATIONS
B&Bs
Hosted private residences: 50.
Many have private baths.
Plus
Some unhosted private residences for overnight or weekend lodging.
Some hosted and unhosted short-term housing.

OTHER SERVICES: Pickup at transportation points.

   LOCATIONS *West Vancouver, North Vancouver, Vancouver, Victoria, Burnaby, Richmond, Surrey, Langley.*

SETTINGS: "We have a wide variety—hopefully wide enough to accommodate everyone's requests."

HOSTS: Travel agent, retirees, accountant, nurse, ex-Army officer. . . .

BREAKFAST: Varies according to host. Could include omelets or quiche.

RESERVATIONS
If arrangements can be made, last-minute reservations accepted.

RATES
Singles $20–$45. Doubles $35–$65.

For hospital program guests (see below): $15 for one, $5 for each additional person in room. In some homes the rate is a little lower after several days.

Deposit required: One night's lodging for every five nights reserved.

Credit cards: MasterCard and VISA.

Cancellation policy: If notice received 72 hours before expected arrival date, 85 percent of deposit is refunded.

Barbara's interest in B&B extends beyond her own service. As president of the West Coast Bed & Breakfast Association of British Columbia, she has been working on the issues of standards. It was her idea to institute a hospital program for her own service; it is a concept that she hopes other services will adopt. The hospital program acknowledges that B&B guests may come for other than sightseeing or business. Recognizing that many travelers come to the Vancouver area for medical reasons, some of Western Comfort's selected hosts have stipulated that they especially enjoy providing a home-away-from-home for those guests.

British Columbia B&Bs are also represented by:
Northwest Bed & Breakfast in Oregon, page 264.
Travellers' Bed & Breakfast in Washington, page 338.
Pacific Bed & Breakfast in Washington, page 340.
Bed & Breakfast Bureau—Canadian Care, page 396.

Index

This index lists the bed and breakfast reservation services (and clearinghouses) according to the states or provinces they are based in. The United States appears first, then Canada.

DATE DUE

JUN 3 0 1989			
NOV 1 8 1994			
FEB 0 2 1995			
APR 28 '96			
AUG 1 8 '97			